Henry F.H. Norfolk, John Henry Newman

**The Pope**

How far Does He Control Conscience? How far Does He Interfere with Citizenship?

Henry F.H. Norfolk, John Henry Newman

**The Pope**
*How far Does He Control Conscience? How far Does He Interfere with Citizenship?*

ISBN/EAN: 9783744727648

Printed in Europe, USA, Canada, Australia, Japan

Cover: Foto ©Lupo / pixelio.de

More available books at **www.hansebooks.com**

# ~~CARD~~INAL NEWMAN ON THE

## THE PO~~PE~~

### HOW FAR DOES HE CONTROL ~~~~?
### HOW FAR DOES HE INTERFERE ~~~~SHIP?

BY

CARDINAL JOHN HENR~~Y NEWMAN~~

Being his Answer to Right Honorable W~~~~ ~~pa~~mphlet entitled "Vaticani~~sm"~~

The Ca~~~~
12~~~~

THE COLUMBUS PRESS,
120 WEST 60TH STREET,
· NEW YORK.

# CONTENTS.

|  | PAGE |
|---|---|
| PREFACE, . . . . . . . . . . | v |
| LETTER TO THE DUKE OF NORFOLK, . . . . | 7 |

## CHAPTER I.

INTRODUCTORY: The Case stated: Has the Pope such a hold on Catholics as to interfere with Citizenship?—Remarks on the Political Reasons for Gladstone's Attack.—Relation of the Pope to Irish Politics.—Views of the Irish Bishops Fifty Years ago on Papal Infallibility.—The Meeting of the Vatican Council in 1870. . . 11

## CHAPTER II.

THE BISHOP OF ROME IN THE ANCIENT CHURCH: Gladstone's Accusation is the same as that of ancient Rome: Catholics are too independent of the State in Religious Matters.—The Study of this Historical Lesson created the Oxford Movement.—Independence of the Church among the Converted Nations.—Its universal Recognition.—Testimony of the Protestant Historian Ranke. . . . . . . . . . . 26

## CHAPTER III.

THE CHRISTIAN CHURCH IS HISTORICALLY PAPAL: If Christ founded a visible Society, it has ceased to exist, or it is the Church in communion with Rome.—The Objection to the Pope's Independence would apply to any Church claiming Divine Authority.—Necessity of a high Development of Papal Power for the civilizing of

Modern Europe.—Testimony of Dean Milman, and of Alison.—Reflections on the Papal Power in relation to present Civil and Religious Conditions. . . . 36

## CHAPTER IV.

DIVIDED ALLEGIANCE: Obedience to Spiritual Guides as taught in Scripture.—Comparison between the Interference of Civil and of Religious Authority in Daily Life.—Essential Difference between control of *every* Act and of *any* Act.—Control of the Pope compared with that of a Physician, of Public Opinion, or of the Press.—The Pope's Power exists to aid Religion.—Disputes between the Pope and the Nation considered.—Cases supposed in which Catholics would obey the Pope against the Law of the State.—Cases in which they would Disobey the Pope and Obey the State.—Theologians cited to prove that it is sometimes lawful to Disobey the Pope. . . . . . . . . 51

## CHAPTER V.

AUTHORITY OF CONSCIENCE: Understood in the same sense by both Catholics and Protestants.—The Aboriginal Vicar of Christ.—False Notions of Conscience among the Sceptical and Worldly.—Self-will is often misnamed Conscience.—In that sense only has the Pope condemned "Liberty of Conscience."—The Pope's whole Office is to enlighten Conscience and establish its Authority.—"He who acts against his Conscience loses his Soul," is a Catholic Maxim affirmed by Pope Benedict XIV. . . . . . . . 72

## CHAPTER VI.

THE ENCYCLICAL OF 1864: Reflections on the Movement in England towards Universal Toleration.—The Encyclical does not condemn Liberty in any different sense than does English Law.—The real and practical Meaning of the Encyclical. . . . . . . 87

## CHAPTER VII.

THE SYLLABUS: Description of this Document.—Why it was issued, and how.—It was sent by the Pope's direction, but without His Name or Seal affixed.—It lacks the formal Authentication of a Dogmatic Instrument.—Its Meaning to be learned only from the Papal Declarations to which it refers.— Discussion of the Propositions of the Syllabus most violently attacked.—Explanation of the Opposition to the Syllabus. . . . . . 100

## CHAPTER VIII.

THE VATICAN COUNCIL: A Personal Explanation.—Reasons for and against accepting the Council's Definition of Papal Infallibility.—The Vatican compared with early Councils of the Church.—Objections against it considered.—Does the Definition of Infallibility conflict with Historical Facts? . . . . . . 120

## CHAPTER IX.

THE VATICAN DEFINITION; Summary of Scripture Evidence for the Church's Right to Teach.—The Vatican Council has defined that the Pope has the same Right.—Signs and Conditions of the exercise of this Right.—Neither Council nor Pope is inspired.—Detailed Examination of the Uses and Methods of Papal Infallibility.—Meaning of the Maxim "Out of the Church there is no Salvation."—Contrast between rigorous Interpretation and loyal Moderation of Views on disputed Questions. . . . . . . 139

## CHAPTER X.

CONCLUSION: The Definition of Infallibility has not increased the Pope's Power.—Remarks on Freedom of Opinion among Catholics.—Catholics acknowledge but one Pope, and tolerate no self-assumed Power of Anathema. . . . . . . . . 158

## CHAPTER XI.

POSTSCRIPT : Rejoinder to Gladstone's Answer.—" From the Day on which I became a Catholic to this Day, now close upon Thirty Years, I have never had a Moment's Misgiving."—Gladstone's withdrawal of the Accusation of Disloyalty.—Re-examination of Accusation of former Disbelief in Papal Infallibility among some Classes of Catholics.—Papal Supremacy and the Supremacy of Conscience.—Example from the Life of M. Emery.—Further Remarks on the grade of Authority possessed by the Syllabus.—Difference between receiving it with Obedience and as an Act of Infallibility. —How the Church regards Marriages of non-Catholics.   164

# PUBLISHER'S PREFACE.

IN 1870 the General Council of the Vatican, composed of almost the entire Catholic Episcopate, defined as an article of faith that our divine Redeemer had invested the Roman Pontiff, in the person of the Apostle St. Peter, with the same infallibility in matters concerning faith and morals with which He had invested the Church itself. As a result of this the Prussian government, controlled at the time by Prince Bismarck, passed a series of laws against the Catholic clergy and people, with the hope of compelling German Catholics to substitute the authority of the State for that of the Pope. More than ten years of fierce persecution and courageous resistance ended in Bismarck finally giving up the struggle and causing the repeal of nearly all the obnoxious laws.

In England in 1874 Mr. Gladstone, chagrined and angered by the defeat of his Irish University bill by the opposition of the Catholic clergy and laity of Ireland, and by his consequent expulsion from power, launched against Catholic British subjects his "Expostulation." It was a vehement accusation that Catholics could not be loyal to their country if they were faithful to the Vatican decree.

Among the many answers which it provoked Cardinal Newman's ranks highest, and was without doubt the chief means of drawing from Gladstone—as frank as he is vehement—an acknowledgment that he had mistaken the mental attitude of his Catholic fellow-subjects towards Pope and country respectively.

The value of Newman's splendid exposition is that his name and office give him an authority in the religious world similar to that which his supreme literary genius won for him in the world of letters. Also, that his treatment of the question is throughout practical, touching the daily conduct and the common habit of mind of Catholics true to both church and country.

As Cardinal Newman has not expressly discussed the Scripture reasons for holding Papal Infallibility we here give the three principal texts for convenience of reference, using the Protestant version:

St. Luke xxii. 31 : "And the Lord said, Simon, Simon, behold, Satan hath desired to have you, that he may sift you as wheat : But I have prayed for thee, that thy faith fail not : and when thou art converted, strengthen thy brethren."

St. Matthew xvi. 13 : "When Jesus came into the coasts of Cæsarea Philippi, he asked his disciples, saying, Whom do men say that I, the Son of man, am? And they said, Some say that thou art John the Baptist : some, Elias ; and others, Jeremias, or one of the prophets. He saith unto them, But whom say ye that I am? And Simon Peter answered and said, Thou art the Christ, the Son of the living God. And Jesus answered and said unto him, Blessed art thou, Simon Barjona : for flesh and blood hath not revealed it unto thee, but my Father which is in heaven. And I say also unto thee, That thou art Peter (*kephas*, a rock), and upon this rock I will build my church ; and the gates of hell shall not prevail against it. And I will give unto thee the keys of the kingdom of heaven : and whatsoever thou shalt bind on earth shall be bound in heaven ; and whatsoever thou shalt loose on earth shall be loosed in heaven."

St. John xxi. 15 : "So when they had dined, Jesus saith to Simon Peter, Simon, son of Jonas, lovest thou me more than these? He saith unto him, Yea, Lord, thou knowest that I love thee. He saith unto him, Feed my lambs. He saith to him again the second time, Simon, Son of Jonas, lovest thou me? He saith unto him, Yea, Lord, thou knowest that I love thee. He saith unto him, Feed my sheep. He saith unto him the third time, Simon, son of Jonas, lovest thou me? Peter was grieved because he said unto him the third time, Lovest thou me? And he said unto him, Lord, thou knowest all things; thou knowest that I love thee. Jesus saith unto him, Feed my sheep."

To facilitate the use of this most valuable exposition of Catholic doctrine and sentiment, we have marked its divisions off as chapters, prefixing to each a summary

TO

# HIS GRACE THE DUKE OF NORFOLK,

HEREDITARY EARL MARSHAL OF ENGLAND,
ETC., ETC.

---

MY DEAR DUKE OF NORFOLK:

When I yielded to the earnest wish which you, together with many others, urged upon me, that I should reply to Mr. Gladstone's recent expostulation, a friend suggested that I ought to ask your Grace's permission to address my remarks to you.  Not that for a moment he or I thought of implicating you, in any sense or measure, in a responsibility which is solely and entirely my own; but on a very serious occasion, when such heavy charges had been made against the Catholics of England by so powerful and so earnest an adversary, it seemed my duty, in meeting his challenge, to gain the support, if I could, of a name which is the special representative and the fitting sample of a laity as zealous for the Catholic Religion as it is patriotic.

You consented with something of the reluctance which I had felt myself when called upon to write ; for it was hard to be summoned at any age, early or late, from a peaceful course of life and the duties of one's station, to a scene of war.  Still, you consented; and for myself, it is the compensation for a very unpleasant task, that I, who belong to a generation that is fast flitting away, am thus enabled, in what is likely to be my last publication, to associate myself with one, on many accounts so dear to me, so full of young promise —whose career is before him.

I deeply grieve that Mr. Gladstone has felt it his duty to speak with such extraordinary severity of our Religion and of ourselves. I consider he has committed himself to a representation of ecclesiastical documents which will not hold, and to a view of our position in the country which we have neither deserved nor can be patient under. None but the *Schola Theologorum* is competent to determine the force of Papal and Synodal utterances, and the exact interpretation of them is a work of time. But so much may be safely said of the decrees which have lately been promulgated, and of the faithful who have received them, that Mr. Gladstone's account, both of them and of us, is neither trustworthy nor charitable.

Yet not a little may be said in explanation of a step which so many of his admirers and well-wishers deplore. I own to a deep feeling, that Catholics may in good measure thank themselves, and no one else, for having alienated from them so religious a mind. There are those among us, as it must be confessed, who for years past have conducted themselves as if no responsibility attached to wild words and overbearing deeds; who have stated truths in the most paradoxical form, and stretched principles till they were close upon snapping; and who at length, having done their best to set the house on fire, leave to others the task of putting out the flame. The English people are sufficiently sensitive of the claims of the Pope, without having them, as if in defiance, flourished in their faces. Those claims most certainly I am not going to deny;

I have never denied them. I have no intention, now that I have to write upon them, to conceal any part of them. And I uphold them as heartily as I recognize my duty of loyalty to the constitution, the laws, and the government of England. I see no inconsistency in my being at once a good Catholic and a good Englishman. Yet it is one thing to be able to satisfy myself as to my consistency, quite another to satisfy others; and, undisturbed as I am in my own conscience, I have great difficulties in the task before me. I have one difficulty to overcome in the present excitement of the public mind against our Religion, caused partly by the chronic extravagances of knots of Catholics here and there, partly by the vehement rhetoric which is the occasion and subject of this Letter. A worse difficulty lies in getting people, as they are commonly found, to put off the modes of speech and language which are usual with them, and to enter into scientific distinctions and traditionary rules of interpretation, which as being new to them, appear evasive and unnatural. And a third difficulty, as I may call it, is this—that in so very wide a subject, opening as great a variety of questions, and of opinions upon them, while it will be simply necessary to take the objections made against us and our faith, one by one, readers may think me trifling with their patience, because they do not find those points first dealt with on which they lay most stress themselves.

But I have said enough by way of preface, and without more delay turn to Mr. Gladstone's pamphlet.

# THE POPE.

## CHAPTER I.

### INTRODUCTORY.

THE CASE STATED: HAS THE POPE SUCH A HOLD ON CATHOLICS AS TO INTERFERE WITH CITIZENSHIP?—REMARKS ON THE POLITICAL REASONS FOR GLADSTONE'S ATTACK.—RELATION OF THE POPE TO IRISH POLITICS.—VIEWS OF THE IRISH BISHOPS FIFTY YEARS AGO ON PAPAL INFALLIBILITY.—THE MEETING OF THE VATICAN COUNCIL IN 1870.

THE main question which Mr. Gladstone has started I consider to be this: Can Catholics be trustworthy subjects of the State? has not a foreign Power a hold over their consciences such, that it may at any time be used to the serious perplexity and injury of the civil government under which they live? Not that Mr. Gladstone confines himself to these questions, for he goes out of his way, I am sorry to say, to taunt us with our loss of mental and moral freedom, a vituperation which is not necessary for his purpose at all. He informs us too that we have "repudiated ancient history," and are rejecting modern "thought," and that our Church has been "refurbishing her rusty tools," and has been lately aggravating, and is likely still more to aggravate, our state of bondage. I think it unworthy of Mr. Gladstone's high character thus to have inveighed against us; what intellectual manliness is left to us according to him? Yet his circle of acquaintance is too wide, and his knowledge of his countrymen on the other hand too accurate, for him not to know that he is bringing a great amount of odium and bad feeling upon excellent men, whose only offence is their religion. The more intense is the prejudice with which we are regarded by whole classes of men, the less is there of generosity in his pouring upon us superfluous reproaches. The graver the charge which is the direct occasion of his writing against us, the more careful should he be not to prejudice judge and jury to our disadvantage. No rhetoric is needed in England against an unfortunate Catholic at any time; but so little is Mr. Gladstone conscious of his treatment of us, that in one place of his pamphlet, strange as it may seem, he makes it his boast that he has been careful to "do nothing towards importing passion into what is matter of pure argument" (pp. 15, 16). I venture to think he will one day be sorry for what he has said.

However, we must take things as we find them ; and what I propose to do is this—to put aside, unless it comes directly in my way, his accusation against us of repudiating ancient history, rejecting modern thought, and renouncing our mental freedom, and to confine myself for the most part to what he principally insists upon, that Catholics, if they act consistently with their principles, cannot be loyal subjects; I shall not, however, omit notice of his attack upon our moral uprightness.

The occasion and the grounds of Mr. Gladstone's impeachment of us, if I understand him, are as follows:—

He was alarmed, as a statesman, ten years ago by the Pope's Encyclical of December 8, and by the Syllabus of Erroneous Propositions which, by the Pope's authority, accompanied its transmission to the bishops. Then came the Definitions of the Vatican Council in 1870, upon the universal jurisdiction and doctrinal infallibility of the Pope. And lastly, as the event which turned alarm into indignation, and into the duty of public remonstrance, "the Roman Catholic Prelacy of Ireland thought fit to procure the rejection of" the Irish University Bill of February, 1873, "by the direct influence which they exercised over a certain number of Irish members of Parliament," etc. (p. 60). This step on the part of the bishops showed, if I understand him, the new and mischievous force which had been acquired at Rome by the late acts there, or at least left him at liberty, by causing his loss of power, to denounce it. "From that time forward the situation was changed," and an opening was made for a "broad political discussion" on the subject of the Catholic religion and its professors, and a "debt to the country had to be disposed of." That debt, if I am right, will be paid, if he can ascertain, on behalf of the country, that there is nothing in the Catholic Religion to hinder its professors from being as loyal as other subjects of the State, and that the See of Rome cannot interfere with their civil duties so as to give the civil power trouble or alarm. The main ground on which he relies for the necessity of some such inquiry is, first, the text of the authoritative documents of 1864 and 1870; next, and still more, the *animus* which they breathe, and the sustained aggressive spirit which they disclose; and thirdly, the daring deed of aggression in 1873, when the Pope, acting (as it is alleged) upon the Irish members ministry who, besides past benefits, were at that very time doing for Irish Catholics, and therefore ousted for doing, a special service.

Now, it would be preposterous and officious in me to put myself forward as champion for the Venerable Prelacy of Ireland, or to take upon myself the part of advocate and representative of the Holy See. "Non tali auxilio"; in neither character could I come forward without great presumption; not the least for this reason, because I cannot know the exact points which are really the *gist* of the affront, which Mr. Gladstone conceives he has sustained, whether from the one quarter or from the other; yet in a question so nearly interesting myself as that February bill, which he brought into the House, in great sincerity and kindness, for the benefit of the Catholic University in Ireland, I may be allowed to say thus much—that I, who now have no official relation to the Irish Bishops, and am not in any sense in the counsels of Rome, felt at once, when I first saw the outline of that bill, the greatest astonishment on reading one of its provisions, and a dread which painfully affected me, lest Mr. Gladstone perhaps was acting on an understanding with the Catholic Prelacy. I did not see how in honor they could accept it. It was possible, did the question come over again, to decide in favor of the Queen's Colleges, and to leave the project of a Catholic University alone. The Holy See might so have decided in 1847. But at or about that date three rescripts had come from Rome in favor of a distinctively Catholic Institution; a National Council had decided in its favor; large offers of the Government had been rejected; great commotions had been caused in the political world; munificent contributions had been made; all on the sole principle that Catholic teaching was to be upheld in the country inviolate. If, then, for the sake of a money grant, or other secular advantage, this ground of principle was deserted, and Catholic youths after all were allowed to attend the lectures of men of no religion, or of the Protestant, the contest of thirty years would have been stultified, and the Pope and the Bishops would seem to have been playing a game, while putting forward the plea of conscience and religious duty. I hoped that the clause in the bill, which gave me such uneasiness, could have been omitted from it; but, anyhow, it was an extreme relief to me when the papers announced that the Bishops had expressed their formal dissatisfaction with it.

They determined to decline a gift laden with such a condition, and who can blame them for so doing? who can be surprised that they should now do what they did in 1847? what new move in politics was it, if they so determined? what was there in it of a factious character? Is the Catholic Irish interest the only one which is not to be represented in the House of Commons? Why is not that interest as much a matter of right as any other? I fear to expose my own ignorance of Parliamentary rules and proceedings, but I had supposed that the railway interest, and what is called the publican interest, were very powerful there: in Scotland, too, I believe, a government has a formidable party to deal with; and, to revert to Ireland, there are the Home-rulers, who have objects in view quite distinct from, or contrary to, those of the Catholic hierarchy. As to the Pope, looking at the surface of things, there is nothing to suggest that he interfered, there was no necessity of interference on so plain a lights, I altogether disbelieve the interpositon of Rome in the matter. In the proceedings which they adopted, the Bishops were only using civil rights, common to all, which others also used and in their own way. Why might it not be their duty to promote the interests of their religion by means of their political opportunities? Is there no Exeter Hall interest? I thought it was a received theory of our Reformed Constitution that members of Parliament were representatives, and in some sort delegates of their constituents, and that the strength of each interest was shown, and the course of the nation determined, by the divisions in the House of Commons. I recollect the *Times* intimating its regret, after one general election, that there was no English Catholic in the new House, on the ground that every class and party should be represented there. Surely the Catholic religion has not a small party in Ireland; why then should it not have a corresponding number of exponents and defenders at Westminster? So clear does this seem to me, that I think there must be some defect in my knowledge of facts to explain Mr. Gladstone's surprise and displeasure at the conduct of the Irish Prelacy in 1873; yet I suspect none; and, if there be none, then his unreasonableness in this instance of Ireland makes it not unlikely that he is unreasonable also in his judgment of the Encyclical, Syllabus, and Vatican Decrees.

However, the Bishops, I believe, not only opposed Mr. Gladstone's bill, but, instead of it, they asked for some money grant towards the expenses of their University. If so, their obvious argument was this—that Catholics formed the great majority of the population of Ireland, and it was not fair that the Protestant minority should have all that was bestowed in endowment or otherwise upon education. To this the reply, I suppose, would be, that it was not Protestantism, but liberal education that had the money, and that, if the Bishops chose to give up their own principles and act as Liberals, they might have the benefit of it too. I am not concerned here with these arguments, but I wish to notice the position which the Bishops would occupy in urging such a request: I must not say that they were Irishmen first and Catholics afterwards, but I do say that in such a demand they spoke not simply as Catholic Bishops, but as the Bishops of a Catholic nation. They did not speak from any promptings of the Encyclical, Syllabus, or Vatican Decrees. They claimed as Irishmen a share in the endowments of the country; and has not Ireland surely a right to speak in such a matter, and might not her Bishops fairly represent her? It seems to me a great mistake to think that everything that is done by the Irish Bishops and clergy is done on an ecclesiastical motive; why not on a national? but if so, such acts have nothing to do with Rome. I know well what simple, firm faith the great body of the Irish people have, and how they put the Catholic Religion before anything else in the world. It is their comfort, their joy, their treasure, their boast, their compensation for a hundred worldly disadvantages; but who can deny that in politics their conduct at times—nay more than at times—has had a flavor rather of their nation than of their Church? Only in the last general election this was said, when they were so earnest for Home Rule. Why, then, must Mr. Gladstone come down upon the Catholic Religion, because the Irish love dearly the Green Island, and its interests? Ireland is not the only country in which politics, or patriotism, or party, has been so closely associated with religion in the nation or a class, that it is difficult to say which of the various motive principles was uppermost. "The Puritan," says Macaulay, "prostrated himself in the dust before his Maker, but he set his foot on the neck of his king"; I am not accusing such a man of hypocrisy on account of this; having great wrongs, as he considered, both in religious and temporal matters, and the authors of these distinct wrongs being the same persons, he did not nicely discriminate between the acts which he did as a patriot and the acts which he did as a Puritan. And so as regards Irishmen, they do not, cannot, distinguish between their love of Ireland and their love of religion; their patriotism is religious, and their religion is strongly tinctured with patriotism; and it is hard to recognize the abstract and Ideal Ultramontane, pure and simple, in the concrete exhibition of him in flesh and blood as found in the polling-booth or in his chapel. I do not see how the Pope can be made answerable for him in any of his political acts during the last fifty years.

This leads me to a subject, of which Mr. Gladstone makes a good deal in his pamphlet. I will say of a great man, whom he quotes, and for whose memory I have a great respect, I mean Bishop Doyle, that there was just a little tinge of patriotism in the way in which, on one occasion, he speaks of the Pope. I dare say any of us would have done the same, in the heat of a great struggle for national liberty, for he said nothing but what was true and honest; I only mean that the energetic language which he used was not exactly such as would have suited the atmosphere of Rome. He says to Lord Liverpool: "We are taunted with the proceedings of Popes. What, my Lord, have we Catholics to do with the proceedings of Popes, or why should we be made accountable for them?" (p. 27). Now, with some proceedings of Popes, we Catholics have very much to do indeed; but, if the context of his words is consulted, I make no doubt it would be found that he was referring to certain proceedings of certain Popes, when he said that Catholics had no part of their responsibility. Assuredly there are certain acts of Popes in which no one would like to have part. Then, again, his words require some pious interpretation when he says that "the allegiance due to the king and the allegiance due to the Pope are as distinct and as divided in their nature as any two things can possibly be" (p. 30). Yes, in their nature, in the abstract, but not in the particular case; for a heathen State might bid me throw incense upon the altar of Jupiter, and the Pope would bid me not to do so. I venture to make the same remark on the Address of the Irish Bishops to their clergy and laity in 1826 (quoted at p. 31), and on the Declaration of the Vicars-Apostolic in England, *ibid.*

But I must not be supposed for an instant to mean, in what I have said, that the venerable men, to whom I have referred, were aware of any ambiguity either in such statements as the above, or in others which were denials of the Pope's infallibility. Indeed, one of them at an earlier date, 1793, Dr. Troy, Archbishop of Dublin, had introduced into one of his pastorals the subject which Mr. Gladstone considers they so summarily disposed of. The Archbishop says: "Many Catholics contend that the Pope, when teaching the universal Church, as their supreme visible head and pastor, as successor to St. Peter, and heir to the promises of special assistance made to him by Jesus Christ, is infallible; and that his decrees and decisions in that capacity are to be respected as rules of faith, when they are dogmatical or confined to doctrinal points of faith and morals. Others deny this, and require the expressed or tacit acquiescence of the Church, assembled or dispersed, to stamp infallibility on his dogmatical decrees. Until the Church shall decide upon this question of the Schools, either opinion may be adopted by individual Catholics, without any breach of Catholic communion or peace. The Catholics of Ireland have lately declared that it is not an article of the Catholic faith; nor are they thereby required to believe or profess that the Pope is infallible, without adopting or abjuring either of the recited opinions which are open to discussion, while the Church continues silent about them." The Archbishop thus addressed his flock, at the time when he was informing them that the Pope had altered the oath which was taken by the Catholic Bishops.

As to the language of the Bishops in 1826, we must recollect that at that time the clergy, both of Ireland and England, were educated in Gallican opinions. They took those opinions for granted, and they thought, if they went so far as to ask themselves the question, that the definition of Papal Infallibility was simply impossible. Even among those at the Vatican Council, who, themselves personally believed in it, I believe there were Bishops who, until the actual definition had been passed, thought that such a definition could not be made. Perhaps they would argue that, though the historical evidence was sufficient for their own personal conviction, it was not sufficiently clear of difficulties to be made the ground of a Catholic dogma. Much more would this be the feeling of the Bishops in 1826. "How," they would ask, "can it ever come to pass that a majority of our order should find it their duty to relinquish their prime prerogative, and to make the Church take the shape of a pure monarchy?" They would think its definition as much out of the question, as the prospect that, in twenty-five years after their time, there would be a hierarchy of thirteen Bishops in England, with a cardinal for Archbishop.

But, all this while, such modes of thinking were foreign altogether to the minds of the *entourage* of the Holy See. Mr. Gladstone himself says, and the Duke of Wellington and Sir Robert Peel must have known it as well as he: "The Popes have kept up, with comparatively little intermission, for well-nigh a thousand years, their claim to dogmatic infallibility" (p. 28). Then, if the Pope's claim to infallibility was so patent a fact, could they ever suppose that he could be brought to admit that it was hopeless to turn that claim into a dogma? In truth, Wellington and Peel were very little interested in that question; as was said in a Petition or Declaration, signed among others by Dr. Troy, it was "immaterial, in a political light"; but, even if they thought it material, or if there were other questions they wanted to ask, why go to Bishop Doyle? If they wanted to obtain some real information about the probabilities of the future, why did they not go to headquarters? Why did they potter about the halls of Universities in this matter of Papal exorbitances, or rely upon the pamphlets or examinations of Bishops whom they never asked for their credentials? Why not go at once to Rome?

The reason is plain: it was a most notable instance, with a grave consequence, of what is a fixed tradition with us the English people, and a great embarrassment to every administration in its dealings with Catholics. I recollect, years ago, Dr. Griffiths, Vicar-Apostolic of the London District, giving me an account of an interview he had with the late Lord Derby, then I suppose Colonial Secretary. I understood him to say that Lord Derby was in perplexity at the time, on some West India matter, in which Catholics were concerned, because he could not find their responsible representative. He wanted Dr. Griffiths to undertake the office, and expressed something of disappointment when the Bishop felt obliged to decline it. A chronic malady has from time to time its paroxysms, and the history on which I am now engaged is a serious instance of it. I think it is impossible that the British government could have entered into formal negotiations with the Pope, without its transpiring in the course of them, and its becoming perfectly clear that Rome could never be a party to such a pledge as England wanted, and that no pledge from Catholics was of any value to which Rome was not a party.

But no; they persisted in an enterprise which was hopeless in its first principle, for they thought to break the indissoluble tie which bound together the head and the members,—and doubtless Rome felt the insult, though she might think it prudent not to notice it. France was not the keystone of the œcumenical power, though her Church was so great and so famous; nor could the hierarchy of Ireland, in spite of its fidelity to the Catholic faith, give any pledge of the future to the statesmen who required one; there was but one See whose word was worth anything in the matter, "that church" (to use the language of the earliest of our Doctors) "to which the faithful all round about are bound to have recourse." Yet for three hundred years it has been the official rule with England to ignore the existence of the Pope, and to deal with Catholics in England, not as his children, but as sectaries of the Roman Catholic persuasion. Napoleon said to his envoy: "Treat with the Pope as if he were master of one hundred thousand men." So clearly did he, from mere worldly sagacity, comprehend the Pope's place in the then state of European affairs, as to say that "if the Pope had not existed, it would have been well to have created him for that occasion as the Roman consuls created a dictator in difficult circumstances" (Alison's *Hist.*, ch. 35). But we, in the instance of the greatest, the oldest power in Europe, a church whose grandeur in past history demanded, one would think, some reverence in our treatment of her; the mother of English Christianity, who, whether her subsequent conduct had always been motherly or not, had been a true friend to us in the beginning of our history, her we have not only renounced, but, to use a familiar word, we have absolutely cut. Time has gone on and we have no relentings; to-day, as little as yesterday, do we understand that pride was not made for man, nor the cuddling of resentments for a great people. I am entering into no theological question: I am speaking all along of mere decent secular intercourse between England and Rome. A hundred grievances would have been set right on their first uprising, had there been a frank diplomatic understanding between two great powers; but, on the contrary, even within the last few weeks, the present ministry has destroyed any hope of a better state of things by withdrawing from the Vatican the makeshift channel of intercourse which had of late years been permitted there.

The world of politics has its laws; and such abnormal courses as England has pursued have their *Nemesis*. An event has taken place which, alas! already makes itself felt in issues, unfortunate for English Catholics certainly, but also, as I think, for our country. A great Council has been called; and as England has for so long a time ignored Rome, Rome, I suppose, it must be said, has in turn ignored England. I do not mean of set purpose ignored, but as the natural consequence of our act. Bishops brought from the

corners of the earth, in 1870, what could they know of
English blue-books and Parliamentary debates in the
years 1826 and 1829? It was an extraordinary gather-
ing, and its possibility, its purpose, and its issue were
alike marvellous, as depending on a coincidence of
strange conditions, which, as might be said beforehand,
never could take place. Such was the long reign of
the Pope, in itself a marvel, as being the sole exception
to a recognized ecclesiastical tradition. Only a Pontiff
so unfortunate, so revered, so largely loved, so popular
even with Protestants, with such a prestige of long
sovereignty, with such claims on the Bishops around
him, both of age and of paternal gracious acts, only
such a man could have harmonized and guided to the
conclusion which he pointed out an assembly so
variously composed. And, considering the state of
theological opinion seventy years before, not less
marvellous was the concurrence of all but a few out of
so many hundred Bishops in the theological judgment,
so long desired at Rome; the protest made by some
eighty or ninety, at the termination of the Council,
against the proceedings of the vast majority lying, not
against the truth of the doctrine then defined, but
against the fact of its definition. Nor less to be noted
is the neglect of the Catholic powers to send representatives to the Council, who might have laid before the
Fathers its political bearings. For myself, I did not
call it inopportune, for times and seasons are known to
God alone, and persecution may be as opportune,
though not so pleasant as peace; nor, in accepting as a
dogma what I had ever held as a truth, could I be
doing violence to any theological view or conclusion of
my own; nor has the acceptance of it any logical or
practical effect whatever, as I considered, in weakening
my allegiance to Queen Victoria; but there are few

Catholics, I think, who will not deeply regret, though no one be in fault, that the English and Irish Prelacies of 1826 did not foresee the possibility of the Synodal determinations of 1870, nor can we wonder that Statesmen should feel themselves aggrieved, that stipulations, which they considered necessary for Catholic emancipation, should have been, as they may think, rudely cast to the winds.

And now I must pass from the mere accidents of the controversy to its essential points, and I cannot treat them to the satisfaction of Mr. Gladstone, unless I go back a great way, and be allowed to speak of the ancient Catholic Church.

# CHAPTER II.

## THE BISHOP OF ROME IN THE ANCIENT CHURCH.

Gladstone's Accusation is the same as that of Ancient Rome: Catholics are too Independent of the State in Religious Matters.—The Study of this Historical Lesson created the Oxford Movement.—Independence of the Church among the Converted Nations.—Its Universal Recognition.—Testimony of the Protestant Historian Ranke.

WHEN Mr. Gladstone accuses us of "repudiating ancient history," he means the ancient history of the Church; also, I understand him to be viewing that history under a particular aspect. There are many aspects in which Christianity presents itself to us; for instance, the aspect of social usefulness, or of devotion, or again of theology; but, though he in one place glances at the last of these aspects, his own view of it is its relation towards the civil power. He writes "as one of the world at large"; as a "layman who has spent most and the best years of his life in the observation and practice of politics" (p. 7); and, as a statesman, he naturally looks at the Church on its political side. Accordingly, in his title-page, in which he professes to be expostulating with us for accepting the Vatican Decrees, he does so, not for any reason whatever but because of their incompatibility with our civil allegiance. This is the key-note of his impeachment of us. As a public man, he has only to do with the public action and effect of our Religion, its aspect upon national affairs, on our civil duties, on our foreign interests; and he tells us that our Religion has a bearing and behavior towards the State utterly unlike that of ancient Christianity, so unlike that we may be even said to repudiate what Christianity was in its first centuries, so unlike to what it was then that we have actually forfeited the proud boast of being "Ever one and the same"; unlike, I say, in this, that our action is so antagonistic to the State's action, and our claims so menacing to civil peace and prosperity.

Indeed! then I suppose that St. Ignatius of Antioch, and St. Polycarp of Smyrna, and St. Cyprian of Carthage, and St. Laurence of Rome, that St. Alexander and St. Paul of Constantinople, that St. Ambrose of Milan, that Popes Leo, John, Sylverian, Gregory, and Martin, all members of the "undivided Church," cared supremely and labored successfully to cultivate peaceful relations with the government of Rome. They had no doctrines and precepts, no rules of life, no isolation and aggressiveness, which caused them to be considered, in spite of themselves, the enemies of the human race! May I not, without disrespect, submit to Mr. Gladstone that this is very paradoxical? Surely it is our fidelity to the history of our forefathers, and not its repudiation, which Mr. Gladstone dislikes in us. When, indeed, was it in ancient times that the State did not show jealousy of the Church? Was it when Decius and Dioclesian slaughtered their thousands who had abjured the religion of old Rome? or was it when Athanasius was banished to Treves? or when Basil, on the imperial prefect's crying out, "Never before did any man before fell in with a Bishop"? or when Chrysostom was sent off to Cucusus, to be worried to death by an empress? Go through the long annals of Church History, century after century, and say, was there ever a time when her Bishops, and notably the Bishop of Rome, were slow to give their testimony in behalf of the moral and revealed law, and to suffer for their obedience to it? ever a time when they forgot that they had a message to deliver to the world—not the task merely of administering spiritual consolation, or of making the sick-bed easy, or of training up good members of society, or of "serving tables" (though all this was included in their range of duty)—but specially and directly, a definite message to high and low, from the world's Maker, whether men would hear or whether they would forbear? The history surely of the Church in all past times, ancient as well as mediæval, is the very embodiment of that tradition of Apostolical independence and freedom of speech which in the eyes of man is her great offence now.

Nay, that independence, I may say, is even one of her Notes or credentials; for where shall we find it except in the Catholic Church? "I spoke of Thy testimonies," says the Psalmist, "even before kings, and I was not ashamed." This verse, I think Dr. Arnold used to say, rose up in judgment against the Anglican Church, in spite of its real excellences. As to the Oriental Churches, every one knows in what bondage they lie, whether they are under the rule of the Czar or of the Sultan. Such is the actual fact that, whereas it is the very mission of Christianity to bear witness to the Creed and Ten Commandments in a world which is averse to them, Rome is now the one faithful representative, and thereby is heir and successor, of that free-spoken, dauntless Church of old, whose political and social traditions Mr. Gladstone says the said Rome has repudiated.

I have one thing more to say on the subject of the "semper eadem." In truth, this fidelity to the ancient Christian system, seen in modern Rome, was the luminous fact which more than any other turned men's minds at Oxford forty years ago to look towards her with reverence, interest, and love. It affected individual minds variously of course; some it even brought on eventually to conversion, others it only restrained from active opposition to her claims; but none of us could read the Fathers, and determine to be their disciples, without feeling that Rome, like a faithful steward, had kept in fulness and in vigor what our own communion had let drop. The Tracts for the Times were founded on a deadly antagonism to what in these last centuries has been called Erastianism or Cæsarism. Their writers considered the Church to be a divine creation, "not of men, neither by man, but by Jesus Christ," the Ark of Salvation, the Oracle of Truth, the Bride of Christ, with a message to all men everywhere, and a claim on their love and obedience; and, in relation to the civil power, the object of that promise of the Jewish prophets: "Behold, I will lift up My Hand to the Gentiles, and will set up My standard to the peoples: kings and their queens shall bow down to thee with their face toward the earth, and they shall lick up the dust of thy feet." No Ultramontane (so called) could go beyond those writers in the account which they gave of her from the Prophets, and that high notion is recorded beyond mistake in a thousand passages of their writings.

There is a fine passage of Mr. Keble's in the *British Critic*, in animadversion upon a contemporary reviewer. Mr. Hurrell Froude, speaking of the Church of England, had said that "she was 'united' to the State as Israel to Egypt." This shocked the reviewer in question, who exclaimed in consequence: "The Church is *not* united to the State as Israel to Egypt; it is united as a believing *wife* to a *husband* who threatened to apostatize; and, as a Christian wife so placed would act . . . clinging to the connection . . . so the Church must struggle even now, and save, not herself, but the State, from the crime of a *divorce*." On this Mr. Keble says: "We had thought that the Spouse of the Church was a very different Person from any or all States, and her relation to the State through him *very unlike that of hers, whose duties are summed up in ' love, service, cherishing, and obedience.'* And since the one is exclusively of this world, the other essentially of the eternal world, *such an Alliance* as the above sentence describes would have seemed to us, *not only fatal, but monstrous!*" \* And he quotes the lines—

> "Mortua quinetiam jungebat corpora vivis,
> Componens manibusque manus, atque oribus ora:
> Tormenti genus !"

It was this same conviction that the Church had rights which the State could not touch, and was prone to ignore, and which in consequence were the occasion of great troubles between the two, that led Mr. Froude at the beginning of the movement to translate the letters of St. Thomas Becket, and Mr. Bowden to write the Life of Hildebrand. As to myself, I will but refer, as to one out of many passages with the same drift, in the books and tracts which I published at that time, to my Whit-Monday and Whit-Tuesday Sermons.

I believe a large number of members of the Church

\* Review of Gladstone's " The State in its Relations with the Church," October, 1839.

of England at this time are faithful to the doctrine which was proclaimed within its pale in 1833, and following years; the main difference between them and Catholics being, not as to the existence of certain high prerogatives and spiritual powers in the Christian Church, but that the powers which we give to the Holy See, they lodge in her Bishops and Priests, whether as a body or individually. Of course, this is a very important difference, but it does not interfere with my argument here. It does seem to me preposterous to charge the Catholic Church of to-day with repudiating ancient history by certain political acts of hers, and thereby losing her identity, when it was her very likeness in political action to the Church of the first centuries that has in our time attracted even to her communion, and at least to her teaching, not a few educated men, who made those first centuries their special model.

But I have more to say on this subject, perhaps too much, when I go on, as I now do, to contemplate the Christian Church, when persecution was exchanged for establishment, and her enemies became her children. As she resisted and defied her persecutors, so she ruled her convert people. And surely this was but natural, and will startle those only to whom the subject is new. If the Church is independent of the State, so far as she is a messenger from God, therefore, should the State, with its high officials and its subject masses, come into her communion, it is plain that they must at once change hostility into submission. There was no middle term; either they must deny her claim to divinity or humble themselves before it—that is, as far as the domain of religion extends, and that domain is a wide

We see this principle carried out among themselves in all sects every day, though with greater or less exactness of application, according to the supernatural power which they ascribe to their ministers or clergy. It is a sentiment of nature, which anticipates the inspired command, "Obey them that have the rule over you, and submit yourselves, for they watch for your souls."

As regards the Roman emperors, immediately on their becoming Christians, their exaltation of the hierarchy was in proportion to its abject condition in the heathen period. Grateful converts felt that they could not do too much in its honor and service. Emperors bowed the head before the Bishops, kissed their hands and asked their blessing. When Constantine entered into the presence of the assembled Prelates at Nicæa his eyes fell, the color mounted up into his cheek, and his mien was that of a suppliant; he would not sit till the Bishops bade him, and he kissed the wounds of the Confessors. Thus he set the example for the successors of his power, nor did the Bishops decline such honors. Royal ladies served them at table; victorious generals did penance for sin and asked forgiveness. When they quarrelled with them, and would banish them, their hand trembled when they came to sign the order, and after various attempts they gave up their purpose. Soldiers raised to sovereignty asked their recognition and were refused it. Cities under imperial displeasure sought their intervention, and the master of thirty legions found himself powerless to withstand the feeble voice of some aged, travel-stained stranger.

Laws were passed in favor of the Church; Bishops could only be judged by Bishops, and the causes of their clergy were withdrawn from the secular courts. Their sentence was final, as if it were the emperor's own, and the governors of provinces were bound to put it in execution. Litigants everywhere were allowed the liberty of referring their causes to the tribunal of the Bishops, who, besides, became arbitrators on a large scale in private quarrels; and the public, even heathens, wished it so. St. Ambrose was sometimes so taken up with business of this sort, that he had time for nothing else. St. Austin and Theodoret both complain of the weight of such secular engagements as were forced upon them by the importunity of the people. Nor was this all; the emperors showed their belief in the divinity of the Church and of its creed by acts of what we should now call persecution. Jews were forbidden to proselytize a Christian; Christians were forbidden to become pagans; pagan rites were abolished; the books of heretics and infidels were burned wholesale; their chapels were razed to the ground, and even their private meetings were made illegal.

These characteristics of the convert Empire were the immediate, some of them the logical, consequences of its new faith. Had not the emperors honored Christianity in its ministers and in its precepts, they would not properly have deserved the name of converts. Nor was it unreasonable in litigants voluntarily to frequent the episcopal tribunals, if they got justice done to them there better than in the civil courts. As to the prohibition of heretical meetings, I cannot get myself quite to believe that Pagans, Marcionites, and Manichees had much tenderness of conscience in their religious profession, or were wounded seriously by the imperial rescripts to their disadvantage. Many of these sects were of a most immoral character, whether in doctrine or practice; others were forms of witchcraft; often they were little better than paganism. The Novatians would be most unjust to class such wild, impure, inhuman rites with even the most extravagant and grotesque of American sectaries now. They could entertain no bitter feeling that injustice was done them in their repression. They did not make free thought or private judgment their watch-words. The populations of the Empire did not rise in revolt when its religion was changed. There were two broad conditions which accompanied the grant of all this ecclesiastical power and privilege, and made the exercise of it possible; first, that the people consented to it; secondly, that the law of the Empire enacted and enforced it. Thus high and low opened the door to it. The Church of course would say that such prerogatives were justly hers, as being at least congruous grants made to her, on the part of the State, in return for the benefits which she bestowed upon it. It was her right to demand them, and the State's duty to concede them. This seems to have been the basis of the new state of society. And in fact these prerogatives were in force and in exercise all through those troublous centuries which followed the break-up of the Imperial sway; and, though the handling of them at length fell into the hands of one see exclusively (on which I shall remark presently), the See of Peter, yet the substance and character of these prerogatives, and the Church's claim to possess them, remained untouched. The change in the internal allocation of power did not affect the existence and the use of the power itself.

Ranke, speaking of this development of ecclesiastical supremacy upon the conversion of the Empire, remarks as follows:

"It appears to me that this was the result of an internal necessity. The rise of Christianity involved the liberation of religion from all political elements.

From this followed the growth of a distinct ecclesiastical class with a peculiar constitution. In this separation of the Church from the State consists perhaps the greatest, the most pervading and influential, peculiarity of all Christian times. The spiritual and secular powers may come into near contact, may even stand in the closest community; but they can be thoroughly incorporated only at rare conjunctures and for a short period. Their mutual relations, their positions with regard to each other, form, from this time forward, one of the most important considerations in all history" (*The Popes*, vol. i. p. 10, *translation*).

# CHAPTER III.

## THE CHRISTIAN CHURCH IS HISTORICALLY PAPAL.

IF CHRIST FOUNDED A VISIBLE SOCIETY IT HAS CEASED TO EXIST, OR IT IS THE CHURCH IN COMMUNION WITH ROME.—THE OBJECTION TO THE POPE'S INDEPENDENCE WOULD APPLY TO ANY CHURCH CLAIMING DIVINE AUTHORITY.—NECESSITY OF A HIGH DEVELOPMENT OF PAPAL POWER FOR THE CIVILIZATION OF MODERN EUROPE.—TESTIMONY OF DEAN MILMAN, AND OF ALISON.—REFLECTIONS ON THE PAPAL POWER IN RELATION TO PRESENT CIVIL AND RELIGIOUS CONDITIONS.

NOW we come to the distinctive doctrine of the Catholic Religion, the doctrine which separates us from all other denominations of Christians, however near they may approach to us in other respects, the claims of the See of Rome, which have given occasion to Mr. Gladstone's pamphlet and to the remarks which I am now making upon it. Of those rights, prerogatives, privileges, and duties, which I have been surveying in the ancient Church, the Pope is historically the heir. I shall dwell now upon this point, as far as it is to my purpose to do so, not treating it theologically (else I must define and prove from Scripture and the Fathers the "Primatus jure divino Romani Pontificis," which of course I firmly hold), but historically,\* because Mr.

---

\* History never serves as the measure of dogmatic truth in its fulness.—*Vid. infr.* § 8.

Gladstone appeals to history. Instead of treating it theologically I wish to look with (as it were) secular, or even non-Catholic, eyes at the powers claimed during the last thousand years by the Pope—that is, only as they lie in the nature of the case, and on the surface of the facts which come before us in history.

1. I say the Pope is the heir of the Ecumenical Hierarchy of the fourth century, as being, what I may call, heir by default. No one else claims or exercises its rights or its duties. Is it possible to consider the Patriarch of Moscow or of Constantinople heir to the historical pretensions of St. Ambrose or St Martin? Does any Anglican Bishop for the last 300 years recall to our minds the image of St. Basil? Well, then, has all that ecclesiastical power, which makes such a show in the Christian Empire, simply vanished, or, if not, where is it to be found? I wish Protestants would throw themselves into our minds upon this point; I am not holding an argument with them; I am only wishing them to understand where we stand and how we look at things. There is this great difference of belief between us and them: they do not believe that Christ set up a visible society, or rather kingdom, for the propagation and maintenance of His religion, for a necessary home and a refuge for His people; but we do. We know the kingdom is still on earth: where is it? If all that can be found of it is what can be discerned at Constantinople or Canterbury, I say it has disappeared; and either there was a radical corruption of Christianity from the first, or Christianity came to an end, in proportion as the type of the Nicene Church faded out of the world: for all that we know of Christianity, in ancient history, as a concrete fact, is the Church of Athanasius and his

bundle of phenomena, that combination of claims, prerogatives, and corresponding acts, some of which I have recounted above. There is no help for it then; we cannot take as much as we please, and no more, of an institution which has a monadic existence. We must either give up the belief in the Church as a divine institution altogether, or we must recognize it at this day in that communion of which the Pope is the head. With him alone and round about him are found the claims, the prerogatives and duties which we identify with the kingdom set up by Christ. We must take things as they are; to believe in a Church, is to believe in the Pope. And thus this belief in the Pope and his attributes, which seems so monstrous to Protestants, is bound up with our being Catholics at all; as our Catholicism is bound up with our Christianity. There is nothing then of wanton opposition to the powers that be, no dinning of novelties in their startled ears in what is often unjustly called Ultramontane doctrine; there is no pernicious servility to the Pope in our admission of his pretensions. I say, we cannot help ourselves—Parliament may deal as harshly with us as it will; we should not believe in the Church at all, unless we believe in its visible head.

So it is; the course of ages has fulfilled the prophecy and promise, "Thou art Peter, and upon this rock I will build My Church; and whatsoever thou shalt bind on earth shall be bound in heaven, and whatsoever thou shalt loose on earth shall be loosed in heaven." That which in substance was possessed by the Nicene Hierarchy, that the Pope claims now. I do not wish to put difficulties in my way: but I cannot conceal or smooth over what I believe to be a simple truth, though the avowal of it will be very unwelcome to Protestants, and, as I fear, to some Catholics. However, I do not call upon another to believe all that I believe on the subject myself. I declare it, as my own judgment, that the prerogatives, such as, and in the way in which, I have described them in substance, which the Church had under the Roman power, those she claims now, and never, never will relinquish; claims them, not as having received them from a dead Empire, but partly by the direct endowment of her Divine Master, and partly as being a legitimate outcome of that endowment; claims them, but not except from Catholic populations, not as if accounting the more sublime of them to be of every-day use, but holding them as a protection or remedy in great emergencies or on supreme occasions, when nothing else will serve, as extraordinary and solemn acts of her religious sovereignty. And our Lord, seeing what would be brought about by human means, even had He not willed it, and recognizing, from the laws which He Himself had imposed upon human society, that no large community could be strong which had no head, spoke the word in the beginning, as he did to Judah, "Thou art he whom thy brethren shall praise," and then left it to the course of events to fulfil it.

2. Mr. Gladstone ought to have chosen another issue for attack upon us than the Pope's special power. His real difficulty lies deeper; as little permission as he allows to the Pope, would he allow to any ecclesiastic who would wield the weapons of St. Ambrose and St. Augustine. That concentration of the Church's powers which history brings before us ought not to be the simple object of his indignation. It is not the existence of a Pope, but of a Church, which is his aversion. It is the powers themselves, and not their distribution and allocation in the ecclesiastical body, which he writes against. A triangle is the same in its substance and

nature, whichever side is made its base. "The
Pontiffs," says Mr. Bowden, who writes as an Anglican, "exalted to the kingly throne of St. Peter, did not
so much claim new privileges for themselves, as deprive their episcopal brethren of privileges originally
common to the hierarchy. Even the titles by which
those autocratical prelates in the plenitude of their power delighted to style themselves, 'Summus Sacerdos,'
'Pontifex Maximus,' 'Vicarius Christi,' 'Papa' itself,
had, nearer to the primitive times, been the honorable
appellations of every bishop; as 'Sedes Apostolica'
had been the description of every bishop's throne.
The ascription of these titles, therefore, to the Pope only
gave to the terms new force, because that ascription
became exclusive; because, that is, the bishops in
general were stripped of honors to which their claims
were as well founded as those of their Roman brother,
who became, by the change, not so strictly universal as
sole Bishop" (*Greg. VII.*, vol. i. p. 64).

Say that the Christian polity now remained as history represents it to us in the fourth century, or that
it was, if that were possible, now to revert to such
a state, would politicians have less trouble with
eighteen hundred centres of power than they have
with one? Instead of one, with traditionary rules, the
trammels of treaties and engagements, public opinion to
consult and manage, the responsibility of great interests, and the guarantee for his behavior in his temporal
possessions, there would be a legion of ecclesiastics,
each bishop with his following, each independent of the
others, each with his own views, each with extraordinary powers, each with the risk of misusing them, all
over Christendom. It would be the Anglican theory
made real. It would be an ecclesiastical communism;
and, if it did not benefit religion, at least it would

not benefit the civil power. Take a small illustration: what interruption at this time to Parliamentary proceedings does a small, zealous party occasion, which its enemies call a mere "handful of clergy"; and why? Because its members are responsible for what they do to God alone and to their conscience as His voice. Even suppose it was only here or there that episcopal autonomy was vigorous; yet consider what zeal is kindled by local interests and national spirit. One John of Tuam, with a Pope's full Apostolic powers, would be a greater trial to successive ministries than an Ecumenical Bishop at Rome. Parliament understands this well, for it exclaims against the sacerdotal principle. Here, for a second reason, if our divine Master has given those great powers to the Church, which ancient Christianity testifies, we see why His Providence has also brought it about that the exercise of them should be concentrated in one see.

But, anyhow, the progress of concentration was not the work of the Pope; it was brought about by the changes of times and the vicissitudes of nations. It was not his fault that the Vandals swept away the African sees, and the Saracens those of Syria and Asia Minor, or that Constantinople and its dependencies became the creatures of Imperialism, or that France, England, and Germany would obey none but the author of their own Christianity, or that clergy and people at a distance were obstinate in sheltering themselves under the majesty of Rome against their own fierce kings and nobles or imperious bishops, even to the imposing forgeries on the world and on the Pope in justification of their proceedings. All this will be fact, whether the Popes were ambitious or not; and still it will be fact that the issue of that great change was a great benefit to the whole of Europe. No one but a master, who was a thousand bishops in himself at once, could have tamed and controlled, as the Pope did, the great and little tyrants of the middle age.

3. This is generally confessed now, even by Protestant historians, viz., that the concentration of ecclesiastical power in those centuries was simply necessary for the civilization of Europe. Of course it does not follow that the benefits rendered then to the European commonwealth by the political supremacy of the Pope, would, if he was still supreme, be rendered in time to come. I have no wish to make assumptions; yet conclusions short of this will be unfavorable to Mr. Gladstone's denunciation of him. We reap the fruit at this day of his services in the past. With the purpose of showing this I make a rather long extract from Dean Milman's *Latin Christianity;* he is speaking of the era of Gregory I., and he says, the Papacy "was the only power which lay not entirely and absolutely prostrate before the disasters of the times—a power which had an inherent strength, and might resume its majesty. It was this power which was most imperatively required to preserve all which was to survive out of the crumbling wreck of Roman civilization. To Western Christianity was absolutely necessary a centre, standing alone, strong in traditionary reverence, and in acknowledged claims to supremacy. Even the perfect organization of the Christian hierarchy might in all human probability have fallen to pieces in perpetual conflict: it might have degenerated into a half-secular feudal caste, with hereditary benefices more and more entirely subservient to the civil authority, a priesthood of each nation or each tribe, gradually sinking to the intellectual or religious level of the nation or tribe. On the rise of a power both controlling and conservative hung, humanly speaking, the life and death of Chris-

tianity—of Christianity as a permanent, aggressive, expansive, and, to a certain extent, uniform system. There must be a counterbalance to barbaric force, to the unavoidable anarchy of Teutonism, with its tribal, or at the utmost national independence, forming a host of small, conflicting, antagonistic kingdoms. All Europe would have been what England was under the Octarchy, what Germany was when her emperors were weak; and even her emperors she owed to Rome, to the Church, to Christianity. Providence might have otherwise ordained; but it is impossible for man to imagine by what other organizing or consolidating force the commonwealth of the Western nations could have grown up to a discordant, indeed, and conflicting league, but still a league, with that unity and conformity of manners, usages, laws, religion, which have made their rivalries, oppugnancies, and even their long ceaseless wars, on the whole to issue in the noblest, highest, most intellectual form of civilization known to man. . . . It is impossible to conceive what had been the confusion, the lawlessness, the chaotic state of the middle ages, without the mediæval Papacy; and of the mediæval Papacy the real father is Gregory the Great. In all his predecessors there was much of the uncertainty and indefiniteness of a new dominion. . . . Gregory is the Roman altogether merged in the Christian Bishop. It is a Christian dominion of which he lays the foundations in the Eternal City, not the old Rome, associating Christian influence to her ancient title of sovereignty" (vol. i. pp. 401, 402).

4. From Gregory I. to Innocent III. is six hundred years; a very fair portion of the world's history, to have passed in doing good of primary importance to a whole continent, and that the continent of Europe;

statesmen and legislatures, are the gainers. And, again, should it not occur to Mr. Gladstone that these services were rendered to mankind by means of those very instruments of power on which he thinks it proper to pour contempt as "rusty tools"? The right to warn and punish powerful men, to excommunicate kings, to preach aloud truth and justice to the inhabitants of the earth, to denounce immoral doctrines, to strike at rebellion in the garb of heresy, were the very weapons by which Europe was brought into a civilized condition; yet he calls them "rusty tools" which need "refurbishing." Does he wish then that such high expressions of ecclesiastical displeasure, such sharp penalties, should be of daily use? If they are rusty, because they have been long without using, then have they ever been rusty. Is a Council a rusty tool, because none had been held, till 1870, since the sixteenth century? or because there have been but nineteen in 1900 years? How many times is it in the history of Christianity that the Pope has solemnly drawn and exercised his sword upon a king or an emperor? If an extraordinary weapon must be a rusty tool, I suppose Gregory VII.'s sword was not keen enough for the German Henry; and the seventh Pius too used a rusty tool in his excommunication of Napoleon. How could Mr. Gladstone ever "fondly think that Rome had disused" her weapons, and that they had hung up as antiquities and curiosities in her celestial armory, or, in his own words, as "hideous mummies" (p. 46)—when the passage of arms between the great Conqueror and the aged Pope was so close upon his memory! Would he like to see a mummy come to life again? That unexpected miracle actually took place in the first years of this century. Gregory was considered to have done an astounding deed in the middle ages when he brought

Henry, the German Emperor, to do penance and shiver in the snow at Canossa; but Napoleon had his snow-penance too, and that with an actual interposition of Providence in the infliction of it. I describe it in the words of Alison:

"'What does the Pope mean,' said Napoleon to Eugene, in July, 1807, 'by the threat of excommunicating me? Does he think the world has gone back a thousand years? does he suppose the arms will fall from the hands of my soldiers?'" Within two years after these remarkable words were written the Pope did excommunicate him, in return for the confiscation of his whole dominions, and in less than four years more the arms did fall from the hands of his soldiers; and the hosts, apparently invincible, which he had collected were dispersed and ruined by the blasts of winter. 'The weapons of the soldiers,' says Segur, in describing the Russian retreat, 'appeared of an insupportable weight to their stiffened arms. During their frequent falls they fell from their hands, and destitute of the power of raising them from the ground, they were left in the snow. They did not throw them away: famine and cold tore them from their grasp.' 'The soldiers could no longer hold their weapons,' says Salgues, 'they fell from the hands even of the bravest and most robust. The muskets dropped from the frozen arms of those who bore them'" (*Hist.*, ch. lx. 9th ed.)

Alison adds: "There is something in these marvellous coincidences beyond the operations of chance, and which even a Protestant historian feels himself bound to mark for the observation of future ages. The world had not gone back a thousand years, but that Being existed with whom a thousand years are as one day, and one day as a thousand years." As He was with will be with some future Pope again, when the necessity shall come.

5. In saying this, I am far from saying that Popes are never in the wrong, and are never to be resisted; or that their excommunications always avail. I am not bound to defend the policy or the acts of particular Popes, whether before or after the great revolt from their authority in the sixteenth century. There is no reason that I should contend, and I do not contend, for instance, that they at all times have understood our own people, our natural character and resources, and our position in Europe; or that they have never suffered from bad counsellors or misinformation. I say this the more freely because Urban VIII., about the year 1641 or 1642, seems to have blamed the policy of some Popes of the preceding century in their dealings with our country.*

But, whatever we are bound to allow to Mr. Gladstone on this head, that does not warrant the passionate invective against the Holy See and us individually, which he has carried on through sixty-four pages. What we have a manifest right to expect from him is lawyer-like exactness and logical consecutiveness in his impeachment of us. The heavier that is, the less does it need the exaggerations of a great orator. If the Pope's conduct towards us three centuries ago has righteously wiped out the memory of his earlier benefits, yet

---

* "When he was urged to excommunicate the Kings of France and Sweden, he made answer, 'We may declare them excommunicate, as Pius V. declared Queen Elizabeth of England, and before him Clement VII., the King of England, Henry VIII., . . . but with what success? The whole world can tell. We yet bewail it with tears of blood. Wisdom does not teach us to imitate Pius V. or Clement VII., but Paul V., who, in the beginning, being many times urged by the Spaniards to excommunicate James, King of England, never would consent to it'" (State Paper Office, *Italy*, 1641-1662). *Vide* Mr. Simpson's very able and careful life of Campion, 1867, p. 371.

he should have a fair trial. The more intoxicating was his solitary greatness, when it was in the zenith, the greater consideration should be shown towards him in his present temporal humiliation, when concentration of ecclesiastical functions in one man does but make him, in the presence of the haters of Catholicism, what a Roman Emperor contemplated, when he wished all his subjects had but one neck that he might destroy them by one blow. Surely, in the trial of so august a criminal, one might have hoped, at least, to have found gravity and measure in language, and calmness in tone —not a pamphlet written as if on impulse, in defence of an incidental parenthesis in a previous publication, and then, after being multiplied in twenty-two thousand copies, appealing to the lower classes in the shape of a sixpenny tract, the lowness of the price indicating the width of the circulation. Surely Nana Sahib will have more justice done to him by the English people than has been shown to the Father of European civilization.

6. I have been referring to the desolate state in which the Holy See has been cast during the last years, such that the Pope, humanly speaking, is at the mercy of his enemies, and morally a prisoner in his palace. That state of secular feebleness cannot last for ever; sooner or later there will be, in the divine mercy, a change for the better, and the Vicar of Christ will no longer be a mark for insult and indignity. But one thing, except by an almost miraculous interposition, cannot be; and that is, a return to the universal religious sentiment, the public opinion, of the mediæval time. The Pope himself calls those centuries "the ages of faith." Such endemic faith may certainly be decreed for some future time; but, as far as we have the means of judging at present, centuries must run out first. Even in the fourth century the ecclesiastical privileges, claimed on

the one hand, granted on the other, came into effect more or less under two conditions, that they were recognized by public law, and that they had the consent of the Christian populations. Is there any chance whatever, except by miracles which were not granted then, that the public law and the inhabitants of Europe will allow the Pope that exercise of his rights which they allowed him as a matter of course in the eleventh and twelfth centuries? If the whole world will at once answer No, it is surely inopportune to taunt us this day with the acts of mediæval Popes towards certain princes and nobles, when the sentiment of Europe was radically Papal. How does the past bear upon the present in this matter? Yet Mr. Gladstone is in earnest alarm, earnest with the earnestness which distinguishes him as a statesman, at the harm which society may receive from the Pope, at a time when the Pope can do nothing. He grants (p. 46) that "the fears are visionary . . . that either foreign foe or domestic treason can, at the bidding of the Court of Rome, disturb these peaceful shores"; he allows that "in the middle ages the Popes contended, not by direct action of fleets and armies," but mainly "by interdicts" (p. 35). Yet, because men then believed in interdicts, though now they don't, therefore the civil Power is to be roused against the Pope. But his *animus* is bad; his *animus*! what can *animus* do without matter to work upon? Mere *animus*, like big words, breaks no bones.

As if to answer Mr. Gladstone by anticipation, and to allay his fears, the Pope made a declaration three years ago on the subject, which, strange to say, Mr. Gladstone quotes without perceiving that it tells against the very argument which he brings it to corroborate; that is except as the Pope's *animus* goes. Doubtless he which his predecessors had, because it was given to him by Providence, and is conducive to the highest interests of mankind; but he distinctly tells us in the declaration in question that he has not got it, and cannot have it, till a time comes, which we can speculate about as well as he, and which we say cannot come at least for centuries. He speaks of what is his highest political power, that of interposing in the quarrel between a prince and his subjects, and of declaring, upon appeal made to him from them, that the prince had or had not forfeited their allegiance. This power, most rarely exercised, and on very extraordinary occasions, it is not necessary for any Catholic to acknowledge; and I suppose, comparatively speaking, few Catholics do acknowledge it; to be honest, I may say I do; that is, under the conditions which the Pope himself lays down in the declaration to which I have referred, his answer to the address of the Academia. He speaks of his right "to depose sovereigns, and release the people from the obligation of loyalty, a right which had undoubtedly sometimes been exercised in crucial circumstances," and he says: "This right (*diritto*) in those ages of faith (which discerned in the Pope, what he is, that is to say, the Supreme Judge of Christianity, and recognized the advantages of his tribunal in the great contests of peoples and sovereigns) was freely extended—(aided indeed as a matter of duty by the public law (*diritto*) and by the common consent of peoples)—to the most important (*i più gravi*) interest of states and their rulers" (*Guardian*, Nov. 11, 1874).

Now let us observe how the Pope restrains the exercise of this right. He calls it his right—that is, in the sense in which right in one party is correlative with duty in the other, so that, when the duty is not observed, the right cannot be brought into exercise; and lays down the conditions of that exercise. First, it can only be exercised in rare and critical circumstances (*supreme circonstanze, i più gravi interessi*). Next he refers to his being the supreme judge of Christendom, and to his decision as coming from a tribunal; his prerogative then is not a mere arbitrary power, but must be exercised by a process of law and a formal examination of the case, and in the presence and the hearing of the two parties interested in it. Also in this limitation is implied that the Pope's definite sentence involves an appeal to the supreme standard of right and wrong, the moral law, as its basis and rule, and must contain the definite reasons on which it decides in favor of the one party or the other. Thirdly, the exercise of this right is limited to the ages of faith; ages which, on the one hand, inscribed it among the provisions of the *jus publicum*, and, on the other, so fully recognized the benefits it conferred as to be able to enforce it by the common consent of the peoples. These last words should be dwelt on: it is no consent which is merely local, as of one country, of Ireland or of Belgium, if that were probable; but a united consent of various nations of Europe, for instance, as a commonwealth, of which the Pope was the head. Thirty years ago we heard much of the Pope being made the head of an Italian confederation: no word came from England against such an arrangement. It was possible, because the members of it were all of one religion; and in like manner a European commonwealth would be reasonable, if Europe were of one religion. Lastly, the Pope declares with indignation that a Pope is not infallible in the exercise of this right; such a notion is an invention of the enemy; he calls it "malicious."

What is there in all this to arouse the patriotic anxieties of Mr. Gladstone?

# CHAPTER IV.

## DIVIDED ALLEGIANCE.

OBEDIENCE TO SPIRITUAL GUIDES AS TAUGHT IN SCRIPTURE.—COMPARISON BETWEEN THE INTERFERENCE OF CIVIL AND OF RELIGIOUS AUTHORITY IN DAILY LIFE.—ESSENTIAL DIFFERENCE BETWEEN CONTROL OF *every* ACT AND OF *any* ACT.—CONTROL OF THE POPE COMPARED WITH THAT OF A PHYSICIAN, OF PUBLIC OPINION, OR OF THE PRESS.—THE POPE'S POWER EXISTS TO AID RELIGION.—DISPUTES BETWEEN THE POPE AND THE NATION CONSIDERED.—CASES SUPPOSED IN WHICH CATHOLICS WOULD OBEY THE POPE AGAINST THE LAW OF THE STATE.—CASES IN WHICH THEY WOULD DISOBEY THE POPE AND OBEY THE STATE.—THEOLOGIANS CITED TO PROVE THAT IT IS SOMETIMES LAWFUL TO DISOBEY THE POPE.

BUT one attribute the Church has, and the Pope as head of the Church, whether he be in high estate, as this world goes, or not, whether he has temporal possessions or not, whether he is in honor or dishonor, whether he is at home or driven about, whether those special claims of which I have spoken are allowed or not,—and that is Sovereignty. As God has sovereignty, though He may be disobeyed or disowned, so has His Vicar upon earth; and farther than this, since Catholic populations are found everywhere, he ever will be in fact lord of a vast empire; as large in numbers, as far spreading as the British; and all his acts are sure to be such as are in keeping with the position of one who is thus supremely exalted.

I beg not to be interrupted here, as many a reader will interrupt me in his thoughts, for I am using these words, not at random, but as the commencement of a long explanation, and, in a certain sense, limitation, of what I have hitherto been saying concerning the Church's and the Pope's power. To this task the remaining pages will be directed; and I trust that it will turn out, when I come to the end of them, that, by first stating fully what the Pope's claims are, I shall be able most clearly to show what he does not claim.

Now the main point of Mr. Gladstone's pamphlet is this: that, since the Pope claims infallibility in faith and morals, and since there are no "departments and functions of human life which do not and cannot fall within the domain of morals" (p. 36), and since he claims also "the domain of all that concerns the government and discipline of the Church," and moreover "claims the power of determining the limits of those domains," and "does not sever them, by any acknowledged or intelligible line, from the domains of civil duty and allegiance" (p. 45), therefore Catholics are moral and mental slaves, and "every convert and member of the Pope's Church places his loyalty and civil duty at the mercy of another" (p. 45).

I admit Mr. Gladstone's premises, but I reject his conclusion; and now I am going to show why I reject it.

In doing this I shall, with him, put aside for the present and at first the Pope's prerogative of infallibility in general enunciations, whether of faith or morals, and confine myself to the consideration of his authority (in respect to which he is not infallible) in matters of conduct, and of our duty of obedience to him. "There is something wider still," he says (than the claim of infallibility), "and that is the claim to an Absolute and entire Obedience" (p. 37). "Little does it matter to me whether my Superior claims infallibility, so long as he is entitled to demand and exact conformity" (p. 39). He speaks of a third province being opened, "not indeed to the abstract assertion of Infallibility, but to the far more practical and decisive demand of Absolute Obedience" (p. 41), "the Absolute Obedience, at the peril of salvation, of every member of his communion" (p. 42).

Now, I proceed to examine this large, direct, religious sovereignty of the Pope, both in its relation to his subjects and to the Civil Power; but first, I beg to be allowed to say just one word on the principle of obedience itself, that is, by way of inquiring whether it is or is not now a religious duty.

Is there then such a duty at all as obedience to ecclesiastical authority now? or, is it one of those obsolete ideas, which are swept away, as unsightly cobwebs, by the New Civilization? Scripture says: "Remember them which have the *rule* over you, who have spoken unto you the word of God, whose faith follow." And, "*Obey* them that have the *rule* over you, and *submit yourselves;* for they watch *for your souls* as they that must give account, that they may do it with joy and not with grief; for that is unprofitable for you." The margin in the Protestant Version reads, "those who are your *guides*"; and the word may also be translated "leaders." Well, as rulers, or guides and leaders, whichever word be right, they are to be *obeyed*. Now Mr. Gladstone dislikes our way of fulfilling this precept; whether as regards our choice of ruler and leader, or our "Absolute Obedience" to him; but he does not give us his own. Is there any liberalistic reading of the Scripture passage? Or are the words only for the benefit of the poor and ignorant, not for the *Schola* (as it may be called) of political and periodical writers, not for individual members of Parliament, not for statesmen and cabinet ministers, and people of Progress? Which party then is the more "Scriptural," those who recognize and carry out in their conduct texts like these, or those who don't? May not we Catholics claim some mercy from Mr. Gladstone, though we be faulty in the object and the manner of our obedience, since in a lawless day an object and a manner of obedience we have? Can we be blamed, if, arguing from those texts which say that ecclesiastical authority comes from above, we obey it in that one form in which alone we find it on earth, in that one person who, of all the notabilities of this nineteenth century into which we have been born, alone claims it of us? The Pope has no rival in his claim upon us; nor is it our doing that his claim has been made and allowed for centuries upon centuries, and that it was he who made the Vatican decrees, and not they him. If we give him up, to whom shall we go? Can we dress up any civil functionary in the vestments of divine authority? Can I, for instance, follow the faith, can I put my soul into the hands, of our gracious Sovereign? or of the Archbishop of Canterbury? or of the Bishop of Lincoln, albeit he is not broad and low, but high? Catholics have "done what they could"—all that any one could: and it should be Mr. Gladstone's business before telling us that we are slaves, because we obey the Pope, first of all to tear away those texts from the Bible.

With this preliminary remark, I proceed to consider whether the Pope's authority is either a slavery to his subjects, or a menace to the Civil Power; and first, as to his power over his flock.

1. Mr. Gladstone says that "the Pontiff declares to belong to him the *supreme direction* of Catholics in respect to all duty" (p. 37). Supreme direction; true, but "supreme" is not "minute," nor does "direction" mean "supervision" or "management." Take the parallel of human law; the Law is *supreme*, and the Law *directs* our conduct under the manifold circumstances in which we have to act, and may and must be absolutely obeyed; but who therefore says that the Law has the "supreme direction" of us? The State, as well as the Church, has the power at its will of imposing laws upon us, laws bearing on our moral duties, our daily conduct, affecting our actions in various ways, and circumscribing our liberties; yet no one would say that the Law, after all, with all its power in the abstract and its executive vigor in fact, interferes either with our comfort or our conscience. There are numberless laws about property, landed and personal, titles, tenures, trusts, wills, convenants, contracts, partnerships, money transactions, life-insurances, taxes, trade, navigation, education sanitary measures, trespasses, nuisances, all in addition to the criminal law. Law, to apply Mr. Gladstone's words, "is the shadow that cleaves to us, go where we will." Moreover, it varies year after year, and refuses to give any pledge of fixedness or finality. Nor can any one tell what restraint is to come next, perhaps painful personally to himself. Nor are its enactments easy of interpretation; for actual cases, with the opinions and speeches of counsel, and the decisions of judges, must prepare the raw material, as it proceeds from the Legislature, before it can be rightly understood; so that "the glorious uncertainty of the Law" has become a proverb. And, after all, no one is sure of escaping its

such private and personal matters that the lawyers are, as by an imperative duty, bound to a secrecy which even courts of justice respect. And then, besides the Statute Law, there is the common and traditional; and, below this, usage. Is not all this enough to try the temper of a free-born Englishman, and to make him cry out with Mr. Gladstone, "Three-fourths of my life are handed over to the Law; I care not to ask if there be dregs or tatters of human life, such as can escape from the description and boundary of Parliamentary tyranny?" Yet, though we may dislike it, though we may at times suffer from it ever so much, who does not see that the thraldom and irksomeness is nothing compared with the great blessings which the Constitution and Legislature secure to us?

Such is the jurisdiction which the Law exercises over us. What rule does the Pope claim which can be compared to its strong and its long arm? What interference with our liberty of judging and acting in our daily work, in our course of life, comes to us from him? Really, at first sight, I have not known where to look for instances of his actual interposition in our private affairs, for it is our routine of personal duties about which I am now speaking. Let us see how we stand in this matter.

We are guided in our ordinary duties by the books of moral theology, which are drawn up by theologians of authority and experience, as an instruction for our Confessors. These books are based on the three Christain foundations of Faith, Hope, and Charity, on the Ten Commandments, and on the six Precepts of the Church, which relate to the observance of Sunday, of fast days, of confession and communion, and, in one shape or other, to paying tithes. A great number of possible cases are noted under these heads, and in difficult questions a variety of opinions are given, with plain directions, when it is that private Catholics are at liberty to choose for themselves whatever answer they like best, and when they are bound to follow some one of them in particular. Reducible as these directions in detail are to the few and simple heads which I have mentioned, they are little more than reflections and memoranda of our moral sense, unlike the positive enactments of the Legislature; and, on the whole, present to us no difficulty—though now and then some critical question may arise, and some answer may be given (just as by the private conscience itself) which it is difficult to us or painful to accept. And again, cases may occur now and then, when our private judgment differs from what is set down in theological works, but even then it does not follow at once that our private judgment must give way, for those books are no utterance of Papal authority.

And this is the point to which I am coming. So little does the Pope come into this whole system of moral theology by which (as by our conscience) our lives are regulated, that the weight of his hand upon us, as private men, is absolutely unappreciable. I have had a difficulty where to find a measure or gauge of his interposition. At length I have looked through Busenbaum's *Medulla*, to ascertain what light such a book would throw upon the question. It is a book of casuistry for the use of Confessors, running to 700 pages, and is a large repository of answers made by various theologians on points of conscience, and generally of duty. It was first published in 1645—my own edition is of 1844—and in this latter are marked those propositions, bearing on subjects treated in it, which have been condemned by Popes in the intermediate two hundred years. On turning over the pages I find they are in all between fifty and sixty. This list includes matters sacramental, ritual, ecclesiastical, monastic, and disciplinarian, as well as moral—relating to the duties of ecclesiastics and regulars, of parish priests, and of professional men, as well as of private Catholics. And these condemnations relate for the most part to mere occasional details of duty, and are in reprobation of the lax or wild notions of speculative casuists, so that they are rather restraints upon theologians than upon laymen. For instance, the following are some of the propositions condemned: "The ecclesiastic who on a certain day is hindered from saying Matins and Lauds, is not bound to say, if he can, the remaining hours"; "Where there is good cause, it is lawful to swear without the purpose of swearing, whether the matter is of light or grave moment"; "Domestics may steal from their masters, in compensation for their service, which they think greater than their wages"; "It is lawful for a public man to kill an opponent, who tries to fasten a calumny upon him, if he cannot otherwise escape the ignominy." I have taken these instances at random. It must be granted, I think, that in the long course of two hundred years the amount of the Pope's authoritative enunciations has not been such as to press heavily on the back of the private Catholic. He leaves us surely far more than that "one-fourth of the department of conduct" which Mr. Gladstone allows us. Indeed, if my account and specimens of his sway over us in morals be correct, I do not see what he takes away at all from our private consciences.

But here Mr. Gladstone will object, that the Pope does really exercise a claim over the whole domain of conduct, inasmuch as he refuses to draw any line across it in limitation of his interference, and *therefore* it is that we are his slaves: let us see if another illustration or parallel will not show this to be a *non sequitur*. Suppose a man, who is in the midst of various and important lines of business, has a medical adviser, in whom he has full confidence, as knowing well his constitution. This adviser keeps a careful and anxious eye upon him; and, as an honest man, says to him, "You must not go off on a journey to-day," or, "You must take some days' rest," or "You must attend to your diet." Now, this is not a fair parallel to the Pope's hold upon us; for the Pope does not speak to us personally, but to all, and, in speaking definitively on ethical subjects, what he propounds must relate to things good and bad in themselves, not to things accidental, changeable, and of mere expedience; so that the argument which I am drawing from the case of a medical adviser is *à fortiori* in its character. However, I say that though a medical man exercises a "supreme direction" over those who put themselves under him, yet we do not therefore say, even of him, that he interferes with our daily conduct, and that we are his slaves. He certainly does thwart many of our wishes and purposes; and in a true sense we are at his mercy: he may interfere any day, suddenly; he will not, he cannot, draw any intelligible line between the acts which he has a right to forbid us, and the acts which he has not. The same journey, the same press of business, the same indulgence at table, which he passes over one year, he sternly forbids the next. Therefore if Mr. Gladstone's argument is good, he has a finger in all the commercial transactions of the great trader or financier who has chosen him. But surely there is a simple fallacy here. Mr. Gladstone asks us whether our political and civil life is not at the Pope's mercy; every act, he says, of at least three-quarters of the day, is under his control. No, not *every*, but *any*, and this is all the difference—that is, we have no guarantee given us that there will never be a case when the Pope's general utterances may come to have a bearing upon some personal act of ours. In the same way we are all of us in this age under the control of public opinion and the public prints; nay, much more intimately so. Journalism can be and is very personal; and, when it is in the right, more powerful just now than any Pope; yet we do not go into fits, as if we were slaves, because we are under a *surveillance* much more like tyranny than any sway so indirect, so practically limited, so gentle, as his is.

But it seems the cardinal point of our slavery lies, not simply in the domain of morals, but in the Pope's general authority over us in all things whatsoever. This count in his indictment Mr. Gladstone founds on a passage in the third chapter of the *Pastor æternus*, in which the Pope, speaking of the Pontifical jurisdiction, says: "Towards it (erga quam) pastors and people of whatsoever rite or dignity, each and all, are bound by the duty of hierarchical subordination and true obedience, not only in matters which pertain to faith and morals, but also in those which pertain to the *discipline* and the *regimen* of the Church spread throughout the world; so that, unity with the Roman Pontiff (both of communion and of profession of the same faith) being preserved, the Church of Christ may be one flock under one supreme Shepherd. This is the doctrine of Catholic truth, from which no one can deviate without loss of faith and salvation."

On Mr. Gladstone's use of this passage I observe first, that he leaves out a portion of it which has much to do with the due understanding of it (ita ut custoditâ, etc.) Next, he speaks of "*absolute* obedience" so often, that any reader, who had not the passage before him, would think that the word "absolute" was the Pope's word, not his. Thirdly, three times (at pp. 38, 41, and 42) does he make the Pope say that no one can *disobey* him without risking his salvation, whereas what the Pope does say is, that no one can *disbelieve* the *duty* of obedience and unity without such risk. And fourthly, in order to carry out this false sense, or rather to hinder its being evidently impossible, he mistranslates, p. 38, "doctrina" (Hæc est doctrina) by the word "rule."

But his chief attack is directed to the words "disciplina" and "regimen." "Thus," he says, "are swept into the Papal net whole multitudes of facts, whole systems of government, prevailing, though in different degrees, in every country of the world" (p. 41). That is, *disciplina* and *regimen* are words of such lax, vague, indeterminate meaning, that under them any matters can be slipped in, which may be required for the Pope's purpose in this or that country, such as, to take Mr. Gladstone's instances, blasphemy, poor-relief, incorporation, and mortmain; as if no definitions were contained in our theological and ecclesiastical works of words in such common use, and as if in consequence the Pope was at liberty to give them any sense of his own. As to discipline, Fr. Perrone says: "Discipline comprises the exterior worship of God, the liturgy, sacred rites, psalmody, the administration of the sacraments, the canonical form of sacred elections and the institution of ministers, vows, feast-days, and the like"; all of them (observe) matters internal to the Church, and without any relation to the Civil Power and civil affairs. Perrone adds: "Ecclesiastical discipline is a practical and external rule, prescribed by the Church, in order to retain the faithful in their *faith*, and the more easily lead them on to *eternal happiness*"

(*Præl. Theol.*, t. 2, p. 381, 2d ed., 1841). Thus discipline is in no sense a political instrument, except as the profession of our faith may accidentally become political. In the same sense Zallinger: "The Roman Pontiff has by divine right the power of passing universal laws pertaining to the *discipline* of the Church; for instance, to divine worship, sacred rites, the ordination and manner of life of the clergy, the order of the ecclesiastical regimen, and the right administration of the temporal possessions of the church" (*Jur. Eccles.*, lib. i. t. 2, § 121).

So too the word "regimen" has a definite meaning, relating to a matter strictly internal to the Church: it means government, or the mode or form of government, or the course of government; and as, in the intercourse of nation with nation, the nature of a nation's government, whether monarchical or republican, does not come into question, so the constitution of the Church simply belongs to its nature, not to its external action. Certainly there are aspects of the Church which involve relations toward secular powers and to nations, as, for instance, its missionary office; but regimen has relation to one of its internal characteristics, viz., its form of government, whether we call it a pure monarchy or, with others, a monarchy tempered by aristocracy. Thus Tournely says: "Three kinds of regimen or government are set down by philosophers, monarchy, aristocracy, and democracy" (*Theol.*, t. 2, p. 100. Bellarmine says the same, *Rom. Pont.*, i. 2; and Perrone takes it for granted, *ibid.* pp. 70, 71).

Now, why does the Pope speak at this time of regimen and discipline? He tells us in that portion of the sentence which, thinking it of no account, Mr. Gladstone has omitted. The Pope tells us that all Catholics should recollect their duty of obedience to him, not only in faith and morals, but in such matters of regimen and discipline as belong to the universal Church, "so that unity with the Roman Pontiff, both of communion and of profession of the same faith being preserved, the Church of Christ may be one flock under one supreme Shepherd." I consider this passage to be especially aimed at Nationalism. "Recollect," the Pope seems to say, "the Church is one, and that, not only in faith and morals, for schismatics may profess as much as this, but one, wherever it is, all over the world; and not only one, but one and the same, bound together by its one regimen and discipline and by the same regimen and discipline—the same rites, the same sacraments, the same usages, and the same one Pastor; and in these bad times it is necessary for all Catholics to recollect, that this doctrine of the Church's individuality, and, as it were, personality, is not a mere received opinion or understanding, which may be entertained or not, as we please, but is a fundamental, necessary truth." This being, speaking under correction, the drift of the passage, I observe that the words "spread throughout the world" or "universal" are so far from turning "discipline and regimen" into what Mr. Gladstone calls a "net," that they contract the range of both of them, not including, as he would have it, "marriage" here, "blasphemy" there, and "poor-relief" in a third country, but noting and specifying that one and the same structure of laws, rites, rules of government, independency, everywhere, of which the Pope himself is the centre and life. And surely this is what every one of us will say as well as the Pope, who is not an Erastian, and who believes that the Gospel is no mere philosophy thrown upon the world at large, no mere quality of mind and thought, no mere beautiful and deep sentiment or subjective opinion, but a substantive message from above, guarded and preserved in a visible polity.

2. And now I am naturally led on to speak of the Pope's supreme authority, such as I have described it, in its bearing towards the Civil Power all over the world—a power which as truly comes from God as his own does, though diverse, as the Church is invariable.

That collisions can take place between the Holy See and national governments, the history of fifteen hundred years sufficiently teaches us; also, that on both sides there may occur grievous mistakes. But my question all along lies, not with "quicquid delirant reges," but with what, under the circumstance of such a collision, is the duty of those who are both children of the Pope and subjects of the Civil Power. As to the duty of the Civil Power, I have already intimated in my first section that it should treat the Holy See as an independent sovereign, and if this rule had been observed, the difficulty to Catholics in a country not Catholic would be most materially lightened. Great Britain recognizes and is recognized by the United States; the two powers have ministers at each other's court; here is one standing prevention of serious quarrels. Misunderstandings between the two co-ordinate powers may arise; but there follow explanations, removals of the causes of offence, acts of restitution. In actual collisions, there are conferences, compromises, arbitrations. Now the point to observe here is, that in such cases neither party gives up its abstract rights, but neither party practically insists on them. And each party thinks itself in the right in the particular case, protests against any other view, but still concedes. Neither party says: "I will not make it up with you, till you draw an intelligible line between your domain and mine." I suppose in the Geneva arbitration, though we gave way, we still thought that, in our conduct in the American civil war, we had acted within our rights. I say all this in answer to Mr. Gladstone's challenge to us to draw the line between the Pope's domain and the State's domain in civil or political questions. Many a private American, I suppose, lived in London and Liverpool, all through the correspondence between our Foreign Office and the government of the United States, and Mr. Gladstone never addressed any expostulation to them, or told them they had lost their moral freedom because they took part with their own government. The French, when their late war began, did sweep their German sojourners out of France (the number, as I recollect, was very great), but they were not considered to have done themselves much credit by such an act. When we went to war with Russia, the English in St. Petersburg made an address, I think to the Emperor, asking for his protection, and he gave it; I don't suppose they pledged themselves to the Russian view of the war, nor would he have called them slaves instead of patriots, if they had refused to do so. Suppose England were to send her ironclads to support Italy against the Pope and his allies, English Catholics would be very indignant, they would take part with the Pope before the war began, they would use all constitutional means to hinder it; but who believes that, when they were once in the war, their action would be anything else than prayers and exertions for a termination of it? What reason is there for saying that they would commit themselves to any step of a treasonable nature, any more than loyal Germans, had they been allowed to remain in France? Yet, because those Germans would not relinquish their allegiance to their country, Mr. Gladstone, were he consistent, would at once send them adrift.

Of course it will be said that in these cases there is no double allegiance, and again that the German government did not call upon Germans in France, as the Pope might call upon English Catholics, nay command them, to take a side; but my argument at least shows this, that till there comes to us a special, direct command from the Pope to oppose our country, we need not be said to have "placed our loyalty and civil duty at the mercy of another" (p. 45). It is strange that a great statesman, versed in the new and true philosophy of compromise, instead of taking a practical view of the actual situation, should proceed against us, like a professor in the schools, with the "parade" of his "relentless" (and may I add "rusty"?) "logic" (p. 23).

I say, *till* the Pope told us to exert ourselves for his cause in a quarrel with this country, as in the time of the Armada, we need not attend to an abstract and hypothetical difficulty: then and not till then. I add, as before, that, if the Holy See were frankly recognized by England, as other sovereignties are, direct quarrels between the two powers would in this age of the world be rare indeed; and still rarer, their becoming so energetic and urgent as to descend into the hearts of the community, and to disturb the consciences and the family unity of private Catholics.

But now, lastly, let us suppose one of these extraordinary cases of direct and open hostility between the two powers actually to occur; here first, we must bring before us the state of the case. Of course we must recollect, on the one hand, that Catholics are not only bound by allegiance to the British Crown, but have special privileges as citizens, can meet together, speak and pass resolutions, can vote for members of Parliament, and sit in Parliament, and can hold office, all which are denied to foreigners sojourning among us; while on the other hand there is the authority of the Pope, which, though not "absolute" even in religious matters, as Mr. Gladstone would have it to be, has a call, a supreme call on our obedience. Certainly in the event of such a collision of jurisdictions, there are cases in which we should obey the Pope and disobey the State. Suppose, for instance, an act was passed in Parliament bidding Catholics to attend Protestant service every week, and the Pope distinctly told us not to do so, for it was to violate our duty to our faith : I should obey the Pope and not the law. It will be said by Mr. Gladstone, that such a case is impossible. I know it is; but why ask me for what I should do in extreme and utterly improbable cases such as this, if my answer cannot help bearing the character of an axiom? It is not my fault that I must deal in truisms. The circumferences of State jurisdiction and of Papal are for the most part quite apart from each other ; there are just some few degrees out of the 360 in which they intersect, and Mr. Gladstone, instead of letting these cases of intersection alone, till they occur actually, asks me what I should do if I found myself placed in the space intersected. If I must answer then, I should say distinctly that did the State tell me in a question of worship to do what the Pope told me not to do, I should obey the Pope, and should think it no sin if I used all the power and the influence I possessed as a citizen to prevent such a bill passing the Legislature, and to effect its repeal if it did.

But now, on the other hand, could the case ever occur in which I should act with the Civil Power, and not with the Pope? Now, here again, when I begin to imagine instances, Catholics will cry out (as Mr. Gladstone, in the case I supposed, cried out in the interest of the other side), that instances never can occur. I know they cannot; I know the Pope never can do what I am going to suppose; but then, since it cannot possibly happen in fact, there is no harm in just saying what I should (hypothetically) do, if it did happen. I say then in certain (impossible) cases I should side, not with the Pope, but with the Civil Power. For instance, let us suppose members of Parliament, or of the Privy Council, took an oath that they would not acknowledge the right of succession of a Prince of Wales, if he became a Catholic: in that case I should not consider the Pope could release me from that oath, had I bound myself by it. Of course, I might exert myself to the utmost to get the act repealed which bound me; again, if I could not, I might retire from parliament or office, and so rid myself of the engagement I had made; but I should be clear that, though the Pope bade all Catholics to stand firm in one phalanx for the Catholic Succession, still, while I remained in office, or in my place in Parliament, I could not do as he bade me.

Again, were I actually a soldier or sailor in her Majesty's service, and sent to take part in a war which I could not in my conscience see to be unjust, and should the Pope suddenly bid all Catholic soldiers and sailors to retire from the service, here again, taking the advice of others, as best I could, I should not obey him.

What is the use of forming impossible cases? One can find plenty of them in books of casuistry, with the answers attached in respect to them. In an actual case, a Catholic would, of course, not act simply on his own judgment; at the same time, there are supposable cases in which he would be obliged to go by it solely—viz., when his conscience could not be reconciled to any of the courses of action proposed to him by others.

In support of what I have been saying, I refer to one or two weighty authorities:

Cardinal Turrecremata says: "Although it clearly follows from the circumstance that the Pope can err at times, and command things which must not be done, that we are not to be simply obedient to him in all things, that does not show that he must not be obeyed by all when his commands are good. To know in what cases he is to be obeyed and in what not . . . it is said in the Acts of the Apostles, 'One ought to obey God rather than man': therefore, were the Pope to command anything against Holy Scripture, or the articles of faith, or the truth of the Sacraments, or the commands of the natural or divine law, *he ought not to be obeyed*, but in such commands is to be passed over (despiciendus)." (*Summ. de Eccl.*, pp. 47, 48.)

Bellarmine, speaking of resisting the Pope, says: "In order to resist and defend oneself no authority is required. . . . Therefore, as it is lawful to resist the Pope, if he assaulted a man's person, so it is lawful to resist him, if he assaulted souls, or *troubled the state* (turbanti rempublicam), and much more if he strove to destroy the Church. It is lawful, I say, to resist him, by not doing what he commands, and hindering the execution of his will" (*De Rom. Pont.*, ii. 29).

Archbishop Kenrick says: "His power was given for edification, not for destruction. If he uses it from the love of domination (quod absit) *scarcely will he meet with obedient populations*" (*Theolog. Moral.*, t. i. p. 158).

When, then, Mr. Gladstone asks Catholics how they can obey the Queen and yet obey the Pope, since it may happen that the commands of the two authorities may clash, I answer, that it is my *rule*, both to obey the one and to obey the other, but that there is no rule in this world without exceptions, and if either the Pope or the Queen demanded of me an "Absolute Obedience," he or she would be transgressing the laws of human society. I give an absolute obedience to neither. Further, if ever this double allegiance pulled me in contrary ways, which in this age of the world I think it never will, then I should decide according to the particular case, which is beyond all rule, and must be decided on its own merits. I should look to see what theologians could do for me, what the Bishops and clergy around me, what my confessor; what friends whom I revered: and if, after all, I could not take their view of the matter, then I must rule myself by my own judgment and my own conscience. But all this is hypothetical and unreal.

Here, of course, it will be objected to me, that I am, after all, having recourse to the Protestant doctrine of Private Judgment; not so; it is the Protestant doctrine that Private Judgment is our *ordinary* guide in religious matters, but I use it, in the case in question, in very extraordinary and rare, nay, impossible emergencies. Do not the highest Tories thus defend the substitution of William for James II.? It is a great mistake to suppose our state in the Catholic Church is so entirely subjected to rule and system, that we are never thrown upon what is called by divines "the Providence of God." The teaching and assistance of the Church does not supply all conceivable needs, but those which are ordinary; thus, for instance, the Sacraments are necessary for dying in the grace of God and hope of heaven, yet, when they cannot be got, acts of faith, hope, and contrition, with the desire for those aids which the dying man has not, will convey in substance what those aids ordinarily convey. And so a Catechumen, not yet baptized, may be saved by his purpose and preparation to receive the rite. And so, again, though "Out of the Church there is no salvation," this does not hold in the case of good men who are in invincible ignorance. And so it is also in the case of our ordinations; Chillingworth and Macaulay say that it is morally impossible that we should have kept up for 1800 years an Apostolical succession of ministers without some breaks in the chain ; and we in answer say that, however true this may be humanly speaking, there has been a special Providence over the Church to secure it. Once more, how else could private Catholics save their souls when there was a Pope and Anti-popes, each severally claiming their allegiance?

# CHAPTER V

## AUTHORITY OF CONSCIENCE.

Understood in the same Sense by both Catholics and Protestants.—The Aboriginal Vicar of Christ.—False Notions of Conscience among the Sceptical and Worldly.—Self-will is often misnamed Conscience.—In that sense only has the Pope condemned "Liberty of Conscience."—The Pope's whole Office is to enlighten Conscience and establish its Authority.—"He who acts against his Conscience loses his Soul" is a Catholic Maxim affirmed by Pope Benedict XIV.

It seems, then, that there are extreme cases in which Conscience may come into collision with the word of a Pope, and is to be followed in spite of that word. Now I wish to place this proposition on a broader basis, acknowledged by all Catholics, and, in order to do this satisfactorily, as I began with the prophecies of Scripture and the primitive Church, when I spoke of the Pope's prerogatives, so now I must begin with the Creator and His creature, when I would draw out the prerogatives and the supreme authority of Conscience.

I say, then, that the Supreme Being is of a certain character, which, expressed in human language, we call ethical. He has the attributes of justice, truth, wisdom, sanctity, benevolence, and mercy, as eternal characteristics in His nature, the very Law of His being, identical with Himself; and next, when he became Creator, He implanted this Law, which is Himself, in the intelligence of all his rational creatures. The divine Law, then, is the rule of ethical truth, the standard of right and wrong, a sovereign, irreversible, absolute authority in the presence of men and Angels. "The eternal law," says St. Augustine, "is the Divine Reason or Will of God, commanding the observance, forbidding the disturbance, of the natural order of things." "The natural law," says St. Thomas, "is an impression of the Divine Light in us, a participation of the eternal law in the rational creature" (Gousset, *Theol. Moral.*, t. i. pp. 24, etc.) This law, as apprehended in the minds of individual men, is called "conscience"; and though it may suffer refraction in passing into the intellectual medium of each, it is not therefore so affected as to lose its character of being the Divine Law, but still has, as such, the prerogative of commanding obedience. "The Divine Law," says Cardinal Gousset, "is the supreme rule of actions; our thoughts, desires, words, acts, all that man is, is subject to the domain of the law of God; and this law is the rule of our conduct by means of our conscience. Hence it is never lawful to go against our conscience; as the fourth Lateran Council says, 'Quidquid fit contra conscientiam, ædificat ad gehennam.'"

This view of conscience, I know, is very different from that ordinarily taken of it, both by the science and literature, and by the public opinion, of this day. It is founded on the doctrine that conscience is the voice of God, whereas it is fashionable on all hands now to consider it in one way or another a creation of man. Of course, there are great and broad exceptions to this statement. It is not true of many or most religious bodies of men; especially not of their teachers and ministers. When Anglicans, Wesleyans, the various

Presbyterian sects in Scotland, and other denominations among us, speak of conscience, they mean what we mean, the voice of God in the nature and heart of man, as distinct from the voice of Revelation. They speak of a principle planted within us, before we have had any training, although training and experience are necessary for its strength, growth, and due formation. They consider it a constituent element of the mind, as our perception of other ideas may be, as our powers of reasoning, as our sense of order and the beautiful, and our other intellectual endowments. They consider it, as Catholics consider it, to be the internal witness of both the existence and the law of God. They think it holds of God, and not of man, as an Angel walking on the earth would be no citizen or dependent of the Civil Power. They would not allow, any more than we do, that it could be resolved into any combination of principles in our nature, more elementary than itself; nay, though it may be called, and is, a law of the mind, they would not grant that it was nothing more; I mean, that it was not a dictate, nor conveyed the notion of responsibility, of duty, of a threat and a promise, with a vividness which discriminated it from all other constituents of our nature.

This, at least, is how I read the doctrine of Protestants as well as of Catholics. The rule and measure of duty is not utility nor expedience, nor the happiness of the greatest number, nor State convenience, nor fitness, order, and the *pulchrum*. Conscience is not a long-sighted selfishness, nor a desire to be consistent with oneself; but it is a messenger from Him who, both in nature and in grace, speaks to us behind a veil, and teaches and rules us by His representatives. Conscience is the aboriginal Vicar of Christ, a prophet in its informations, a monarch in its peremptoriness, a priest in its blessings and anathemas, and, even though the eternal priesthood throughout the Church could cease to be, in it the sacerdotal principle would remain and would have a sway.

Words such as these are idle empty verbiage to the great world of philosophy now. All through my day there has been a resolute warfare, I had almost said conspiracy against the rights of conscience, as I have described it. Literature and science have been embodied in great institutions in order to put it down. Noble buildings have been reared as fortresses against that spiritual, invisible influence which is too subtle for science and too profound for literature. Chairs in universities have been made the seats of an antagonist tradition. Public writers, day after day, have indoctrinated the minds of innumerable readers with theories subversive of its claims. As in Roman times, and in the middle age, its supremacy was assailed by the arm of physical force, so now the intellect is put in operation to sap the foundations of a power which the sword could not destroy. We are told that conscience is but a twist in primitive and untutored man; that its dictate is an imagination; that the very notion of guiltiness, which that dictate enforces, is simply irrational, for how can there possibly be freedom of will, how can there be consequent responsibility, in that infinite eternal network of cause and effect in which we helplessly lie? and what retribution have we to fear, when we have had no real choice to do good or evil?

So much for philosophers; now let us see what is the notion of conscience in this day in the popular mind. There, no more than in the intellectual world, does " conscience " retain the old, true, Catholic meaning of the word. There too the idea, the presence of a Moral Governor is far away from the use of it, frequent and emphatic as that use of it is. When men advocate the rights of conscience, they in no sense mean the rights of the Creator, nor the duty to Him, in thought and deed, of the creature; but the right of thinking, speaking, writing, and acting according to their judgment or their humor, without any thought of God at all. They do not even pretend to go by any moral rule, but they demand, what they think is an Englishman's prerogative, for each to be his own master in all things, and to profess what he pleases, asking no one's leave, and accounting priest or preacher, speaker or writer, unutterably impertinent, who dares to say a word against his going to perdition, if he like it, in his own way. Conscience has rights because it has duties; but in this age, with a large portion of the public, it is the very right and freedom of conscience to dispense with conscience, to ignore a Lawgiver and Judge, to be independent of unseen obligations. It becomes a license to take up any or no religion, to take up this or that and let it go again, to go to church, to go to chapel, to boast of being above all religions and to be an impartial critic of each of them. Conscience is a stern monitor, but in this century it has been superseded by a counterfeit, which the eighteen centuries prior to it never heard of, and could not have mistaken for it, if they had. It is the right of self-will.

And now I shall turn aside for a moment to show how it is that the Popes of our century have been misunderstood by the English people, as if they really were speaking against conscience in the true sense of the word, when in fact they were speaking against it in the various false senses, philosophical or popular, which in this day are put upon the word. Pope Pius IX., in his Encyclical of 1864, *Quantâ curâ*, speaks (as will come before us in the next section) against "liberty of conscience," and he refers to his predecessor, Gregory XVI., who, in his *Mirari vos*, calls it a "deliramentum." It is a rule in formal ecclesiastical proceedings, as I shall have occasion to notice lower down, when books or authors are condemned, to use the very words of the book or author, and to condemn the words in that particular sense which they have in their context and their drift, not in the literal, not in the religious sense, such as the Pope might recognize, were they in another book or author. To take a familiar parallel, among many which occur daily. Protestants speak of the "Blessed Reformation"; Catholics too talk of "the Reformation," though they do not call it blessed. Yet every "reformation" ought, from the very meaning of the word, to be good, not bad; so that Catholics seem to be implying a eulogy on an event which, at the same time, they consider a surpassing evil. Here then they are taking the word and using it in the popular sense of it, not in the Catholic. They would say, if they expressed their full meaning, "the *so-called* reformation." In like manner, if the Pope condemned "the Reformation," it would be utterly sophistical to say in consequence that he had declared himself against all reforms; yet this is how Mr. Gladstone treats him, when he speaks of (so-called) liberty of conscience. To make this distinction clear, viz., between the Catholic sense of the word "conscience," and that sense in which the Pope condemns it, we find in the *Recueil des Allocutions*, etc., the words accompanied with quotation-marks, both in Pope Gregory's and Pope Pius's Encyclicals, thus: Gregory's, "Ex hoc putidissimo 'indifferentismi' fonte" (mind, "indifferentismi" is under quotation-marks, because the Pope will not make himself answerable for so unclassical a word), "absurda illa fluit ac erronea sententia, seu potius deliramentum, asserendam esse ac vindicandam cuilibet 'libertatem conscientiæ.'" And that of Pius, "Haud timent erroneam illam fovere opinionem a Gregorio XVI. deliramentum appellatam, nimirum 'libertatem conscientiæ' esse proprium cujuscunque hominis jus." Both Popes certainly scoff at the so-called "liberty of conscience," but there is no scoffing of any Pope, in formal documents addressed to the faithful at large, at that most serious doctrine, the right and the duty of following that Divine Authority, the voice of conscience, on which in truth the Church herself is built.

So indeed it is; did the Pope speak against Conscience in the true sense of the word, he would commit a suicidal act. He would be cutting the ground from under his feet. His very mission is to proclaim the moral law, and to protect and strengthen that "Light which enlighteneth every man that cometh into the world." On the law of conscience and its sacredness are founded both his authority in theory and his power in fact. Whether this or that particular Pope in this bad world always kept this great truth in view in all he did, it is for history to tell. I am considering here the Papacy in its office and its duties, and in reference to those who acknowledge its claims. They are not bound by the Pope's personal character or private acts, but by its formal teaching. Thus viewing his position, we shall find that it is by the universal sense of right and wrong, the consciousness of transgression, the pangs of guilt, and the dread of retribution, as first principles deeply lodged in the hearts of men—it is thus and only thus that he has gained his footing in the world and achieved his success. It is his claim to come from the Divine Lawgiver, in order to elicit, protect, and enforce those truths which the Lawgiver has sown in our very nature—it is this and this only that is the explanation of his length of life more than antediluvian. The championship of the Moral Law and of conscience is his *raison d'être*. The fact of his mission is the answer to the complaints of those who feel the insufficiency of the natural light; and the insufficiency of that light is the justification of his mission.

All sciences, except the science of Religion, have their certainty in themselves; as far as they are sciences, they consist of necessary conclusions from undeniable premises, or of phenomena manipulated into general truths by an irresistible induction. But the sense of right and wrong, which is the first element in religion, is so delicate, so fitful, so easily puzzled, obscured, perverted, so subtle in its argumentative methods, so impressible by education, so biassed by pride and passion, so unsteady in its course, that, in the struggle for existence amid the various exercises and triumphs of the human intellect, this sense is at once the highest of all teachers, yet the least luminous; and the Church, the Pope, the Hierarchy are, in the Divine purpose, the supply of an urgent demand. Natural Religion, certain as are its grounds and its doctrines as addressed to thoughtful, serious minds, needs, in order that it may speak to mankind with effect and subdue the world, to be sustained and completed by Revelation.

In saying all this, of course I must not be supposed to be limiting the Revelation of which the Church is the keeper to a mere republication of the Natural Law; but still it is true, that, though Revelation is so distinct from the teaching of nature and beyond it, yet it is not independent of it, nor without relations towards it, but is its complement, reassertion, issue, embodiment, and interpretation. The Pope, who comes of Revelation, has no jurisdiction over Nature. If, under the plea of his revealed prerogatives, he neglected his mission of preaching truth, justice, mercy, and peace, much more if he trampled on the consciences of his subjects—if he had done so all along, as Protestants say, then he could not have lasted all these many centuries till now, so as to supply a mark for their reprobation. Dean Milman has told us above how faithful he was to his duty in the mediæval time, and how successful. Afterwards, for a while the Papal chair was filled by men who gave themselves up to luxury, security, and a Pagan kind of Christianity; and we all know what a moral earthquake was the consequence, and how the Church lost, thereby, and has lost to this day, one-half of Europe. The Popes could not have recovered from so terrible a catastrophe, as they have done, had they not returned to their first and better ways, and the grave lesson of the past is in itself the guarantee of the future.

Such is the relation of the ecclesiastical power to the human conscience: however, a contrary view may be taken of it. It may be said that no one doubts that the Pope's power rests on those weaknesses of human nature, that religious sense, which in ancient days Lucretius noted as the cause of the worst ills of our race; that he uses it dexterously, forming under shelter of it a false code of morals for his own aggrandisement and tyranny; and that thus conscience becomes his creature and his slave, doing, as if on a divine sanction, his will; so that in the abstract indeed and in idea it is free, but never free in fact, never able to take a flight of its own, independent of him, any more than birds whose wings are clipped; moreover, that, if it were able to exert a will of its own, then there would ensue a collision more unmanageable than that between the Church and the State, as being in one and the same subject-matter— viz., religion; for what would become of the Pope's "absolute authority," as Mr. Gladstone calls it, if the private conscience had an absolute authority also?

I wish to answer this important objection distinctly.

1. First, I am using the word "conscience" in the high sense in which I have already explained it, not as a fancy or an opinion, but as a dutiful obedience to what claims to be a divine voice, speaking within us; and that this is the view properly to be taken of it, I shall not attempt to prove here, but shall assume it as a first principle.

2. Secondly, I observe that conscience is not a judgment upon any speculative truth, any abstract doctrine, but bears immediately on conduct, on something to be done or not done. "Conscience," says St. Thomas, "is the practical judgment or dictate of reason, by which we judge what *hic et nunc* is to be done as being good, or to be avoided as evil." Hence conscience cannot come into direct collision with the Church's or the Pope's infallibility; which is engaged on general propositions, and in the condemnation of particular and given errors.

3. Next, I observe that, conscience being a practical dictate, a collision is possible between it and the Pope's authority only when the Pope legislates, or gives particular orders, and the like. But a Pope is not infallible in his laws, nor in his commands, nor in his acts of state, nor in his administration, nor in his public policy. Let it be observed that the Vatican Council has left him just as it found him here. Mr. Gladstone's language on this point is to me quite unintelligible. Why, instead of using vague terms, does he not point out precisely the very words by which the Council has made the Pope in his acts infallible? Instead of so doing, he assumes a conclusion which is altogether false. He says (p. 34), "First comes the Pope's infallibility";

then in the next page he insinuates that, under his infallibility, come acts of excommunication, as if the Pope could not make mistakes in this field of action. He says (p. 35) : "It may be sought to plead that the Pope does not propose to invade the country, to seize Woolwich, or burn Portsmouth. He will only, at the worst, excommunicate opponents. . . . Is this a good answer? After all, even in the Middle Ages, it was not by the direct action of fleets and armies of their own that the Popes contended with kings who were refractory; it was mainly by interdicts," etc. What have excommunication and interdict to do with Infallibility? Was St. Peter infallible on that occasion at Antioch when St. Paul withstood him? was St. Victor infallible when he separated from his communion the Asiatic Churches? or Liberius when in like manner he excommunicated Athanasius? And, to come to later times, was Gregory XIII., when he had a medal struck in honor of the Bartholomew massacre? or Paul IV. in his conduct towards Elizabeth? or Sextus V. when he blessed the Armada? or Urban VIII. when he persecuted Galileo? No Catholic ever pretends that these Popes were infallible in these acts. Since then infallibility alone could block the exercise of conscience, and the Pope is not infallible in that subject-matter in which conscience is of supreme authority, no dead-lock, such as is implied in the objection which I am answering, can take place between conscience and the Pope.

4. But, of course, I have to say again, lest I should be misunderstood, that when I speak of Conscience, I mean conscience truly so called. When it has the right of opposing the supreme, though not infallible authority of the Pope, it must be something more than that miserable counterfeit which, as I have said above, now goes by the name. If in a particular case it is to be taken as

a sacred and sovereign monitor, its dictate, in order to prevail against the voice of the Pope, must follow upon serious thought, prayer, and all available means of arriving at a right judgment on the matter in question. And further, obedience to the Pope is what is called "in possession"; that is, the *onus probandi* of establishing a case against him lies, as in all cases of exception, on the side of conscience. Unless a man is able to say to himself, as in the Presence of God, that he must not, and dare not, act upon the Papal injunction, he is bound to obey it, and would commit a great sin in disobeying it. *Primâ facie* it is his bounden duty, even from a sentiment of loyalty, to believe the Pope right and to act accordingly. He must vanquish that mean, ungenerous, selfish, vulgar spirit of his nature, which, at the very first rumor of a command, places itself in opposition to the Superior who gives it, asks itself whether he is not exceeding his right, and rejoices, in a moral and practical matter, to commence with scepticism. He must have no wilful determination to exercise a right of thinking, saying, doing just what he pleases, the question of truth and falsehood, right and wrong, the duty if possible of obedience, the love of speaking as his Head speaks, and of standing in all cases on his Head's side, being simply discarded. If this necessary rule were observed, collisions between the Pope's authority and the authority of conscience would be very rare. On the other hand, in the fact that, after all, in extraordinary cases, the conscience of each individual is free, we have a safeguard and security, were security necessary (which is a most gratuitous supposition), that no Pope ever will be able, as the objection supposes, to create a false conscience for his own ends.

Now, I shall end this part of the subject, for I have not done with it altogether, by appealing to various of our theologians in evidence that, in what I have been saying, I have not misrepresented Catholic doctrine on these important points.

That is, on the duty of obeying our conscience at all hazards.

I have already quoted the words which Cardinal Gousset has adduced from the Fourth Lateran: that "He who acts against his conscience loses his soul." This *dictum* is brought out with singular fulness and force in the moral treatises of theologians. The celebrated school, known as the Salamanticenses, or Carmelites of Salamanca, lays down the broad proposition, that conscience is ever to be obeyed whether it tells truly or erroneously, and that whether the error is the fault of the person thus erring or not.* They say that this opinion is certain, and refer, as agreeing with them, to St. Thomas, St. Bonaventura, Cajetan, Vasquez, Durandus, Navarrus, Corduba, Layman, Escobar, and fourteen others. Two of them even say this opinion is *de fide*. Of course, if a man is culpable in being in error, which he might have escaped had he been more in earnest, for that error he is answerable to God, but still he must act according to that error, while he is in it, because he in full sincerity thinks the error to be truth.

Thus, if the Pope told the English Bishops to order their priests to stir themselves energetically in favor of teetotalism, and a particular priest was fully persuaded that abstinence from wine, etc., was practically a Gnostic error, and therefore felt he could not so exert himself without sin; or suppose there was a Papal order to hold

---

* "Aliqui opinantur quod conscientia erronea non obligat; secundam sententiam, et certam, asserentem esse peccatum discordare à conscientiâ erroneâ, invincibili aut vincibili, tenet D. Thomas; quem sequuntur omnes Scholastici."—*Theol. Moral.*, t. v. p. 12, ed. 1728.

lotteries in each mission for some religious object, and a priest could say in God's sight that he believed lotteries to be morally wrong, that priest in either of these cases would commit a sin *hic et nunc* if he obeyed the Pope, whether he was right or wrong in his opinion, and, if wrong, although he had not taken proper pains to get at the truth of the matter.

Busenbaum, of the Society of Jesus, whose work I have already had occasion to notice, writes thus: "A heretic, as long as he judges his sect to be more or equally deserving of belief, has no obligation to believe [in the Church]." And he continues: "When men who have been brought up in heresy, are persuaded from boyhood that we impugn and attack the word of God, that we are idolaters, pestilent deceivers, and therefore are to be shunned as pests, they cannot, while this persuasion lasts, with a safe conscience, hear us" (T. 1. p. 54).

Antonio Corduba, a Spanish Franciscan, states the doctrine with still more point, because he makes mention of Superiors. "In no manner is it lawful to act against conscience, even though a Law, or a Superior commands it" (*De Conscient.*, p. 138).

And the French Dominican, Natalis Alexander: "If, in the judgment of conscience, though a mistaken conscience, a man is persuaded that what his Superior commands is displeasing to God, he is bound not to obey" (*Theol.*, t. 2, p. 32).

The word "Superior" certainly includes the Pope; Cardinal Jacobatius brings out this point clearly in his authoritative work on Councils, which is contained in Labbe's Collection, introducing the Pope by name. "If it were doubtful," he says, "whether a precept [of the Pope] be a sin or not, we must determine thus: that, if he to whom the precept is addressed has a conscientious sense that it is a sin and injustice, first it is duty to put off that sense; but, if he cannot, nor conform himself to the judgment of the Pope, in that case it is his duty to follow his own private conscience, and patiently to bear it, if the Pope punishes him" (Lib. iv. p. 241).

Would it not be well for Mr. Gladstone to bring passages from our recognized authors as confirmatory of his view of our teaching, as those which I have quoted are destructive of it? and they must be passages declaring, not only that the Pope is ever to be obeyed, but that there are no exceptions to the rule, for exceptions there must be in all concrete matters.

I add one remark. Certainly, if I am obliged to bring religion into after-dinner toasts (which indeed does not seem quite the thing), I shall drink—to the Pope, if you please—still, to Conscience first, and to the Pope afterwards.

# CHAPTER VI.

## THE ENCYCLICAL OF 1864.

REFLECTIONS ON THE MOVEMENT IN ENGLAND TOWARDS UNIVERSAL TOLERATION.—THE ENCYCLICAL DOES NOT CONDEMN LIBERTY IN ANY DIFFERENT SENSE THAN DOES ENGLISH LAW.—THE REAL AND PRACTICAL MEANING OF THE ENCYCLICAL.

THE subject of Conscience leads us to the Encyclical, which is one of the special objects of Mr. Gladstone's attack; and to do justice to it, I must, as in other sections, begin from an earlier date than 1864.

Modern Rome then is not the only place where the traditions of the old Empire, its principles, provisions, and practices, have been held in honor; they have been retained, they have been maintained in substance, as the basis of European civilization down to this day, and notably among ourselves. In the Anglican establishment the king took the place of the Pope; but the Pope's principles kept possession. When the Pope was ignored, the relations between Pope and king were ignored too, and therefore we had nothing to do any more with the old Imperial laws which shaped those relations; but the old idea of a Christian Polity was still in force. It was a first principle with England that there was one true religion, that it was inherited from an earlier time, that it came of direct Revelation, that it was to be supported to the disadvantage, to say the least, of other religions, of private judgment, of personal conscience. The Puritans held these principles as firmly as the school of Laud. As to the Scotch Presbyterians, we read enough about them in the pages of Mr. Buckle. The Stuarts went, but still their principles suffered no dethronement: their action was restrained, but they were still in force, when this century opened.

It is curious to see how strikingly in this matter the proverb has been fulfilled, "Out of sight, out of mind." Men of the present generation, born in the new civilization, are shocked to witness in the abiding Papal system the words, ways, and works of their grandfathers. In my own lifetime has that old world been alive, and has gone its way. Who will say that the plea of conscience was as effectual, sixty years ago, as it is now in England for the toleration of every sort of fancy religion? Had the Press always that wonderful elbow-room which it has now? Might public gatherings be held, and speeches made, and republicanism avowed in the time of the Regency, as is now possible? Were the thoroughfares open to monster processions at that date, and the squares and parks at the mercy of Sunday manifestations? Could *savants* in that day insinuate in scientific assemblies what their hearers mistook for atheism, and artisans practise it in the centres of political action? Could public prints day after day, or week after week, carry on a war against religion, natural and revealed, as now is the case? No; law or public opinion would not suffer it; we may be wiser or better now, but we were then in the wake of the Holy Roman Church, and had been so from the time of the Reformation. We were faithful to the tradition of fifteen hundred years. All this was called Toryism, and men gloried in the name; now it is called Popery and reviled.

When I was young the State had a conscience, and the Chief-Justice of the day pronounced, not as a point of obsolete law, but as an energetic, living truth, that Christianity was the law of the land. And by Christianity was meant pretty much what Bentham calls Church-of-Englandism, its cry being the dinner toast, "Church and king." Blackstone, though he wrote a hundred years ago, was held, I believe, as an authority on the state of the law in this matter, up to the beginning of this century. On the supremacy of Religion he writes as follows, that is, as I have abridged him for my purpose :

" The belief of a future state of rewards and punishments, etc., etc., . . . these are the grand foundation of all judicial oaths. All moral evidence, all confidence in human veracity, must be weakened by irreligion, and overthrown by infidelity. Wherefore all affronts to Christianity, or endeavors to depreciate its efficacy, are highly deserving of human punishment. It was enacted by the statute of William III. that if any person *educated in*, and *having made profession of*, the Christian religion shall by writing, printing, teaching, or advised speaking, deny the Christian religion to be true, or the Holy Scriptures to be of divine authority," or again in like manner, "if any person *educated* in the Christian religion shall by writing, etc., deny any one of the Persons of the Holy Trinity to be God, or maintain that there are more gods than one, he shall on the first offence be rendered incapable to hold any office or place of trust ; and for the second, be rendered incapable of bringing any action, being guardian, executor, legatee, or purchaser of lands, and shall suffer three years' imprisonment without bail. To give room, however, for repentance, if, within four months after the first conviction, the delinquent will in open court publicly renounce his error, he is discharged for that once from all disabilities."

Again: "Those who absent themselves from the divine worship in the established Church, through total irreligion, and attend the service of no other persuasion, forfeit one shilling to the poor every Lord's day they so absent themselves, and £20 to the king if they continue such a default for a month together. And if they keep any inmate, thus irreligiously disposed, in their houses, they forfeit £10 per month."

Further, he lays down that "reviling the ordinances of the Church is a crime of a much grosser nature than the other of non-conformity; since it carries with it the utmost indecency, arrogance, and ingratitude: indecency, by setting up private judgment in opposition to public; arrogance, by treating with contempt and rudeness what has at least a better chance to be right than the singular notions of any particular man; and ingratitude, by denying that indulgence and liberty of conscience to the members of the national Church which the retainers to every petty conventicle enjoy."

Once more: "In order to secure the established Church against perils from non-conformists of all denominations, infidels, Turks, Jews, heretics, papists, and sectaries, there are two bulwarks erected, called the Corporation and Test Acts; by the former, no person can be legally elected to any office relating to the government of any city or corporation, unless, within a twelvemonth before, he has received the sacrament of the Lord's Supper according to the rites of the Church of England; . . . . the other, called the Test Act, directs all officers, civil and military, to make the declaration against transubstantiation within six months after their admission, and also within the same time to receive the sacrament according to the usage of the

Church of England." The same test being undergone by all persons who desired to be naturalized, the Jews also were excluded from the privileges of Protestant churchmen.

Laws, such as these, of course gave a tone to society, to all classes, high and low, and to the publications, periodical or other, which represented public opinion. Dr. Watson, who was the liberal prelate of his day, in his answer to Paine, calls him (unless my memory betrays me) "a child of the devil and an enemy of all righteousness." Cumberland, a man of the world (here again I must trust to the memory of many past years), reproaches a Jewish writer with ingratitude for assailing, as he seems to have done, a tolerant religious establishment; and Gibbon, an unbeliever, feels himself at liberty, in his posthumous Autobiography, to look down on Priestley, whose "Socinian shield," he says, "has been repeatedly pierced by the mighty spear of Horsley, and whose trumpet of sedition may at length awake the magistrates of a free country."

Such was the position of free opinion and dissenting worship in England till quite a recent date, when one after another the various disabilities which I have been recounting, and many others besides, melted away, like snow at spring-tide; and we all wonder how they could ever have been in force. The cause of this great revolution is obvious, and its effect inevitable. Though I profess to be an admirer of the principles now superseded in themselves, mixed up as they were with the imperfections and evils incident to everything human, nevertheless I say frankly I do not see how they could possibly be maintained in the ascendant. When the intellect is cultivated, it is as certain that it will develop into a thousand various shapes, as that infinite hues and tints and shades of color will be reflected from the earth's surface, when the sunlight touches it; and in matters of religion the more, by reason of the extreme subtlety and abstruseness of the mental action by which they are determined. During the last seventy years, first one class of the community, then another, has awakened up to thought and opinion. Their multiform views on sacred subjects necessarily affected and found expression in the governing order. The State in past time had a conscience; George the Third had a conscience; but there were other men at the head of affairs besides him with consciences, and they spoke for others besides themselves, and what was to be done, if he could not work without them, and they could not work with him, as far as religious questions came up at the council-board? This brought on a dead-lock in the time of his successor. The ministry of the day could not agree together in the policy or justice of keeping up the state of things which Blackstone describes. The State ought to have a conscience; but what if it happened to have half-a-dozen, or a score, or a hundred, in religious matters, each different from each? I think Mr. Gladstone has brought out the difficulties of the situation himself in his Autobiography. No government could be formed, if religious unanimity was a *sine quâ non*. What then was to be done? As a necessary consequence, the whole theory of Toryism, hitherto acted on, came to pieces and went the way of all flesh. This was in the nature of things. Not a hundred Popes could have hindered it, unless Providence interposed by an effusion of divine grace on the hearts of men, which would amount to a miracle, and perhaps would interfere with human responsibility. The Pope has denounced the sentiment that he ought to come to terms with "progress, liberalism, and the new civilization." I have no thought at all of disputing his words. I leave the great problem to the future. God will guide other Popes to act when Pius goes, as He has guided him. No one can dislike the democratic principle more than I do. No one mourns, for instance, more than I, over the state of Oxford, given up, alas! to "liberalism and progress," to the forfeiture of her great mediæval motto, "Dominus illuminatio mea," and with a consequent call on her to go to Parliament or the Heralds' College for a new one; but what can we do? All I know is, that Toryism, that is, loyalty to persons, "springs immortal in the human breast"; that religion is a spiritual loyalty; and that Catholicity is the only divine form of religion. And thus, in centuries to come, there may be found out some way of uniting what is free in the new structure of society with what is authoritative in the old, without any base compromise with "Progress" and "Liberalism."

But to return: I have noticed the great revolution in the state of the Law which has taken place since 1828 for this reason: to suggest that Englishmen, who within fifty years kept up the Pope's system, are not exactly the parties to throw stones at the Pope for keeping it up still.

But I go further: in fact the Pope has not said on this subject of conscience (for that is the main subject in question) what Mr. Gladstone makes him say. On this point I desiderate that fairness in his Pamphlet which we have a right to expect from him; and in truth his unfairness is wonderful. He says (pp. 15, 16) that the Holy See has "condemned" the maintainers of "the Liberty of the Press, of conscience, and of worship." Again, that the "Pontiff has condemned free speech, free writing, a free press, toleration of nonconformity, liberty of conscience" (p. 42). Now, is not this accusation of a very wholesale character? Who would not understand it to mean that the Pope had pronounced a universal anathema against *all* these liberties *in toto*, and that English law, on the contrary, allowed those liberties *in toto*, which the Pope had condemned? But the Pope has done no such thing. The real question is, in what respect, in what measure, has he spoken against liberty: the grant of liberty admits of degrees. Blackstone is careful to show how much more liberty the law allowed to the subject in his day, how much less severe it was in its safeguards against abuse, than it had used to be; but he never pretends that it is conceivable that liberty should have no boundary at all. The very idea of political society is based upon the principle that each member of it gives up a portion of his natural liberty for advantages which are greater than that liberty; and the question is, whether the Pope, in any act of his which touches us Catholics, in any ecclesiastical or theological statement of his, has propounded any principle, doctrine, or view which is not carried out in fact at this time in British courts of law, and would not be conceded by Blackstone. I repeat, the very notion of human society is a relinquishment, to a certain point, of the liberty of its members individually, for the sake of a common security. Would it be fair on that account to say that the British Constitution condemns *all* liberty of conscience in word and in deed?

We Catholics, on our part, are denied liberty of our religion by English law in various ways, but we do not complain, because a limit must be put to even innocent liberties, and we acquiesce in it for the social compensations which we gain on the whole. Our school-boys cannot play cricket on Sunday, not even in country places, for fear of being taken before a magistrate and fined. In Scotland we cannot play music on Sundays.

Here we cannot sound a bell for church. I have had before now a lawyer's authority for saying that a religious procession is illegal even within our own premises. Till the last year or two we could not call our Bishops by the titles which our Religion gave them. A mandate from the Home Secretary obliged us to put off our cassocks when we went out of doors. We are forced to pay rates for the establishment of secular schools which we cannot use, and then we have to find means over again for building schools of our own. Why is not all this as much an outrage on our conscience as the prohibition upon Protestants at Rome, Naples, and Malaga, before the late political changes (*not*, to hold their services in a private house, or in the ambassador's, or outside the walls), but to flaunt them in public and thereby to irritate the natives? Mr. Gladstone seems to think it is monstrous for the Holy See to sanction such a prohibition. If so, may we not call upon him to gain for us in Birmingham "the free exercise of our religion," in making a circuit of the streets in our vestments, and chanting the "Pange Lingua," and the protection of the police against the mob which would be sure to gather round us—particularly since we are English born, whereas the Protestants at Malaga or Naples were foreigners.\* But we have the good sense neither to feel such disabilities a hardship, nor to protest against them as a grievance.

But now for the present state of English Law: I say seriously Mr. Gladstone's accusation of us avails quite as much against Blackstone's four volumes, against laws in general, against the social contract, as against the Pope. What the Pope has said, I will show pre-

---

\* "Hominibus illuc immigrantibus." These words Mr. Gladstone omits; also he translates "publicum" "free," pp. 17, 18, as if worship could not be free without being public.

sently: first let us see what the statute book has to tell us about the present state of English liberty of speech, of the press, and of worship.

First, as to public speaking and meetings: do we allow of seditious language, or of insult to the sovereign, or his representatives? Blackstone says that a misprision is committed against him by speaking or writing against him, cursing or wishing him ill, giving out scandalous stories concerning him, or doing anything that may tend to lessen him in the esteem of his subjects, may weaken his government, or may raise jealousies between him and his people. Also he says, that "threatening and reproachful words to any judge sitting in the courts" involve "a high misprision, and have been punished with large fines, imprisonment, and corporal punishment." And we may recollect quite lately the judges of the Queen's Bench prohibited public meetings and speeches which had for their object the issue of a case then proceeding in court.

Then, again, as to the Press, there are two modes of bridling it, one before the printed matter is published, the other after. The former is the method of censorship, the latter that of the law of libel. Each is a restriction on the liberty of the Press. We prefer the latter. I never heard it said that the law of libel was of a mild character; and I never heard that the Pope, in any brief or rescript, had insisted on a censorship.

Lastly, liberty of worship: as to the English restriction of it, we have had a notable example of it in the last session of Parliament, and we shall have still more edifying illustrations of it in the next, though certainly not from Mr. Gladstone. The ritualistic party, in the free exercise of their rights, under the shelter of the Anglican rubrics, of certain of the Anglican offices, of the teaching of their great divines, and of their conscientious interpretation of the Thirty-nine Articles have, at their own expense, built churches for worship after their own way; and, on the other hand, Parliament and the newspapers are attempting to put them down, not so much because they are acting against the tradition and the law of the Establishment, but because of the national dislike and dread of the principles and doctrines which their worship embodies.

When Mr. Gladstone has a right to say broadly, by reason of these restrictions, that British law and the British people condemn the maintainers of liberty of conscience, of the press, and of worship, *in toto*, then may he say so of the Encyclical, on account of those words which to him have so frightful a meaning.

But now let us see, on the other hand, what the proposition really is, the condemnation of which leads him to say, that the Pope has unrestrictedly " condemned those who maintain *the* liberty of the Press, *the* liberty of conscience and of worship, and *the* liberty of speech " (p. 16), has " condemned free speech, free writing, and a free press (p. 42). The condemned proposition speaks as follows:

" 1. Liberty of conscience and worship is the *inherent right* of all men. 2. It ought to be proclaimed in *every* rightly constituted society. 3. It is a right to *all sorts of liberty* (omnimodam libertatem) such, that it ought not to be restrained by any authority, ecclesiastical *or civil*, as far as public speaking, printing, or any other public manifestation of opinions is concerned."

Now, is there any government on earth that could stand the strain of such a doctrine as this? It starts by taking for granted that there are certain Rights of man; Mr. Gladstone so considers, I believe; but other deep thinkers of the day are quite of another opinion; however, if the doctrine of the proposition is true, then the right of conscience, of which it speaks, being inherent in man, is of universal force—that is, all over the world; also, says the proposition, it is a right which must be recognized by all rightly constituted governments. Lastly, what is the right of conscience thus inherent in our nature, thus necessary for all states? The proposition tells us. It is the liberty of *every* one to give *public* utterance, in *every* possible shape, by *every* possible channel, without *any* let or hindrance from God or man, to *all* his notions *whatsoever*.\*

Which of the two in this matter is peremptory and sweeping in his utterance, the author of this thesis himself, or the Pope who has condemned what the other has uttered? Which of the two is it who would force upon the world a universal? All that the Pope has done is to deny a universal, and what a universal!—a universal liberty to all men to say out whatever doctrines they may hold by preaching, or by the press, uncurbed by church or civil power. Does not this bear out what I said in the foregoing section of the sense in which Pope Gregory denied a "liberty of conscience"? It is a liberty of self-will. What if a man's conscience embraces the duty of regicide? or infanticide? or free love? You may say that in England the good sense of the nation would stifle and extinguish such atrocities. True, but the proposition says that it is the very right of every one, by nature, in *every* well constituted society. If so, why have we gagged the Press in Ireland on the ground of its being seditious? Why is not India brought within the British constitution? It seems a light epithet for the Pope to use, when he calls

---

\* "Jus civibus *inesse* ad *omnimodam* libertatem, *nullâ* vel ecclesiasticâ vel civili auctoritate coarctandam, quo suos conceptus *quoscunque* sive voce, sive typis, sive aliâ ratione, *palam publiceque* manifestare ac declarare valeant."

such a doctrine of conscience *deliramentum :* of all conceivable absurdities it is the wildest and most stupid. Has Mr. Gladstone really no better complaint to make against the Pope's condemnations than this?

Perhaps he will say, Why should the Pope take the trouble to condemn what is so wild?* But he does: and to say that he condemns something which he does not condemn, and then to inveigh against him on the ground of that something else, is neither just nor logical.

\* This question is directly answered in the Postscript on this Section.

## CHAPTER VII.

### THE SYLLABUS.

DESCRIPTION OF THIS DOCUMENT.—WHY IT WAS ISSUED, AND HOW.—IT WAS SENT BY THE POPE'S DIRECTION, BUT WITHOUT HIS NAME OR SEAL AFFIXED.—IT LACKS THE FORMAL AUTHENTICATION OF A DOGMATIC INSTRUMENT.—ITS MEANING IS TO BE LEARNED ONLY FROM THE PAPAL DECLARATIONS TO WHICH IT REFERS.—DISCUSSION OF THE PROPOSITIONS OF THE SYLLABUS MOST VIOLENTLY ATTACKED.—EXPLANATION OF THE OPPOSITION TO THE SYLLABUS.

NOW I come to the Syllabus of "Errors," the publication of which has been exclaimed against in England as such a singular enormity, and especially by Mr. Gladstone. The condemnation of theological statements which militate against the Catholic Faith is of long usage in the Church. Such was the condemnation of the heresies of Wickliffe in the Council of Constance; such those of Huss, of Luther, of Baius, of Jansenius; such the condemnations which were published by Sixtus IV., Innocent XI., Clement XI., Benedict XIV., and other Popes. Such condemnations are no invention of Pius IX. The Syllabus is a collection of such erroneous propositions as he has noted during his Pontificate; there are eighty of them.

What does the word "Syllabus" mean? A collection; the French translation calls it a "*Résumé*"; a Collection of what? I have already said, of propositions—propositions which the Pope in his various allocutions, encyclicals, and like documents, since he has been Pope, has pronounced to be errors. Who gathered the propositions out of these Papal documents, and put them together in one? We do not know; all we know is that, by the Pope's command, this Collection of Errors was sent by his Foreign Minister to the Bishops. He, Cardinal Antonelli, sent to them at the same time the Encyclical of December, 1864, which is a document of dogmatic authority. The Cardinal says, in his circular to them, that the Pope ordered him to do so. The Pope thought, he says, that perhaps the Bishops had not seen some of his Allocutions, and other authoritative letters and speeches of past years; in consequence the Pope had had the Errors which, at one time or other he had therein noted, brought together into one, and that for the use of the Bishops.

Such is the Syllabus and its object. There is not a word in it of the Pope's own writing; there is nothing in it at all but the Erroneous Propositions themselves—that is, except the heading "A Syllabus, containing the principal Errors of our times, which are noted in the Consistorial Allocutions, in the Encyclicals, and in other Apostolical Letters of our most Holy Lord, Pope Pius IX." There is one other addition—viz., after each Error a reference is given to the Allocution, Encyclical, or other document in which it is proscribed.

The Syllabus, then, is to be received with profound submission, as having been sent by the Pope's authority to the Bishops of the world. It certainly comes to them with his indirect extrinsic sanction; but intrinsically, and viewed in itself, it is nothing more than a digest of certain Errors made by an anonymous writer. There would be nothing on the face of it to show that the Pope had ever seen it, page by page, unless the "Imprimatur " implied in the Cardinal's letter had been an evidence of this. It has no mark or seal put upon it which gives it a direct relation to the Pope. Who is its author? Some select theologian or high official doubtless; can it be Cardinal Antonelli himself? No surely: anyhow it is not the Pope, and I do not see my way to accept it for what it is not. I do not speak as if I had any difficulty in recognizing and condemning the Errors which it catalogues, did the Pope himself bid me; but he has not as yet done so, and he cannot delegate his *Magisterium* to another. I wish with St. Jerome to "speak with the Successor of the Fisherman and the Disciple of the Cross." I assent to that which the Pope propounds in faith and morals, but it must be he speaking officially, personally, and immediately, and not any one else, who has a hold over me. The Syllabus is not an official act, because it is not signed, for instance, with " Datum Romæ, Pius P. P. IX.," or " sub annulo Piscatoris," or in some other way; it is not a personal, for he does not address his "Venerabiles Fratres," or " Dilecto Filio," or speak as " Pius Episcopus "; it is not an immediate, for it comes to the Bishops only through the Cardinal Minister of State.

If, indeed, the Pope should ever make that anonymous compilation directly his own, then of course I should bow to it and accept it as strictly his. He might have done so; he might do so still; again, he might issue a fresh list of Propositions in addition, and pronounce them to be Errors, and I should take that condemnation to be of dogmatic authority, because I believe him appointed by his Divine Master to determine in the detail of faith and morals what is true and what is false. But such an act of his he would formally authenticate; he would speak in his own name, as Leo X. or Innocent

XI. did, by Bull or Letter Apostolic. Or, if he wished to speak less authoritatively, he would speak through a Sacred Congregation; but the Syllabus makes no claim to be acknowledged as the word of the Pope. Moreover, if the Pope drew up that catalogue, as it may be called, he would have pronounced in it some definite judgment on the propositions themselves. What gives cogency to this remark is, that a certain number of Bishops and theologians, when a Syllabus was in contemplation, did wish for such a formal act on the part of the Pope, and in consequence they drew up for his consideration the sort of document on which, if he so willed, he might suitably stamp his infallible sanction; but he did not accede to their prayer. This composition is contained in the "*Recueil des Allocutions,*" etc., and is far more than a mere "collection of errors." It is headed, "Theses ad Apostolicam Sedem delatæ *cum censuris,*" etc., and each error from first to last has the ground of its condemnation marked upon it. There are sixty-one of them. The first is "impia, injuriosa religioni," etc.; the second is "complexivè sumpta, falsa," etc.; the third the same; the fourth, "hæretica," and so on, the epithets affixed having a distinct meaning, and denoting various degrees of error. Such a document, unlike the Syllabus, has a substantive character.

Here I am led to interpose a remark; it is plain, then, that there are those near, or with access, to the Holy Father, who would, if they could, go much further in the way of assertion and command than the divine *Assistentia*, which overshadows him, wills or permits: so that his acts and his words on doctrinal subjects must be carefully scrutinized and weighed, before we can be sure what really he has said. Utterances which must be received as coming from an Infallible Voice are not made every day, indeed they are very rare; and those which are by some persons affirmed or assumed to be such, do not always turn out what they are said to be; nay, even such as are really dogmatic must be read by definite rules and by traditional principles of interpretation, which are as cogent and unchangeable as the Pope's own decisions themselves. What I have to say presently will illustrate this truth; meanwhile I use the circumstance which has led to my mentioning it, for another purpose here. When intelligence which we receive from Rome startles and pains us from its seemingly harsh or extreme character, let us learn to have some little faith and patience, and not take for granted that all that is reported is the truth. There are those who wish and try to carry measures, and declare they have carried, when they have not carried them. How many strong things, for instance, have been reported with a sort of triumph on one side and with irritation and despondency on the other, of what the Vatican Council has done; whereas the very next year after it, Bishop Fessler, the Secretary General of the Council, brings out his work on "True and False Infallibility," reducing what was said to be so monstrous to its true dimensions. When I see all this going on, those grand lines in the Greek Tragedy always rise on my lips—

> Oupote tan Dios armonian
> Thnaton parexiasi Boulai—

and still more the consolation given us by a Divine Speaker that, though the swelling sea is so threatening to look at, yet there is One who rules it and says, "Hitherto shalt thou come and no further, and here shall thy proud waves be stayed!"

But to return: the Syllabus then has no dogmatic force; it addresses us, not in its separate portions, but as a whole, and is to be received from the Pope by an act of obedience, not of faith, that obedience being shown by having recourse to the original and authoritative documents (allocutions and the like) to which it pointedly refers. Moreover, when we turn to those documents, which *are* authoritative, we find the Syllabus cannot even be called an echo of the Apostolic Voice; for, in matters in which wording is so important, it is not an exact transcript of the words of the Pope, in its account of the errors condemned—just as is natural in what is professedly an index for reference.

Mr. Gladstone indeed wishes to unite the Syllabus to that Encyclical which so moved him in December, 1864, and says that the Errors noted in the Syllabus are all brought under the infallible judgment pronounced on certain errors specified in the Encyclical. This is an untenable assertion. He says of the Pope and of the Syllabus (p. 20) : " These are not mere opinions of the Pope himself, nor even are they opinions which he might paternally recommend to the pious consideration of the faithful. With the promulgation of his opinions is unhappily combined, in the Encyclical Letter *which virtually, though not expressly, includes the whole*, a *command* to all his spiritual children (from which command we, the disobedient children, are in no way excluded) *to hold them*," and Mr. Gladstone appeals in proof of this to the language of the Encyclical; but let us see what that language is. The Pope speaks thus, as Mr. Gladstone himself quotes him: " All and each of the wrong opinions and doctrines, *mentioned one by one in this Encyclical* (*hisce litteris*), by our Apostolical authority, we reprobate, etc." He says then, as plainly as words can speak, that the wrong opinions which in this passage he condemns, are specified *in* the Encyclical, not outside of it; and, when we look into the earlier part of it, there they are, about ten of them; there is not a single word in the Encyclical to show that the Pope in it was alluding to the Syllabus. The Syllabus does not exist, as far as the language of the Encyclical is concerned. This gratuitous assumption seems to me marvellously unfair.

The only connection between the Syllabus and the Encyclical is one external to them both, the connection of time and organ; Cardinal Antonelli sending them both to the Bishops with the introduction of one and the same letter. In that letter he speaks to the Bishops thus, as I paraphrase his words: *"The Holy Father sends you by me a list, which he has caused to be drawn up and printed, of the errors which he has in various formal documents, in the course of the last eighteen years, noted. With that list of errors, he is also sending you a new Encyclical, which he has judged it *apropos* to write to the Catholic Bishops; so I send you both at once."

The Syllabus, then, is a list, or rather an index, of the Pope's Encyclical or Allocutional "proscriptions," an index *raisonné* (not alphabetical, as is found, for instance, in Bellarmine's or Lambertini's works), drawn up by the Pope's orders, out of his paternal care for the flock of Christ, and conveyed to the Bishops through his Minister of State. But we can no more accept it as *de fide*, as a dogmatic document, than any other index or

* His actual words (abridged) are these: "Notre T. S. S. Pius IX., n'a jamais cessé de proscrire les principales erreurs de notre trèsmalheureuse époque, par ses Encycliques, et par ses Allocutions, etc. Mais comme il peut arriver que tous les actes pontificaux ne perviennent pas à chacun des Ordinaires, le même Souverain Pontife a voulu que l'on rédigeât un Syllabus de ces mêmes erreurs, destiné à être envoyé à tous les Evêques, etc. Il m'a ensuite ordonné de veiller à ce que ce Syllabus imprimé fût envoyé à V. E. R. dans ce temps où le même Souverain Pontife a jugé à propos d'écrire un autre Lettre Encyclique. Ainsi, je m'empresse d'envoyer à V. E. ce Syllabus avec ces Lettres."

table of contents. Take a parallel case, *mutatis mutandis:* Counsel's opinion being asked on a point of law, he goes to his law books, writes down his answer, and, as authority, refers his client to 23 George III., c. 5, s. 11 ; 11 Victoria, c. 12, s. 19, and to Thomas *v.* Smith, Att. Gen. *v.* Roberts, and Jones *v.* Owen. Who would say that that sheet of foolscap has force of law, when it was nothing more than a list of references to the Statutes of the Realm, or judges' decisions, in which the Law's voice really was found ?

The value of the Syllabus, then, lies in its references ; but of these Mr. Gladstone has certainly availed himself very little. Yet, in order to see the nature and extent of the blame cast on any proposition of the Syllabus, it is absolutely necessary to turn out the passage of the Allocution, Encyclical, or other document in which the error is noted ; for the wording of the errors which the Syllabus contains is to be interpreted by its references. Instead of this Mr. Gladstone uses forms of speech about the Syllabus which only excite in me fresh wonder. Indeed, he speaks upon these ecclesiastical subjects generally in a style in which priests and parsons are accused by their enemies of speaking concerning geology. For instance, the Syllabus, as we have seen, is a list or index ; but he calls it "extraordinary declarations" (p. 21). How can a list of errors be a series of Pontifical "Declarations" ?

However, perhaps he would say that, in speaking of "Declarations," he was referring to the authoritative allocutions, etc., which I have accused him of neglecting. With all my heart ; but then let us see how the statements in these allocutions fulfil the character he gives of them. He calls them "Extraordinary declarations on personal and private duty" (p. 21), and "stringent condemnations" (p. 19). Now, I certainly must grant that some are stringent, but only some. One of the most severe that I have found among them is that in the Apostolic Letter of June 10, 1851, against some heretic priest out at Lima, whose elaborate work in six volumes against the Curia Romana, is pronounced to be in its various statements "scandalous, rash, false, schismatical, injurious to the Roman Pontiffs and Ecumenical Councils, impious and heretical." It well deserved to be called by these names, which are not terms of abuse, but each with its definite meaning; and, if Mr. Gladstone, in speaking of the condemnations, had confined his epithet "stringent" to it, no one would have complained of him. And another severe condemnation is that of the works of Professor Nuytz.' But let us turn to some other of the so-called condemnations, in order to ascertain whether they answer to his general description of them.

1. For instance, take his own 16th (the 77th of the "erroneous Propositions"), that "It is no longer expedient that the Catholic Religion should be established to the exclusion of all others." When we turn to the Allocution, which is the ground of its being put into the Syllabus, what do we find there? First, that the Pope was speaking, not of States universally, but of one particular State, Spain, definitely Spain; secondly, that he was not noting the erroneous proposition directly, or categorically, but was protesting against the breach in many ways of the Concordat on the part of the Spanish government; further, that he was not referring to any work containing the said proposition, nor contemplating any proposition at all; nor, on the other hand, using any word of condemnation whatever, nor using any harsher terms of the government in question than an expression of "his wonder and distress." And again, taking the Pope's remonstrance as it stands, is it any great cause

of complaint to Englishmen, who so lately were severe in their legislation upon Unitarians, Catholics, unbelievers, and others, that the Pope merely does *not* think it expedient for *every* state *from this time forth* to tolerate *every* sort of religion on its territory, and to disestablish the Church at once? for this is all that he denies. As in the instance in the foregoing section, he does but deny a universal, which the "erroneous proposition" asserts without any explanation.

2. Another of Mr. Gladstone's "stringent Condemnations" (his 18th) is the Pope's denial of the proposition that "the Roman Pontiff can and ought to come to terms with Progress, Liberalism, and the New Civilization." I turn to the Allocution of March 18, 1861, and find there no formal condemnation of this Proposition at all. The Allocution is a long *argument* to the effect that the moving parties in that Progress, Liberalism, and New Civilization, make use of it so seriously to the injury of the Faith and the Church that it is both out of the power, and contrary to the duty, of the Pope to come to terms with them. Nor would those prime movers themselves differ from him here; certainly in this country it is the common cry that Liberalism is and will be the Pope's destruction, and they wish and mean it so to be. This Allocution on the subject is at once beautiful, dignified, and touching: and I cannot conceive how Mr. Gladstone should make stringency his one characteristic of these condemnations, especially when after all there is here no condemnation at all.

3. Take, again, Mr. Gladstone's 15th—"That the abolition of Temporal Power of the Popedom would be highly advantageous to the Church." Neither can I find in the Pope's Allocution any formal condemnation whatever of this proposition, much less a "stringent" one. Even the Syllabus does no more in the case of

any one of the eighty than to call it an "error"; and what the Pope himself says of this particular error is only this: "We cannot but in particular *warn* and *reprove* (monere et redarguere) those who applaud the decree by which the Roman Pontiff has been despoiled of all the honor and dignity of his civil rule, and assert that the said decree, more than anything else, conduces to the liberty and prosperity of the Church itself" (*Alloc.*, April 20, 1849).

4. Take another of his instances, the 17th, the "error" that "in countries called Catholic the public exercise of other religions may laudably be allowed." I have had occasion to mention already his mode of handling the Latin text of this proposition—viz., that whereas the men who are forbidden the public exercise of their religion were foreigners, who had no right to be in a country not their own at all, and might fairly have conditions imposed upon them during their stay there, nevertheless Mr. Gladstone (apparently through haste) has left out the word "hominibus illuc immigrantibus," on which so much turns. Next, as I have observed above, it was only the sufferance of their *public* worship, and again of all worships whatsoever, however many and various, which the Pope blamed; and further, the Pope's words do not apply to all States, but specially, and, as far as the Allocution goes, definitely, to New Granada.

However, the point I wish to insist upon here is, that there was in this case no condemned proposition at all, but it was merely, as in the case of Spain, an act of the government which the Pope protested against. The Pope merely told that government that that act, and other acts which they had committed, gave him very great pain; that he had expected better things of them; that the way they went on was all of a piece; and they had his best prayers. Somehow, it seems to me strange for any one to call an expostulation like this one of a set of "extraordinary declarations" "stringent condemnations."

I am convinced that the more the propositions and the references contained in the Syllabus are examined, the more signally will the charge break down, brought against the Pope on occasion of it: as to those Propositions which Mr. Gladstone specially selects, some of them I have already taken in hand, and but few of them present any difficulty.

5. As to those on Marriage, I cannot follow Mr. Gladstone's meaning here, which seems to me very confused, and it would be going out of the line of remark which I have traced out for myself (and which already is more extended than I could wish), were I to treat of them.*

6. His fourth Error (taken from the Encyclical), that "Papal judgments and decrees may, without sin, be disobeyed or differed from," is a denial of the principle of Hooker's celebrated work on Ecclesiastical Polity, and would be condemned by him as well as by the Pope. And it is plain to common sense that no society can stand if its rules are disobeyed. What club or union would not expel members who refused so to be bound?

7. And the 5th,† 8th, and 9th propositions are necessarily errors, if the Sketch of Church Polity drawn out in my former sections is true, and are necessarily considered to be such by those, as the Pope, who maintain that Polity.

\* I have observed on them in Postscript on § 7.
† Father Coleridge, in his Sermon on "The Abomination of Desolation," observes that, whereas Proposition 5th speaks of "jura," Mr. Gladstone translates "*civil* jura." Vid. also the *Month* for December, but above all Mgr. Dupanloup's works on the general subject.

8. The 10th Error, as others which I have noticed above, is a *universal* (that "in the conflict of laws, civil and ecclesiastical, the civil law should prevail"), and the Pope does but deny a universal.

9. Mr. Gladstone's 11th, which I do not quite understand in his wording of it, runs thus: "Catholics can approve of that system of education for youth which is separated from the Catholic faith and the Church's power, and which regards the science only of physical things, and the outlines (fines) of earthly social life alone or at least primarily." How is this not an "Error"? Surely there are Englishmen enough who protest against the elimination of religion from our schools; is such a protest so dire an offence to Mr. Gladstone?

10. And the 12th Error is this: That "the science of philosophy and of morals, also the laws of the State, can and should keep clear of divine and ecclesiastical authority." This too will not be anything short of an error in the judgment of great numbers of our own people. Is Benthamism so absolutely the truth, that the Pope is to be denounced because he has not yet become a convert to it?

11. There are only two of the condemnations which really require a word of explanation; I have already referred to them. One is that of Mr. Gladstone's sixth Proposition, "Roman Pontiffs and Ecumenical Councils have departed from the limits of their power, have usurped the rights of princes, and even in defining matters of faith and morals have erred." These words are taken from the Lima Priest's book. We have to see then what *he* means by "the rights of princes," for the proposition is condemned in *his* sense of the word. It is a rule of the Church in the condemnation of a book to state the proposition condemned in the words of the book

itself, without the Church being answerable for those words as employed.* I have already referred to this rule in my 5th Section. Now this priest includes among the rights of Catholic princes that of deposing Bishops from their sacred ministry, of determining the impediments to marriage, of forming episcopal sees, and of being free from episcopal authority in spiritual matters. When, then, the Proposition is condemned "that Popes had usurped the rights of princes," what is meant is, "the so-called rights of princes," which were really the rights of the Church, in assuming which there was no usurpation at all.

12. The other proposition, Mr. Gladstone's seventh, the condemnation of which requires a remark, is this: "The Church has not the power to employ force (vis inferendæ) nor any temporal power direct or indirect."

This is one of a series of Propositions found in the work of Professor Nuytz, entitled *Juris Ecclesiastici Institutiones*, all of which are condemned in the Pope's Apostolic Letter of August 22, 1851. Now here "employing force" is not the Pope's phrase but Professor Nuytz's, and the condemnation is meant to run thus, "It is an error to say, with Professor Nuytz, that what *he* calls 'employing force' is not allowable to the Church." That this is the right interpretation of the "error" depends of course on a knowledge of the professor's work, which I have never had an opportunity

\* Propositiones, de quibus Ecclesia judicium suum pronunciat, duobus præsertim modis spectari possunt, vel absolutè ac in se ipsis, vel relativè ad sensum libri et auctoris. In censurâ propositionis alicujus auctoris vel libri, Ecclesia attendit ad sensum ab eo intentum, qui quidem ex verbis, ex totâ doctrinæ ipsius serie, libri textura et confirmatione, consilio, institutoque elicitur. Propositio libri vel auctoris *æquivoca* esse potest, duplicemque habere sensum, rectum unum et alterum malum. *Ubi contingit Ecclesiam propositiones hujusmodi æquivocas absque prævia distinctione sensuum configere, censura unicè cadit in sensum perversum libri vel auctoris* (Tournely, t. 2, p. 170, ed. 1752).

of seeing; but here I will set down what the received doctrine of the Church is on ecclesiastical punishments, as stated in a work of the highest authority, since it comes to us with letters of approval from Gregory XVI. and Pius IX.

"The opinion," says Cardinal Soglia, "that the coercive power divinely bestowed upon the Church consists in the infliction of spiritual punishments alone, and not in corporal or temporal, seems more in harmony with the gentleness of the Church. Accordingly I follow their judgment who withdraw from the Church the corporal sword, by which the body is destroyed or blood is shed. Pope Nicholas thus writes: 'The Church has no sword but the spiritual. She does not kill, but gives life, hence that well-known saying 'Ecclesia abhorret a sanguine.' But the lighter punishments, though temporal and corporal, such as shutting up in a monastery, prison, flogging, and others of the same kind, short of effusion of blood, the Church *jure suo* can inflict" (*Institut. Jur.*, pp. 167-8, Paris).

And the Cardinal quotes the words of Fleury: "The Church has enjoined on penitent sinners almsgivings, fastings, and other corporal inflictions. . . . Augustine speaks of beating with sticks, as practised by the Bishops, after the manner of masters in the case of servants, parents in the case of children, and schoolmasters in that of scholars. Abbots flogged monks in the way of paternal and domestic chastisement. . . . Imprisonment for a set time or for life is mentioned among canonical penances; priests and other clerics, who had been deposed for their crimes, being committed to prison in order that they might pass the time to come in penance for their crime, which thereby was withdrawn from the memory of the public."

But now I have to answer one question. If what I have said is substantially the right explanation to give to the drift and contents of the Syllabus, have not I to account for its making so much noise, and giving such deep and wide offence on its appearance? It has already been reprobated by the voice of the world. Is there not, then, some reason at the bottom of the aversion felt by educated Europe towards it, which I have not mentioned? This is a very large question to entertain, too large for this place; but I will say one word upon it.

Doubtless one of the reasons of the excitement and displeasure which the Syllabus caused and causes so widely, is the number and variety of the propositions marked as errors, and the systematic arrangement to which they were subjected. So large and elaborate a work struck the public mind as a new law, moral, social, and ecclesiastical, which was to be the foundation of a European code, and the beginning of a new world in opposition to the social principles of the nineteenth century; and there certainly were persons in high station who encouraged this idea. When this belief was once received, it became the interpretation of the whole collection through the eighty Propositions, of which it recorded the erroneousness; as if it had for its object in all its portions one great scheme of aggression. Then, when the public mind was definitively directed to the examination of these erroneous *Theses*, they were sure to be misunderstood, from their being read apart from the context, occasion, and drift of each. They had been noted as errors in the Pope's Encyclicals and Allocutions in the course of the preceding eighteen years, and no one had taken any notice of them; but now, when they were brought all together, they made a great sensation. Why were they brought together (it was asked), except for some purpose sinister and hostile to society? and if they themselves were hard to understand, still more so, and doubly so, was their proscription.

Another circumstance, which I am not theologian enough to account for, is this—that the wording of many of the erroneous propositions, as they are drawn up in the Syllabus, gives an apparent breadth to the matter condemned which is not found in the Pope's own words in his Allocutions and Encyclicals. Not that really there is any difference between the Pope's words and Cardinal Antonelli's, for (as I have shown in various instances) what the former says in the concrete, the latter does but repeat in the abstract. Or, to speak logically, when the Pope enunciates as true the particular affirmative, "Spain ought to keep up the establishment of the Catholic Religion," then (since its contradictory is necessarily false) the Cardinal declares, "To say that no State should keep up the establishment of the Catholic Religion is an error." But there is a dignity and beauty in the Pope's own language which the Cardinal's abstract Syllabus cannot have, and this gave to opponents an opportunity to declaim against the Pope, which opportunity was in no sense afforded by what he said himself.

Then, again, it must be recollected, in connection with what I have said, that theology is a science, and a science of a special kind; its reasoning, its method, its modes of expression, and its language are all its own. Every science must be in the hands of a comparatively few persons—that is, of those who have made it a study. The courts of law have a great number of rules in good measure traditional; so has the House of Commons, and, judging by what one reads in the public prints, men must have a noviceship there before they can be at perfect ease in their position. In like manner young theologians, and still more those who are none, are sure to mistake in matters of detail; indeed a really first-rate theologian is rarely to be found. At Rome the rules of interpreting authoritative documents are known with a perfection which at this time is scarcely to be found elsewhere. Some of these rules, indeed, are known to all priests; but even this general knowledge is not possessed by laymen, much less by Protestants, however able and experienced in their own several lines of study or profession. One of those rules I have had several times occasion to mention. In the censure of books, which offend against doctrine or discipline, it is a common rule to take sentences out of them in the author's own words, whether those are words in themselves good or bad, and to affix some note of condemnation to them in the sense in which they occur in the book in question. Thus it may happen that even what seems at first sight a true statement is condemned for being made the shelter of an error; for instance: "Faith justifies when it works," or "There is no religion where there is no charity," may be taken in a good sense; but each proposition is condemned in Quesnell, because it is false as he uses it.

A further illustration of the necessity of a scientific education in order to understand the value of Propositions, is afforded by a controversy which has lately gone on among us as to the validity of Abyssinian Orders. In reply to a document urged on one side of the question, it was allowed on the other that, "if that document was to be read in the same way as we should read any ordinary judgment, the interpretation which had been given to it was the most obvious and natural." "But it was well known," it was said, "to those who are familiar with the practical working of such decisions, that they are only interpreted with safety in the light of certain rules, which arise out of what is called the *stylus curiæ*." And then some of these rules were given; first, "that to understand the real meaning of a decision, no matter how clearly set forth, we should know the nature of the difficulty or *dubium*, as it was understood by the tribunal that had to decide upon it. Next, nothing but the direct proposition, in its nudest and severest sense, as distinguished from indirect propositions, the grounds of the decision, or implied statements, is ruled by the judgment. Also, if there is anything in the wording of a decision which appears inconsistent with the teaching of an approved body of theologians, etc., the decision is to be interpreted so as to leave such teaching intact"; and so on.* It is plain that the view thus opened upon us has further bearings than that for which I make use of it here.

These remarks on scientific theology apply also, of course, to its language. I have employed myself in illustration in framing a sentence, which would be plain enough to any priest, but I think would perplex any Protestant. I hope it is not of too light a character to introduce here. We will suppose then a theologian to write as follows: "Holding, as we do, that there is only *material* sin in those who, being *invincibly* ignorant, reject the truth, therefore in charity we hope that they have the future portion of *formal* believers, as considering that by *virtue* of their good faith, though not of the *body* of the faithful, they *implicitly* and *interpretatively* believe what they seem to deny." Now let us consider what sense would this statement convey to the mind of a member of some Reformation Society or Protestant League? He would read it as follows, and consider it all the more insidious and dangerous for its being so

* *Month*, Nov. and Dec., 1873.

very unintelligible: "Holding, as we do, that there is only a very considerable sin in those who reject the truth out of contumacious ignorance, therefore in charity we hope that they have the future portion of nominal Christians, as considering, that by the excellence of their living faith, though not in the number of believers, they believe without any hesitation, as interpreters [of Scripture?] what they seem to deny."

Now, considering that the Syllabus was intended for the Bishops, who would be the interpreters of it, as the need rose, to their people, and it got bodily into English newspapers even before it was received at many an episcopal residence, we shall not be surprised at the commotion which accompanied its publication.

I have spoken of the causes intrinsic to the Syllabus, which have led to misunderstandings about it. As to external, I can be no judge myself as to what Catholics who have means of knowing are very decided in declaring, the tremendous power of the Secret Societies. It is enough to have suggested here, how a widespread organization like theirs might malign and frustrate the most beneficial acts of the Pope. One matter I had information of myself from Rome at the time when the Syllabus had just been published, before there was yet time to ascertain how it would be taken by the world at large. Now, the Rock of St. Peter on its summit enjoys a pure and serene atmosphere, but there is a great deal of Roman *malaria* at the foot of it. While the Holy Father was in great earnestness and charity addressing the Catholic world by his Cardinal Minister, there were circles of light-minded men in his city who were laying bets with each other whether the Syllabus would "make a row in Europe" or not. Of course it was the interest of those who betted on the affirmative side to represent the Pope's act to the greatest disadvantage; and it was very easy to kindle a flame in the mass of English and other visitors at Rome which with a very little nursing was soon strong enough to take care of itself.

# CHAPTER VIII.

## THE VATICAN COUNCIL.

A Personal Explanation.—Reasons for and against accepting the Council's Definition of Papal Infallibility.—The Vatican compared with the early Councils of the Church.—Objections against it considered.—Does the Definition of Infallibility conflict with Historical Facts?

IN beginning to speak of the Vatican Council, I am obliged from circumstances to begin by speaking of myself. The most unfounded and erroneous assertions have publicly been made about my sentiments towards it, and as confidently as they are unfounded. Only a few weeks ago it was stated categorically by some anonymous correspondent of a Liverpool paper, with reference to the prospect of my undertaking the task on which I am now employed, that it was, "in fact, understood that at one time Dr. Newman was on the point of uniting with Dr. Döllinger and his party, and that it required the earnest persuasion of several members of the Roman Catholic Episcopate to prevent him from taking that step"—an unmitigated and most ridiculous untruth in every word of it, nor would it be worth while to notice it here, except for its connection with the subject on which I am entering.

But the explanation of such reports about me is easy.

They arise from forgetfulness on the part of those who spread them that there are two sides of ecclesiastical acts, that right ends are often prosecuted by very unworthy means, and that in consequence those who, like myself, oppose a line of action, are not necessarily opposed to the issue for which it has been adopted. Jacob gained by wrong means his destined blessing. "All are not Israelites who are of Israel," and there are partisans of Rome who have not the sanctity and wisdom of Rome herself.

I am not referring to anything which took place within the walls of the Council chambers; of that, of course, we know nothing; but even though things occurred there which it is not pleasant to dwell upon, that would not at all affect, not by a hair's-breadth, the validity of the resulting definition, as I shall presently show. What I felt deeply, and ever shall feel while life lasts, is the violence and cruelty of journals and other publications, which, taking as they professed to do the Catholic side, employed themselves by their rash language (though, of course, they did not mean it so), in unsettling the weak in faith, throwing back inquirers, and shocking the Protestant mind. Nor do I speak of publications only; a feeling was too prevalent in many places that no one could be true to God and His Church who had any pity on troubled souls, or any scruple of "scandalizing those little ones who believe in" Christ, and of "despising and destroying him for whom He died."

It was this most keen feeling, which made me say, as I did continually, "I will not believe that the Pope's Infallibility will be defined, till defined it is."

Moreover, a private letter of mine became public property. That letter, to which Mr. Gladstone has referred with a compliment to me which I have not merited, was one of the most confidential I ever wrote in my life. I wrote it to my own Bishop, under a deep sense of the responsibility I should incur, were I not to speak out to him my whole mind. I put the matter from me when I had said my say, and kept no proper copy of the letter. To my dismay I saw it in the public prints: to this day I do not know, nor suspect, how it got there; certainly from no want of caution in the quarter to which it was addressed. I cannot withdraw it, for I never put it forward, so it will remain on the columns of newspapers whether I will or not; but I withdraw it as far as I can, by declaring that it was never meant for the public eye.

1. So much as to my posture of mind before the Definition: now I will set down how I felt after it. On July 24, 1870, I wrote as follows:

"I saw the new Definition yesterday, and am pleased at its moderation—that is, if the doctrine in question is to be defined at all. The terms are vague and comprehensive; and, personally, I have no difficulty in admitting it. The question is, Does it come to me with the authority of an Ecumenical Council?

"Now the *primâ facie* argument is in favor of its having that authority. The Council was legitimately called; it was more largely attended than any Council before it; and innumerable prayers from the whole of Christendom have preceded and attended it, and merited a happy issue of its proceedings.

"Were it not then for certain circumstances, under which the Council made the definition, I should receive that definition at once. Even as it is, if I were called upon to profess it, I should be unable, considering it came from the Holy Father and the competent local authorities, at once to refuse to do so. On the other hand, it cannot be denied that there are reasons for a

Catholic, till better informed, to suspend his judgment on its validity.

"We all know that ever since the opening of the Council there has been a strenuous opposition to the definition of the doctrine ; and that, at the time when it was actually passed, more than eighty Fathers absented themselves from the Council, and would have nothing to do with its act. But, if the fact be so, that the Fathers were not unanimous, is the definition valid? This depends on the question whether unanimity, at least moral, is or is not necessary for its validity? As at present advised I think it is; certainly Pius IV. lays great stress on the unanimity of the Fathers in the Council of Trent. 'Quibus rebus perfectis,' he says in his Bull of Promulgation, 'concilium tantâ *omnium qui illi interfuerunt* concordiâ peractum fuit, ut consensum plane *a Domino* effectum esse constiterit ; idque in nostris atque omnium oculis valdè mirabile fuerit."

"Far different has been the case now, though the Council is not yet finished. But, if I must now at once decide what to think of it, I should consider that all turned on what the dissentient Bishops now do.

"If they separate and go home without acting as a body, if they act only individually, or as individuals, and each in his own way, then I should not recognize in their opposition to the majority that force, firmness, and unity of view which creates a real case of want of moral unanimity in the Council.

"Again, if the Council continues to sit, if the dissentient Bishops more or less take part in it, and concur in its acts ; if there is a new Pope, and he continues the policy of the present; and if the Council terminates without any reversal or modification of the definition, or any effective movement against it on the part of the dissentients, then again there will be good reason for saying that the want of a moral unanimity has not been made out.

"And further, if the definition is consistently received by the whole body of the faithful as valid, or as the expression of a truth, then too it will claim our assent by the force of the great dictum, 'Securus judicat orbis terrarum.'

"This indeed is a broad principle by which all acts of the rulers of the Church are ratified. But for it, we might reasonably question some of the past Councils or their acts."

Also I wrote as follows to a friend, who was troubled at the way in which the dogma was passed, in order to place before him in various points of view the duty of receiving it:

"July 27, 1870.

"I have been thinking over the subject which just now gives you and me with thousands of others, who care for religion, so much concern.

"First, till better advised, nothing shall make me say that a mere majority in a Council, as opposed to a moral unanimity, in itself creates an obligation to receive its dogmatic decrees. This is a point of history and precedent, and of course on further examination I may find myself wrong in the view which I take of history and precedent; but I do not, cannot see, that a majority in the present Council can of itself *rule* its own sufficiency, without such external testimony.

"But there are other means by which I can be brought under the obligation of receiving a doctrine as a dogma. If I am clear that there is a primitive and uninterrupted tradition, as of the divinity of our Lord; or where a high probability drawn from Scripture or Tradition is partially or probably confirmed by the

Church. Thus a particular Catholic might be so nearly sure that the promise to Peter in Scripture proves that the infallibility of Peter is a necessary dogma, as only to be kept from holding it as such by the absence of any judgment on the part of the Church, so that the present unanimity of the Pope and five hundred Bishops, even though not sufficient to constitute a formal Synodal act, would at once put him in the position, and lay him under the obligation, of receiving the doctrine as a dogma—that is, to receive it with its anathema.

"Or again, if nothing definitely sufficient from Scripture or Tradition can be brought to contradict a definition, the fact of a legitimate Superior having defined it, may be an obligation in conscience to receive it with an internal assent. For myself, ever since I was a Catholic, I have held the Pope's infallibility as a matter of theological opinion; at least, I see nothing in the Definition which necessarily contradicts Scripture, Tradition, or History; and the "Doctor Ecclesiæ" (as the Pope is styled by the Council of Florence) bids me accept it. In this case, I do not receive it on the word of the Council, but on the Pope's self-assertion.

"And I confess, the fact that all along for so many centuries the Head of the Church and Teacher of the faithful and Vicar of Christ has been allowed by God to assert virtually his own infallibility, is a great argument in favor of the validity of his claim.

"Another ground for receiving the dogma, still not upon the direct authority of the Council, or with acceptance of the validity of its act *per se*, is the consideration that our merciful Lord would not care so little for His elect people, the multitude of the faithful, as to allow their visible Head and such a large number of Bishops to lead them into error, and an error so serious, if an error it be. This consideration leads me to accept the doctrine as a dogma, indirectly indeed from the Council, but not so much from a Council, as from the Pope and a very large number of Bishops. The question is not whether they had a right to impose, or even were right in imposing the dogma on the faithful; but whether, having done so, I have not an obligation to accept it, according to the maxim, 'Fieri non debuit, factum valet.'"

This letter, written before the minority had melted away, insists on this principle, that a Council's definition would have a virtual claim on our reception, even though it were not passed *conciliariter*, but in some indirect way; the great object of a Council being in some way or other to declare the judgment of the Church. I think the Third Ecumenical will furnish an instance of what I mean. There the question in dispute was settled and defined, even before certain constituent portions of the Episcopal body had made their appearance; and this, with a protest of sixty-eight of the Bishops then present against the opening of the Council. When the expected party arrived, these did more than protest against the definition which had been carried; they actually anathematized the Fathers who carried it, and in this state of disunion the Council ended. How then was its definition valid? In consequence of after events, which I suppose must be considered complements, and integral portions of the Council. The heads of the various parties entered into correspondence with each other, and at the end of two years their differences with each other were arranged. There are those who have no belief in the authority of Councils at all, and feel no call upon them to discriminate between one Council and another; but Anglicans, who are so fierce against the Vatican, and so respectful towards the Ephesine, should consider what good reason they have for swallowing the third Council, while they strain out the nineteenth.

The Council of Ephesus furnishes us with another remark, bearing upon the Vatican. It was natural for men who were in the minority at Ephesus to think that the faith of the Church had been brought into the utmost peril by the definition of the Council which they had unsuccessfully opposed. They had opposed it on the conviction that the definition gave great encouragement to religious errors in the opposite extreme to those which it condemned; and, in fact, I think that, humanly speaking, the peril was extreme. The event proved it to be so, when twenty years afterwards another Council was held under the successors of the majority at Ephesus and carried triumphantly those very errors whose eventual success had been predicted by the minority. But Providence is never wanting to His Church. St. Leo, the Pope of the day, interfered with this heretical Council, and the innovating party was stopped in its career. Its acts were cancelled at the great Council of Chalcedon, the Fourth Ecumenical, which was held under the Pope's guidance, and which, without of course touching the definition of the Third, which had been settled once for all, trimmed the balance of doctrine by completing it, and excluded for ever from the Church those errors which seemed to have received some sanction at Ephesus. There is nothing, of course, that can be reversed in the definitions of the Vatican Council; but the series of its acts was cut short by the great war, and, should the need arise (which is not likely), to set right a false interpretation, another Leo will be given us for the occasion; "in monte Dominus videbit."

In this remark, made for the benefit of those who need it, as I do not myself, I shelter myself under the following passage of Molina, which a friend has pointed out to me: "Though the Holy Ghost has always been present to the Church, to hinder error in her definitions, and in consequence they are all most true and consistent, yet it is not therefore to be denied, that God, when any matters have to be defined, requires of the Church a co-operation and investigation of those matters, and that, in proportion to the quality of the men who meet together in Councils, to the investigation and diligence which is applied, and the greater or less experience and knowledge which is possessed more at one time than at other times, definitions more or less perspicuous are drawn up and matters are defined more exactly and completely at one time than at other times. . . . And, whereas by disputations, persevering reading, meditation, and investigation of matters, there is wont to be increased in course of time the knowledge and understanding of the same, and the Fathers of the later Councils are assisted by the investigation and definitions of the former, hence it arises that the definitions of later Councils are wont to be more luminous, fuller, more accurate and exact than those of the earlier. Moreover, it belongs to the later Councils to interpret and to define more exactly and fully what in earlier Councils have been defined less clearly, fully, and exactly" (*De Concord. Lib. Arbit.*, etc., xiii. 15, p. 59). So much on the circumstances under which the Vatican Council passed its definition.

2. The other main objection made to the Council is founded upon its supposed neglect of history in the decision which its Definition embodies. This objection is touched upon by Mr. Gladstone in the beginning of his Pamphlet, where he speaks of its "repudiation of ancient history," and I have an opportunity given me of noticing it here.

He asserts that, during the last forty years, "more and more have the assertions of continuous uniformity of doctrine" in the Catholic Church "receded into scarcely penetrable shadow. More and more have another series of assertions, of a living authority, ever ready to open, adopt, and shape Christian doctrine according to the times, taken their place." Accordingly, he considers that a dangerous opening has been made in the authoritative teaching of the Church for the repudiation of ancient truth and the rejection of new. However, as I understand him, he withdraws this charge from the controversy he has initiated (though not from his Pamphlet) as far as it is aimed at the pure theology of the Church. So far it "belongs," he says, "to the theological domain," and "is a matter unfit for him to discuss, as it is a question of divinity." It has been, then, no duty of mine to consider it, except as it relates to matters ecclesiastical; but I am unwilling, when a charge has been made against our theology, unsupported indeed, yet unretracted, to leave it altogether without reply; and that the more because, after renouncing "questions of divinity" at p. 14, nevertheless Mr. Gladstone brings them forward again at p. 15, speaking, as he does, of the "deadly blows of 1854 and 1870 at the old, historic, scientific, and moderate school" by the definitions of the Immaculate Conception and Papal Infallibility.

Mr. Gladstone then insists on the duty of "maintaining the truth and authority of history, and the inestimable value of the historic spirit"; and so far of course I have the pleasure of heartily agreeing with him. As the Church is a sacred and divine creation, so in like manner her history, with its wonderful evolution of events, the throng of great actors who have a part in it, and its multiform literature, stained though its annals are with human sin and error, and recorded on no system, and by uninspired authors, still is a sacred work also; and those who make light of it, or distrust its lessons, incur a grave responsibility. But it is not every one that can read its pages rightly; and certainly I cannot follow Mr. Gladstone's reading of it. He is too well informed indeed, too large in his knowledge, too acute and comprehensive in his views, not to have an acquaintance with history far beyond the run of even highly educated men; still when he accuses us of deficient attention to history, one cannot help asking whether he does not, as a matter of course, take for granted as true the principles for using it familiar with Protestant divines, and denied by our own, and in consequence whether his impeachment of us does not resolve itself into the fact that he is Protestant and we are Catholics. Nay, has it occurred to him that perhaps it is the fact, that we have views on the relation of History to Dogma different from those which Protestants maintain? And is he so certain of the facts of History in detail, of their relevancy, and of their drift, as to have a right, I do not say to have an opinion of his own, but to publish to the world, on his own warrant, that we have "repudiated ancient history"? He publicly charges us, not merely with having "neglected" it, or "garbled" its evidence, or with having contradicted certain ancient usages or doctrines to which it bears witness, but he says "repudiated." He could not have used a stronger term, supposing the Vatican Council had, by a formal act, cut itself off from early times, instead of professing, as it does (hypocritically, if you will, but still professing), to speak "supported by Holy Scripture and the decrees both of preceding Popes and General Councils," and "faithfully adhering to the aboriginal tradition of the Church." Ought any one but an *oculatus testis*, a man whose profession was to acquaint himself with the details of history, to claim to himself the right of bringing, on his own authority, so extreme a charge against so august a power, so inflexible and rooted in its traditions through the long past, as Mr. Gladstone would admit the Roman Church to be?

Of course I shall be reminded that, though Mr. Gladstone cannot be expected to speak on so large a department of knowledge with the confidence decorous in one who has made a personal study of it, there are others who have a right to do so; and that by those others he is corroborated and sanctioned. There are authors, it may be said, of so commanding an authority, from their learning and their honesty, that, for the purposes of discussion or of controversy, what they say may be said by any one else without presumption or risk of confutation. I will never say a word of my own against those learned and distinguished men to whom I refer. No: their present whereabout, wherever it is, is to me a thought full of melancholy. It is a tragical event, both for them and for us, that they have left us. It robs us of a great *prestige;* they have left none to take their place. I think them utterly wrong in what they have done and are doing; and, moreover, I agree as little in their view of history as in their acts. Extensive as may be their historical knowledge, I have no reason to think that they, more than Mr. Gladstone, would accept the position which History holds among the *Loci Theologici*, as Catholic theologians determine it; and I am denying not their report of facts, but their use of the facts they report, and that, because of that special stand-point from which they view the relations existing between the records of History and the enunciations of Popes and Councils. They seem to me to expect from History more than History can furnish, and to have too little confidence in the Divine Promise and Providence as guiding and determining those enunciations.

Why should Ecclesiastical History, any more than the text of Scripture, contain in it "the whole counsel of God"? Why should private judgment be unlawful in interpreting Scripture against the voice of authority, and yet be lawful in the interpretation of history? There are those who make short work of questions such as these by denying authoritative interpretation altogether; that is their private concern, and no one has a right to inquire into their reason for so doing; but the case would be different were one of them to come forward publicly, and to arraign others, without first confuting their theological *præambula*, for repudiating history, or for repudiating the Bible.

For myself, I would simply confess that no doctrine of the Church can be rigorously proved by historical evidence: but at the same time that no doctrine can be simply disproved by it. Historical evidence reaches a certain way, more or less, towards a proof of the Catholic doctrines; often nearly the whole way; sometimes it goes only as far as to point in their direction; sometimes there is only an absence of evidence for a conclusion contrary to them; nay, sometimes there is an apparent leaning of the evidence to a contrary conclusion, which has to be explained; in all cases there is a margin left for the exercise of faith in the word of the Church. He who believes the dogmas of the Church only because he has reasoned them out of History is scarcely a Catholic. It is the Church's dogmatic use of History in which the Catholic believes; and she uses other informants also, Scripture, tradition, the ecclesiastical sense or *phronema* and a subtle ratiocinative power, which in its origin is a divine gift. There is nothing of bondage or "renunciation of mental freedom" in this view, any more than in the converts of the Apostles believing what the Apostles might preach to them or teach them out of Scripture.

What has been said of History in relation to the formal Definitions of the Church applies also to the exercise of Ratiocination.  Our logical powers, too, being a gift from God, may claim to have their informations respected ; and Protestants sometimes accuse our theologians, for instance, the mediæval schoolmen, of having used them in divine matters a little too freely.  Still it has ever been our teaching and our protest that, as there are doctrines which lie beyond the direct evidence of history, so there are doctrines which transcend the discoveries of reason ; and, after all, whether they are more or less recommended to us by the one informant or the other, in all cases the immediate motive in the mind of a Catholic for his reception of them is, not that they are proved to him by Reason or by History, but because Revelation has declared them by means of that high ecclesiastical *Magisterium* which is their legitimate exponent.

What has been said applies also to those other truths, with which Ratiocination has more to do than History, which are sometimes called developments of Christian doctrine, truths which are not upon the surface of the Apostolic *depositum*—that is, the legacy of Revelation—but which from time to time are brought into form by theologians, and sometimes have been proposed to the faithful by the Church, as direct objects of faith.  No Catholic would hold that they ought to be logically deduced in their fulness and exactness from the belief of the first centuries, but only this, that, on the assumption of the Infallibility of the Church (which will overcome every objection except a contradiction in thought), there is nothing greatly to try the reason in such difficulties as occur in reconciling those evolved doctrines with the teaching of the ancient Fathers; such development being evidently the new form, explanation, transformation, or carrying out of what, in substance was held from the first, what the Apostles said, but have not recorded in writing, or would necessarily have said under our circumstances, or if they had been asked, or in view of certain uprisings of error, and in that sense being really portions of the legacy of truth, of which the Church, in all her members but especially in her hierarchy, is the divinely appointed trustee.

Such an evolution of doctrine has been, as I would maintain, a law of the Church's teaching from the earliest times, and in nothing is her title of "semper eadem" more remarkably illustrated than in the correspondence of her ancient and modern exhibition of it. As to the ecclesiastical acts of 1854 and 1870, I think with Mr. Gladstone that the principle of doctrinal development, and that of authority, have never in the proceedings of the Church been so freely and largely used as in the Definitions then promulgated to the faithful;—but I deny that at either time the testimony of history was repudiated or perverted. The utmost that can be fairly said by an opponent against the theological decisions of those years is, that antecedently to the event it might appear that there were no sufficient historical grounds in behalf of either of them—I do not mean for a personal belief in either, but—for the purpose of converting a doctrine long existing in the Church into a dogma, and making it a portion of the Catholic Creed. This adverse anticipation was proved to be a mistake by the fact of the definition being made.

3. I will not pass from this question of history without a word about Pope Honorius, whose condemnation

by anathema in the Sixth Ecumenical Council is certainly a strong *primâ facie* argument against the Pope's doctrinal infallibility. His case is this: Sergius, Patriarch of Constantinople, favored, or rather did not condemn, a doctrine concerning our Lord's Person which afterwards the Sixth Council pronounced to be heresy. He consulted Pope Honorius upon the subject, who in two formal letters declared his entire concurrence with Sergius's opinion. Honorius died in peace, but, more than forty years after him, the Sixth Ecumenical Council was held, which condemned him as a heretic on the score of those two letters. The simple question is, whether the heretical documents proceeded from him as an infallible authority or as a private Bishop.

Now I observe that, whereas the Vatican Council has determined that the Pope is infallible only when he speaks *ex cathedrâ*, and that, in order to speak *ex cathedrâ*, he must at least speak "as exercising the office of Pastor and Doctor of all Christians, defining, by virtue of his Apostolical authority, a doctrine whether of faith or of morals for the acceptance of the universal Church" (though Mr. Gladstone strangely says, p. 34, "There is *no* established or accepted definition of the phrase *ex cathedrâ* "), from this Pontifical and dogmatic explanation of the phrase it follows that, whatever Honorius said in answer to Sergius, and whatever he held, his words were not *ex cathedrâ*, and therefore did not proceed from his infallibility.

I say so first, because he could not fulfil the above conditions of an *ex cathedrâ* utterance, if he did not actually *mean* to fulfil them. The question is unlike the question about the Sacraments; external and positive acts, whether material actions or formal words, speak for themselves. Teaching on the other hand has no sacramental visible signs; it is an *opus operantis*, and mainly a question of intention. Who would say that the architriclinus at the wedding-feast, who said "Thou hast kept the good wine until now," was teaching the Christian world, though the words have a great ethical and evangelical sense? What is the worth of a signature, if a man does not consider he is signing? The Pope cannot address his people East and West, North and South, without meaning it, as if his very voice, the sounds from his lips, could literally be heard from pole to pole; nor can he exert his "Apostolical authority" without knowing he is doing so; nor can he draw up a form of words, and use care and make an effort in doing so accurately, without intention to do so; and, therefore, no words of Honorius proceeded from his prerogative of infallible teaching, which were not accompanied with the intention of exercising that prerogative; and who will dream of saying, be he Anglican, Protestant, unbeliever, or on the other hand Catholic, that Honorius on the occasion in question did actually intend to exert that infallible teaching voice which is heard so distinctly in the *Quantâ curâ* and the *Pastor Æternus?*

What resemblance do these letters of his, written almost as private instructions, bear to the "Pius Episcopus, Servus Servorum Dei, Sacro approbante Concilio, ad *perpetuam rei memoriam*," or with the "Si quis huic nostræ definitioni contradicere (quod Deus avertat), præsumpserit, *anathema* sit" of the *Pastor Æternus?* what to the "Venerabilibus fratribus, Patriarchis primatibus, Archiepiscopis, et Episcopis *universis*," etc., with the "reprobamus, proscribimus, atque damnamus," and the date and signature, "Datum Romæ apud Sanctum Petrum, Die 8 Dec. anno 1864, etc., Pius P. P. IX." of the *Quantâ curâ?*

Secondly, it is no part of our doctrine, as I shall say in my next section, that the discussions previous to a Council's definition, or to an *ex cathedrâ* utterance of a Pope, are infallible, and these letters of Honorius on their very face are nothing more than portions of a discussion with a view to some final decision.

For these two reasons the condemnation of Honorius by the Council in no sense compromises the doctrine of Papal Infallibility. At the utmost it only decides that Honorius in his own person was a heretic, which is inconsistent with no Catholic doctrine; but we may rather hope and believe that the anathema fell, not upon him, but upon his letters in their objective sense, he not intending personally what his letters legitimately expressed. ·

4. And I have one remark to make upon the argumentative method by which the Vatican Council was carried on to its definition. The *Pastor Æternus* refers to various witnesses as contributing their evidence towards the determination of the contents of the *depositum*, such as Tradition, the Fathers and Councils, History, but especially Scripture. For instance, the Bull speaks of the Gospel ("juxta Evangelii testimonia," c. 1) and of Scripture ("manifesta S.S. Scripturarum doctrina," c. 1 : "apertis S.S. Literarum testimoniis," c. 3. "S.S. Scripturis consentanea," c. 4). And it lays an especial stress on three passages of Scripture in particular—viz., "Thou art Peter," etc., Matthew xvi. 16-19; "I have prayed for thee," etc., Luke xxii. 32, and "Feed my sheep," etc., John xxi. 15-17. Now I wish all objectors to this method of ours, viz., of reasoning from Scripture, would view it in the light of the following passage in the great philosophical work of Butler, Bishop of Durham.

He writes as follows: "As it is owned the whole

scheme of Scripture is not yet understood, so, if it ever comes to be understood, before the 'restitution of all things,' and without miraculous interpositions, it must be in the same way as natural knowledge is come at, by the continuance and progress of learning and of liberty, and by particular persons attending to, comparing, and pursuing intimations scattered up and down it, which are overlooked and disregarded by the generality of the world. For this is the way in which all improvements are made by thoughtful men tracing on obscure hints, as it were, dropped us by nature accidentally, or which seem to come into our minds by chance. Nor is it at all incredible that a book, which has been so long in the possession of mankind, should contain many truths as yet undiscovered. For all the same phenomena, and the same faculties of investigation, from which such great discoveries in natural knowledge have been made in the present and last age, were equally in the possession of mankind several thousand years before. And possibly it might be intended that events, as they come to pass, should open and ascertain the meaning of several parts of Scripture " (ii. 3, *vide* also ii. 4, fin.)

What has the long history of the contest for and against the Pope's infallibility been but a growing insight through centuries into the meaning of those three texts, to which I just now referred, ending at length by the Church's definitive recognition of the doctrine thus gradually manifested to her?

## CHAPTER IX.

### THE VATICAN DEFINITION.

SUMMARY OF SCRIPTURE EVIDENCE FOR THE CHURCH'S RIGHT TO TEACH.—THE VATICAN COUNCIL HAS DEFINED THAT THE POPE HAS THE SAME RIGHT.—SIGNS AND CONDITIONS OF THE EXERCISE OF THIS RIGHT.—NEITHER COUNCIL NOR POPE IS INSPIRED.—DETAILED EXAMINATION OF THE USES AND METHODS OF PAPAL INFALLIBILITY.—MEANING OF THE MAXIM "OUT OF THE CHURCH THERE IS NO SALVATION."—CONTRAST BETWEEN RIGOROUS INTERPRETATION AND LOYAL MODERATION OF VIEWS ON DISPUTED QUESTIONS.

NOW I am to speak of the Vatican definition, by which the doctrine of the Pope's infallibility has become *de fide*, that is, a truth necessary to be believed, as being included in the original divine revelation, for those terms, revelation, *depositum*, dogma, and *de fide*, are correlatives; and I begin with a remark which suggests the drift of all I have to say about it. It is this: that so difficult a virtue is faith, even with the special grace of God, in proportion as the reason is exercised, so difficult is it to assent inwardly to propositions verified to us neither by reason nor experience, but depending for their reception on the word of the Church as God's oracle, that she has ever shown the utmost care to contract, as far as possible, the range of truths and the sense of propositions of which she demands this absolute reception. "The Church," says Pallavicini, "as far as may be, has ever abstained from imposing upon the minds of men that commandment, the most arduous of the Christian Law—viz., to believe obscure matters without doubting."* To co-operate in this charitable duty has been one special work of her theologians, and rules are laid down by herself, by tradition, and by custom, to assist them in the task. She only speaks when it is necessary to speak; but hardly has she spoken out magisterially some great general principle when she sets her theologians to work to explain her meaning in the concrete, by strict interpretation of its wording, by the illustration of its circumstances, and by the recognition of exceptions, in order to make it as tolerable as possible, and the least of a temptation to self-willed, independent, or wrongly educated minds. A few years ago it was the fashion among us to call writers, who conformed to this rule of the Church, by the name of "Minimizers"; that day of tyrannous *ipse-dixits*, I trust, is over: Bishop Fessler, a man of high authority, for he was Secretary General of the Vatican Council, and of higher authority still in his work, for it has the approbation of the Sovereign Pontiff, clearly proves to us that a moderation of doctrine, dictated by charity, is not inconsistent with soundness in the faith. Such a sanction, I suppose, will be considered sufficient for the character of the remarks which I am about to make upon definitions in general, and upon the Vatican in particular.

The Vatican definition, which comes to us in the shape of the Pope's Encyclical Bull called the *Pastor Æternus*, declares that "the Pope has that same infalli-

* Quoted by Father Ryder (to whom I am indebted for other of my references) in his 'Idealism in Theology," p. 25.

bility which the Church has" : * to determine therefore what is meant by the infallibility of the Pope we must turn first to consider the infallibility of the Church. And again, to determine the character of the Church's infallibility, we must consider what is the characteristic of Christianity, considered as a revelation of God's will.

Our Divine Master might have communicated to us heavenly truths without telling us that they came from Him, as it is commonly thought He has done in the case of heathen nations; but He willed the Gospel to be a revelation acknowledged and authenticated, to be public, fixed, and permanent; and accordingly, as Catholics hold, He framed a society of men to be its home, its instrument, and its guarantee. The rulers of that Association are the legal trustees, so to say, of the sacred truths which He spoke to the Apostles by word of mouth. As He was leaving them, He gave them their great commission, and bade them "teach" their converts all over the earth, "to observe all things whatever he had commanded them"; and then He added, "Lo, I am with you always, even to the end of the world."

Here, first, He told them to "teach" His revealed Truth; next, "to the consummation of all things"; thirdly, for their encouragement, He said that He would be with them "all days," all along, on every emergency or occasion, until that consummation. They had a duty put upon them of teaching their Master's words, a duty which they could not fulfil in the perfection which fidelity required without His help; therefore came His promise to be with them in their performance of it. Nor did that promise of supernatural help end with the

---

\* Romanum Pontificem eâ infallibilitate pollere, quâ divinus Redemptor Ecclesiam suam in definiendâ doctrinâ de fide vel moribus instructam esse voluit.

Apostles personally, for He adds, "to the consummation of the world," implying that the Apostles would have successors, and engaging that He would be with those successors as He had been with them.

The same safeguard of the Revelation—viz., an authoritative, permanent tradition of teaching, is insisted on by an informant of equal authority with St. Matthew, but altogether independent of him; I mean St. Paul. He calls the Church "the pillar and ground of the Truth"; and he bids his convert Timothy, when he had become a ruler in that Church, to "take heed unto his doctrine," to "keep the deposit" of the faith, and to "commit" the things which he had heard from himself "to faithful men who should be fit to teach others."

This is how Catholics understand the Scripture record, nor does it appear how it can otherwise be understood; but when we have got as far as this, and look back, we find that we have by implication made profession of a further doctrine. For, if the Church, initiated in the Apostles and continued in their successors, has been set up for the direct object of protecting, preserving, and declaring the Revelation, and that by means of the Guardianship and Providence of its Divine Author, we are led on to perceive that, in asserting this, we are in other words asserting that, so far as the message entrusted to it is concerned, the Church is infallible; for what is meant by infallibility in teaching but that the teacher in his teaching is secured from error? and how can fallible man be thus secured except by a supernatural infallible guidance? And what can have been the object of the words, "I am with you all along to the end," but to give thereby an answer by anticipation to the spontaneous, silent alarm of the feeble company of fishermen and laborers, to whom they were addressed, on their finding themselves laden with superhuman duties and responsibilities?

Such then being, in its simple outline, the infallibility of the Church, such too will be the Pope's infallibility, as the Vatican Fathers have defined it. And if we find that by means of this outline we are able to fill out in all important respects the idea of a Council's infallibility, we shall thereby be ascertaining in detail what has been defined in 1870 about the infallibility of the Pope. With an attempt to do this I shall conclude.

1. The Church has the office of teaching, and the matter of that teaching is the body of doctrine, which the Apostles left behind them as her perpetual possession. If a question arises as to what the Apostolic doctrine is on a particular point, she has infallibility promised to her to enable her to answer correctly. And as by the teaching of the Church is understood not the teaching of this or that Bishop, but their united voice, and a Council is the form the Church must take, in order that all men may recognize that in fact she is teaching on any point in dispute, so in like manner the Pope must come before us in some special form or posture, if he is to be understood to be exercising his teaching office, and that form is called *ex cathedrâ*. This term is most appropriate, as being on one occasion used by our Lord Himself. When the Jewish doctors taught, they placed themselves in Moses' seat, and spoke *ex cathedrâ;* and then, as He tells us, they were to be obeyed by their people, and that whatever were their private lives or characters. "The Scribes and Pharisees," He says, "are seated on the chair of Moses: all things therefore whatsoever they shall say to you, observe and do; but according to their works do you not, for they say and do not."

2. The forms, by which a General Council is identified as representing the Church herself, are too clear to need drawing out; but what is to be that moral *cathedra*, or teaching chair, in which the Pope sits, when he is to be recognized as in the exercise of his infallible teaching? The new definition answers this question. He speaks *ex cathedrâ*, or infallibly, when he speaks, first, as the Universal Teacher; secondly, in the name and with the authority of the Apostles; thirdly, on a point of faith or morals; fourthly, with the purpose of binding every member of the Church to accept and believe his decision.

3. These conditions of course contract the range of his infallibility most materially. Hence Billuart speaking of the Pope says: "Neither in conversation, nor in discussion, nor in interpreting Scripture or the Fathers, nor in consulting, nor in giving his reasons for the point which he has defined, nor in answering letters, nor in private deliberations, supposing he is setting forth his own opinion, is the Pope infallible" (t. ii. p. 110).\*
And for this simple reason, because on these various occasions of speaking his mind, he is not in the chair of the universal doctor.

4. Nor is this all; the greater part of Billuart's negatives refer to the Pope's utterances when he is out of the *Cathedra Petri*, but even when he is in it, his words do not necessarily proceed from his infallibility. He has no wider prerogative than a Council, and of a Council Perrone says: "Councils are not infallible in the reasons by which they are led, or on which they rely, in making their definition, nor in matters which relate to persons, nor to physical matters which have no necessary con-

---

\* And so the Swiss Bishops: "The Pope is not infallible as a man, or a theologian, or a priest, or a bishop, or a temporal prince, or a judge, or a legislator, or in his political views, or even in his government of the Church."—*Vid.* Fessler, French Trans., p. iv.

nection with dogma" (*Præl. Theol.*, t. 2, p. 492). Thus, if a Council has condemned a work of Origen or Theodoret, it did not in so condemning go beyond the work itself; it did not touch the persons of either. Since this holds of a Council, it also holds in the case of the Pope; therefore, supposing a Pope has quoted the so-called works of the Areopagite as if really genuine, there is no call on us to believe him; nor again, if he condemned Galileo's Copernicanism, unless the earth's immobility has a "necessary connection with some dogmatic truth," which the present bearing of the Holy See towards that philosophy virtually denies.

5. Nor is a Council infallible, even in the prefaces and introductions to its definitions. There are theologians of name, as Tournely and Amort,* who contend that even those most instructive *capitula* passed in the Tridentine Council, from which the Canons with anathemas are drawn up, are not portions of the Church's infallible teaching; and the parallel introductions prefixed to the Vatican anathemas have an authority not greater nor less than that of those capitula.

6. Such passages, however, as these are too closely connected with the definitions themselves not to be what is sometimes called, by a *catachresis*, "proximum fidei"; still, on the other hand, it is true also that, in those circumstances and surroundings of formal definitions, which I have been speaking of, whether on the part of a Council or a Pope, there may be not only no exercise of an infallible voice, but actual error. Thus, in the Third Council, a passage of an heretical author was quoted in defence of the doctrine defined under the belief he was Pope Julius, and narratives, not trustworthy, are introduced into the Seventh.

* *Vid.* Amort, Dem. Cr., pp. 205-6. This applies to the Unam Sanctam, *vid.* Fessler, Engl. Trans., p. 67.

This remark and several before it will become intelligible if we consider that neither Pope nor Council are on a level with the Apostles. To the Apostles the whole revelation was given, by the Church it is transmitted; no simply new truth has been given to us since St. John's death; the one office of the Church is to guard "that noble deposit" of truth, as St. Paul speaks to Timothy, which the Apostles bequeathed to her, in its fulness and integrity. Hence the infallibility of the Apostles was of a far more positive and wide character than that needed by and granted to the Church. We call it, in the case of the Apostles, inspiration; in the case of the Church, *assistentia*.

Of course there is a sense of the word "inspiration" in which it is common to all members of the Church, and therefore especially to its Bishops, and still more directly to those rulers, when solemnly called together in Council, after much prayer throughout Christendom, and in a frame of mind especially serious and earnest by reason of the work they have in hand. The Paraclete certainly is ever with them, and more effectively in a Council, as being "in Spiritu Sancto congregata"; but I speak of the special and promised aid necessary for their fidelity to Apostolic teaching; and, in order to secure this fidelity, no inward gift of infallibility is needed, such as the Apostles had, no direct suggestion of divine truth, but simply an external guardianship, keeping them off from error (as a man's good angel, without at all enabling him to walk, might, on a night journey, keep him from pitfalls in his way), a guardianship saving them, as far as their ultimate decisions are concerned, from the effects of their inherent infirmities, from any chance of extravagance, of confusion of thought, of collision with former decisions or with Scripture, which in seasons of excitement might reason-

"Never," says Perrone, "have Catholics taught that the gift of infallibility is given by God to the Church after the manner of inspiration" (t. 2, p. 253). Again: "[Human] media of arriving at the truth are excluded neither by a Council's nor by a Pope's infallibility, for God has promised it, not by way of an infused" or habitual "gift, but by the way of *assistentia*" (*Ibid.* p. 541).

But since the process of defining truth is human, it is open to the chance of error; what Providence has guaranteed is only this: that there should be no error in the final step, in the resulting definition or dogma.

7. Accordingly, all that a Council, and all that the Pope, is infallible in, is the direct answer to the special question which he happens to be considering; his prerogative does not extend beyond a power, when in his *Cathedra*, of giving that very answer truly. "Nothing," says Perrone, "but the *objects* of dogmatic definitions of Councils are immutable, for in these are Councils infallible, not in their *reasons*," etc. (*Ibid.*)

8. This rule is so strictly to be observed that, though dogmatic statements are found from time to time in a Pope's Apostolic Letters, etc., yet they are not accounted to be exercises of his infallibility if they are said only *obiter*—by the way, and without direct intention to define. A striking instance of this *sine qua non* condition is afforded by Nicholas I., who, in a letter to the Bulgarians, spoke as if baptism were valid, when administered simply in our Lord's Name, without distinct mention of the Three Persons; but he is not teaching and speaking *ex cathedrâ*, because no question on this matter was in any sense the occasion of his writing. The question asked of him was concerning the *minister* of baptism—viz., whether a Jew or Pagan could validly baptize; in answering in the affirmative, he added *obiter*,

as a private doctor, says Bellarmine, "that the baptism was valid, whether administered in the name of the three Persons or in the name of Christ only" (*De Rom. Pont.*, iv. 12).

9. Another limitation is given in Pope Pius's own conditions, set down in the *Pastor Æternus*, for the exercise of infallibility: viz., the proposition defined will be without any claim to be considered binding on the belief of Catholics, unless it is referable to the Apostolic *depositum*, through the channel either of Scripture or Tradition; and, though the Pope is the judge whether it is so referable or not, yet the necessity of his professing to abide by this reference is in itself a certain limitation of his dogmatic action. A Protestant will object indeed that, after his distinctly asserting that the Immaculate Conception and the Papal Infallibility are in Scripture and Tradition, this safeguard against erroneous definitions is not worth much, nor do I say that it is one of the most effective; but anyhow, in consequence of it, no Pope, any more than a Council, could, for instance, introduce Ignatius's Epistles into the Canon of Scripture; and, as to his dogmatic condemnation of particular books, which, of course, are foreign to the *depositum*, I would say that, as to their false doctrine, there can be no difficulty in condemning that, by means of that Apostolic deposit; nor surely in his condemning the very wording, in which they convey it, when the subject is carefully considered. For the Pope's condemning the language, for instance, of Jansenius is a parallel act to the Church's sanctioning the word "Consubstantial," and if a Council and the Pope were not infallible so far in their judgment of language, neither Pope nor Council could draw up a dogmatic definition at all, for the right exercise of words is involved in the right exercise of thought.

10. And in like manner, as regards the precepts concerning moral duties, it is not in every such precept that the Pope is infallible.* As a definition of faith must be drawn from the Apostolic *depositum* of doctrine, in order that it may be considered an exercise of infallibility, whether in the Pope or a Council, so too a precept of morals, if it is to be accepted as from an infallible voice, must be drawn from the Moral Law, that primary revelation to us from God.

That is, in the first place, it must relate to things in themselves good or evil. If the Pope prescribed lying or revenge, his command would simply go for nothing, as if he had not issued it, because he has no power over the Moral Law. If he forbade his flock to eat any but vegetable food, or to dress in a particular fashion (questions of decency and modesty not coming into the question), he would also be going beyond the province of faith, because such a rule does not relate to a matter in itself good or bad. But if he gave a precept all over the world for the adoption of lotteries instead of tithes or offerings, certainly it would be very hard to prove that he was contradicting the Moral Law, or ruling a practice to be in itself good which was in itself evil; and there are few persons but would allow that it is at least doubtful whether lotteries are abstractedly evil, and in a doubtful matter the Pope is to be believed and obeyed.

However there are other conditions besides this necessary for the exercise of Papal infallibility, in moral subjects: for instance, his definition must relate to things necessary for salvation. No one would so speak

---

\* It is observable that the *Pastor Æternus* does not speak of " præcepta " at all in its definition of the Pope's Infallibility, only of his " defining doctrine," and of his " definitions."

of lotteries, nor of a particular dress, nor of a particular kind of food; such precepts, then, did he make them, would be simply external to the range of his prerogative.

And again, his infallibility in consequence is not called into exercise, unless he speaks of the whole world; for, if his precepts, in order to be dogmatic, must enjoin what is necessary to salvation, they must be necessary for all men. Accordingly orders which issue from him for the observance of particular countries, or political or religious classes, have no claim to be the utterance of his infallibility. If he enjoins upon the hierarchy of Ireland to withstand mixed education, this is no exercise of his infallibility.

It may be added that the field of morals contains so little that is unknown and unexplored, in contrast with revelation and doctrinal fact which form the domain of faith, that it is difficult to say what portions of moral teaching in the course of eighteen hundred years actually have proceeded from the Pope, or from the Church, or where to look for such. Nearly all that either oracle has done in this respect has been to condemn such propositions as in a moral point of view are false, or dangerous, or rash; and these condemnations, besides being such as in fact will be found to command the assent of most men, as soon as heard, do not necessarily go so far as to present any positive statements for universal acceptance.

11. With the mention of condemned propositions I am brought to another and large consideration, which is one of the best illustrations that I can give of that principle of minimizing so necessary, as I think, for a wise and cautious theology; at the same time I cannot insist upon it in the connection into which I am going to introduce it, without submitting myself to the cor-

rection of divines more learned than I can pretend to be myself.

The infallibility, whether of the Church or of the Pope, acts principally or solely in two channels, in direct statements of truth, and in the condemnation of error. The former takes the shape of doctrinal definitions, the latter stigmatizes propositions as heretical, next to heresy, erroneous, and the like. In each case the Church, as guided by her Divine Master, has made provision for weighing as lightly as possible on the faith and conscience of her children.

As to the condemnation of propositions, all she tells us is, that the thesis condemned when taken as a whole, or, again, when viewed in its context, is heretical, or blasphemous, or impious, or whatever like epithet she affixes to it. We have only to trust her so far as to allow ourselves to be warned against the thesis, or the work containing it. Theologians employ themselves in determining what precisely it is that is condemned in that thesis or treatise; and doubtless in most cases they do so with success; but that determination is not *de fide;* all that is of faith is that there is in that thesis itself, which is noted, heresy or error, or other like peccant matter, as the case may be, such that the censure is a peremptory command to theologians, preachers, students, and all others whom it concerns, to keep clear of it. But so light is this obligation, that instances frequently occur when it is successfully maintained by some new writer that the Pope's act does not imply what it has seemed to imply, and questions which seemed to be closed are after a course of years reopened. In discussions such as these, there is a real exercise of private judgment and an allowable one; the act of faith, which cannot be superseded or trifled with, being, I repeat, the unreserved acceptance that the thesis in question is heretical, or the like, as the Pope or the Church has spoken of it.*

In these cases, which in a true sense may be called the Pope's *negative* enunciations, the opportunity of a legitimate minimizing lies in the intensely concrete character of the matters condemned; in his affirmative enunciations a like opportunity is afforded by their being more or less abstract. Indeed, excepting such as relate to persons, that is, to the Trinity in Unity, the Blessed Virgin, the Saints, and the like, all the dogmas of Pope or of Council are but general, and so far, in consequence, admit of exceptions in their actual application—these exceptions being determined either by other authoritative utterances, or by the scrutinizing viligance, acuteness, and the subtlety of the *Schola Theologorum*.

One of the most remarkable instances of what I am insisting on is found in a dogma, which no Catholic can ever think of disputing, viz., that "Out of the Church, and out of the faith, is no salvation." Not to go to Scripture, it is the doctrine of St. Ignatius, St. Irenæus, St. Cyprian in the first three centuries, as of St. Augustine and his contemporaries in the fourth and fifth. It can never be other than an elementary truth of Christianity; and the present Pope has proclaimed it as all Popes, doctors, and bishops before him. But that truth has two aspects, according as the force of the negative falls upon the "Church" or upon the "salvation." The main sense is, that there is no other communion or so-called Church, but the Catholic, in which are stored the promises, the sacraments, and other means of salvation; the other and derived sense is, that no one can be saved who is not *in* that one and

* Fessler seems to confine the exercise of infallibility to the *Note* "heretical," p. 11, Engl. Trans.

only Church. But it does not follow, because there is no Church but one, which has the Evangelical gifts and privileges to bestow, that therefore no one can be saved without the intervention of that one Church. Anglicans quite understand this distinction; for, on the one hand, their Article says "They are to be had accursed (anathematizandi) that presume to say, that every man shall be saved *by* (in) the law or sect which he professeth, so that he be diligent to frame his life according to that law and the light of nature"; while on the other hand they speak of and hold the doctrine of the "uncovenanted mercies of God." The latter doctrine in its Catholic form is the doctrine of invincible ignorance—or, that it is possible to belong to the soul of the Church without belonging to the body; and, at the end of eighteen hundred years, it has been formally and authoritatively put forward by the present Pope (the first Pope, I suppose, who has done so), on the very same occasion on which he has repeated the fundamental principle of exclusive salvation itself. It is to the purpose here to quote his words; they occur in the course of his Encyclical, addressed to the Bishops of Italy, under date of August 10, 1863:

"*We and you know*, that those who lie under invincible ignorance as regards our most Holy Religion, and who, diligently observing the natural law and its precepts, which are engraven by God on the hearts of all, and prepared to obey God, lead a good and upright life, are able, by the operation of the power of divine light and grace, to obtain eternal life."\*

---

\* The Pope speaks more forcibly still in an earlier Allocution. After mentioning invincible ignorance, he adds: "Quis tantum sibi arroget, ut hujusmodi ignorantiæ designare limites queat, juxta populorum, regionum, ingeniorum, aliarumque rerum tam multarum rationem et varietatem?" (*Dec.* 9, 1854).

Who would at first sight gather from the wording of so forcible a universal, that an exception to its operation, such as this, so distinct, and, for what we know, so very wide, was consistent with holding it?

Another instance of a similar kind is suggested by the general acceptance in the Latin Church, since the time of St. Augustine, of the doctrine of absolute predestination, as instanced in the teaching of other great saints besides him, such as St. Fulgentius, St. Prosper, St. Gregory, St. Thomas, and St. Buonaventure. Yet, in the last centuries a great explanation and modification of this doctrine has been effected by the efforts of the Jesuit School, which have issued in the reception of a distinction between predestination to grace and predestination to glory; and a consequent admission of the principle that, though our own works do not avail for bringing us under the action of grace here, that does not hinder their availing, when we are in a state of grace, for our attainment of eternal glory hereafter. Two saints of late centuries, St. Francis de Sales and St. Alfonso, seemed to have professed this less rigid opinion, which is now the more common doctrine of the day.

Another instance is supplied by the Papal decisions concerning Usury. Pope Clement V., in the Council of Vienne, declares: "If any one shall have fallen into the error of pertinaciously presuming to affirm that usury is no sin, we determine that he is to be punished as a heretic." However, in the year 1831 the Sacred *Pœnitentiaria* answered an inquiry on the subject, to the effect that the Holy See suspended its decision on the point, and that a confessor who allowed of usury was not to be disturbed, "non esse inquietandum." Here again a double aspect seems to have been realized of the idea intended by the word *usury*.

To show how natural this process of partial and gradually developed teaching is, we may refer to the apparent contradiction of Bellarmine, who says "the Pope, whether he can err or not, is to be obeyed by all the faithful" (*Rom. Pont.*, iv. 2), yet, as I have quoted him above, p. 52–53, sets down (ii. 29) cases in which he is not to be obeyed. An illustration may be given in political history from the discussions which took place years ago as to the force of the Sovereign's Coronation Oath to uphold the Established Church. The words were large and general, and seemed to preclude any act on his part to the prejudice of the Establishment; but lawyers succeeded at length in making a distinction between the legislative and executive action of the Crown, which is now generally accepted.

These instances out of many similar are sufficient to show what caution is to be observed, on the part of private and unauthorized persons, in imposing upon the consciences of others any interpretation of dogmatic enunciations which is beyond the legitimate sense of the words, inconsistent with the principle that all general rules have exceptions, and unrecognized by the Theological *Schola*.

12. From these various considerations it follows that Papal and Synodal definitions, obligatory on our faith, are of rare occurrence; and this is confessed by all sober theologians. Father O'Reilly, for instance, of Dublin, one of the first theologians of the day, says:

"The Papal Infallibility is comparatively seldom brought into action. I am very far from denying that the Vicar of Christ is largely assisted by God in the fulfilment of his sublime office, that he receives great light and strength to do well the great work entrusted to him and imposed on him, that he is continually guided from above in the government of the Catholic

Church. But this is not the meaning of Infallibility. . . . What is the use of dragging in the Infallibility in connection with Papal acts with which it has nothing to do—Papal acts, which are very good and very holy, and entitled to all respect and obedience, acts in which the Pontiff is commonly not mistaken, but in which he could be mistaken and still remain infallible in the only sense in which he has been declared to be so?" (*Irish Monthly*, vol. ii. No. 10, 1874).\*

This great authority goes on to disclaim any desire to minimize, but there is, I hope, no real difference between us here. He, I am sure, would sanction me in my repugnance to impose upon the faith of others more than what the Church distinctly claims of them: and I should follow him in thinking it a more scriptural, Christian, dutiful, happy frame of mind to be easy, than to be difficult, of belief. I have already spoken of that uncatholic spirit, which starts with a grudging faith in the word of the Church, and determines to hold nothing but what it is, as if by demonstration, compelled to believe. To be a true Catholic a man must have a generous loyalty towards ecclesiastical authority, and accept what is taught him with what is called the *pietas fidei*, and only such a tone of mind has a claim, and it certainly has a claim, to be met and to be handled with a wise and gentle *minimism*. Still the fact remains that there has been of late years a fierce and intolerant temper abroad, which scorns and virtually tramples on the little ones of Christ.

I end with an extract from the Pastoral of the Swiss Bishops, a Pastoral which has received the Pope's approbation:

"It in no way depends upon the caprice of the Pope,

---

\* *Vid.* Fessler also; and I believe Father Perrone says the same.

or upon his good pleasure, to make such and such a doctrine the object of a dogmatic definition. He is tied up and limited to the divine revelation, and to the truths which that revelation contains. He is tied up and limited by the Creeds already in existence, and by the preceding definitions of the Church. He is tied up and limited by the divine law, and by the constitution of the Church. Lastly, he is tied up and limited by that doctrine, divinely revealed, which affirms that alongside religious society there is civil society, that alongside the Ecclesiastical Hierarchy there is the power of temporal Magistrates, invested in their own domain with a full sovereignty, and to whom we owe in conscience obedience and respect in all things morally permitted, and belonging to the domain of civil society."

## CHAPTER X.

### CONCLUSION.

THE DEFINITION OF INFALLIBILITY HAS NOT INCREASED THE POPE'S POWER.—REMARKS ON FREEDOM OF OPINION AMONG CATHOLICS.—CATHOLICS ACKNOWLEDGE BUT ONE POPE AND TOLERATE NO SELF-ASSUMED POWER OF ANATHEMA.

I HAVE now said all that I consider necessary in order to fulfil the task which I have undertaken, a task very painful to me and ungracious. I account it a great misfortune that my last words, as they are likely to be, should be devoted to a controversy with one whom I have always so much respected and admired. But I should not have been satisfied with myself, if I had not responded to the call made upon me from such various quarters, to the opportunity at last given me of breaking a long silence on subjects deeply interesting to me, and to the demands of my own honor.

The main point of Mr. Gladstone's charge against us is that in 1870, after a series of preparatory acts, a great change and irreversible was effected in the political attitude of the Church by the third and fourth chapters of the Vatican *Pastor Æternus*, a change which no state or statesman can afford to pass over. Of this cardinal assertion I consider he has given no proof at all; and my object throughout the foregoing pages has been to make this clear. The Pope's infallibility indeed and his supreme authority have in the Vatican *capita* been declared matters of faith; but his prerogative of infallibility lies in matters speculative, and his prerogative of authority is no infallibility in laws, commands, or measures. His infallibility bears upon the domain of thought, not directly of action, and while it may fairly exercise the theologian, philosopher, or man of science, it scarcely concerns the politician. Moreover, whether the recognition of his infallibility in doctrine will increase his actual power over the faith of Catholics remains to be seen, and must be determined by the event; for there are gifts too large and too fearful to be handled freely. Mr. Gladstone seems to feel this, and therefore insists upon the increase made by the Vatican definition in the Pope's authority. But there is no real increase; he has for centuries upon centuries had and used that authority, which the Definition now declares ever to have belonged to him. Before the Council there was the rule of obedience, and there were exceptions to the rule; and since the Council the rule remains, and with it the possibility of exceptions.

It may be objected that a representation such as this is negatived by the universal sentiment, which testifies to the formidable effectiveness of the Vatican decrees, and to the Pope's intention that they should be effective; that it is the boast of some Catholics, and the reproach levelled against us by all Protestants, that the Catholic Church has now become beyond mistake a despotic aggressive Papacy, in which freedom of thought and action is utterly extinguished. But I do not allow that this alleged unanimous testimony exists. Of course Prince Bismarck,* and other statesmen such

* Let me from this accidental mention of Prince Bismarck make for myself an opportunity, which my subject has not given me, of expressing my deep sympathy with the suffering Catholics of Germany. Who can doubt that, in their present resolute disobedience to that statesman's measures, they are only fulfilling their duty to God and his Church? Who can but pray that, were English Catholics in a similar trial, they might have grace to act as bravely in the cause of religion?

as Mr. Gladstone, rest their opposition to Pope Pius on the political ground; but the Old-Catholic movement is based, not upon politics, but upon theology, and Dr. Döllinger has more than once, I believe, declared his disapprobation of the Prussian acts against the Pope, while Father Hyacinth has quarrelled with the anti-Catholic politics of Geneva. The French indeed have shown their sense of the political support which the Holy Father's name and influence would bring to their country; but does any one suppose that they expect to derive support definitely from the Vatican decrees, and not rather from the *prestige* of that venerable Authority which those decrees have rather lowered than otherwise in the eyes of the world? So again the Legitimists and Carlists in France and Spain doubtless wish to associate themselves with Rome; but where and how have they signified that they can turn to profit the special dogma of the Pope's infallibility, and would not have been better pleased to be rid of the controversy which it has occasioned? In fact, instead of there being a universal impression that the proclamation of his infallibility and supreme authority has strengthened the Pope's secular position in Europe, there is room for suspecting that some of the politicians of the day (I do not mean Mr. Gladstone) were not sorry that the Ultramontane party was successful at the Council in their prosecution of an object which those politicians considered to be favorable to the interests of the Civil Power. There is certainly some plausibility in the view, that it is not the "Curia Romana," as Mr. Gladstone considers, or the "Jesuits," who are the "astute" party, but that rather they themselves have fallen into a trap, and are victims of the astuteness of secular statesmen.

The recognition, which I am here implying, of the existence of parties in the Church reminds me of what, while I have been writing these pages, I have all along felt would be at once the *primâ facie* and also the most telling criticism upon me. It will be said that there are very considerable differences in argument and opinion between me and others who have replied to Mr. Gladstone, and I shall be taunted with the evident breakdown, thereby made manifest, of that topic of glorification so commonly in the mouths of Catholics, that they are all of one way of thinking, while Protestant bodies are all at variance with each other, and by reason of that very variation of opinion can have no ground of certainty severally in their own.

This is a showy and serviceable retort in controversy; but it is nothing more. First, as regards the arguments which Catholics use, it has to be considered whether these are really incompatible with each other; if they are not, then surely it is generally granted by Protestants, as well as Catholics, that two distinct arguments for the same conclusion, instead of invalidating that conclusion, actually strengthen it. And next, supposing the difference to be one of conclusions themselves, then it must be considered whether the difference relates to a matter of faith or to a matter of opinion, If a matter of faith is in question, I grant there ought to be absolute agreement, or rather I maintain that there is; I mean to say that only one out of the statements put forth can be true, and that the other statements will be at once withdrawn by their authors, by virtue of their being Catholics, as soon as they learn on good authority that they are erroneous. But if the differences which I have supposed are only in theological opinion, they do but show that after all private judgment is not so utterly unknown among Catholics and in Catholic Schools as Protestants are desirous to establish.

I have written on this subject at some length in Lectures which I published many years ago, but, it would appear, with little practical effect upon those for whom they were intended. "Left to himself," I say, "each Catholic likes and would maintain his own opinion and his private judgment just as much as a Protestant; and he has it and he maintains it, just so far as the Church does not, by the authority of Revelation, supersede it. The very moment the Church ceases to speak, at the very point at which she, that is, God who speaks by her, circumscribes her range of teaching, then private judgment of necessity starts up; there is nothing to hinder it. . . . A Catholic sacrifices his opinion to the Word of God, declared through His Church; but from the nature of the case, there is nothing to hinder him having his own opinion and expressing it, whenever, and so far as, the Church, the oracle of Revelation, does not speak."\*

In saying this, it must not be supposed that I am denying what is called the *pietas fidei*, that is, a sense of the great probability of the truth of enunciations made by the Church, which are not formally and actually to be considered as the "Word of God." Doubtless it is our duty to check many a speculation, or at least many an utterance, even though we are not bound to condemn it as contrary to religious truth. But, after all, the field of religious thought which the duty of faith occupies, is small indeed compared with that which is opened to our free, though of course to our reverent and conscientious, speculation.

I draw from these remarks two conclusions; first as regards Protestants—Mr. Gladstone should not on the one hand declaim against us as having "no mental freedom," if the periodical press on the other hand is to mock us as admitting a liberty of private judgment,

\* *Vide* "Difficulties felt by Anglicans," Lecture X.

purely Protestant. We surely are not open to contradictory imputations. Every note of triumph over the differences which mark our answers to Mr. Gladstone is a distinct admission that we do not deserve his injurious reproach that we are captives and slaves of the Pope.

Secondly, for the benefit of some Catholics, I would observe that, while I acknowledge one Pope, *jure divino*, I acknowledge no other, and that I think it a usurpation, too wicked to be comfortably dwelt upon, when individuals use their own private judgment, in the discussion of religious questions, not simply "abundare in suo sensu," but for the purpose of anathematizing the private judgment of others.

I say there is only one Oracle of God, the Holy Catholic Church and the Pope as her head. To her teaching I have ever desired all my thoughts, all my words to be conformed; to her judgment I submit what I have now written, what I have ever written, not only as regards its truth, but as to its prudence, its suitableness, and its expedience. I think I have not pursued any end of my own in anything that I have published, but I know well that, in matters not of faith, I may have spoken when I ought to have been silent.

And now, my dear Duke, I release you from this long discussion, and, in concluding, beg you to accept the best Christmas wishes and prayers for your present and future from

Your affectionate Friend and Servant,

JOHN HENRY NEWMAN.

*The Oratory, Dec. 27, 1874.*

# CHAPTER XI.

## POSTSCRIPT.

Rejoinder to Gladstone's Answer.—"From the Day on which I became a Catholic to this Day, now close upon Thirty Years, I have never had a Moment's Misgiving."—Gladstone's withdrawal of the Accusation of Disloyalty.—Re-examination of Accusation of former Disbelief in Papal Infallibility among some Classes of Catholics.—Papal Supremacy and the Supremacy of Conscience.—Example from the Life of M. Emery.—Further Remarks on the Grade of Authority possessed by the Syllabus.—Difference between receiving it with Obedience, and as an Act of Infallibility.—How the Church regards Marriages of non-Catholics.

*February 26, 1875.*

MR. GLADSTONE'S new Pamphlet, which has just appeared, is only partially directed against the foregoing Letter, and, when he remarks on what I have written, he does so with a gentleness which may be thought to be unfair to his argument. Moreover, he commences with some pages about me personally of so special a character that, did I dare dwell upon them in their direct import, they would of course gratify me exceedingly. But I cannot do so, because I believe that, with that seriousness which is characteristic of him, he has wished to say what he felt to be true, not what was complimentary; and because, looking on beyond his words to what they imply, I see in them, though he did not mean it so himself, a grave, or almost severe question addressed to me, which effectually keeps me from taking pleasure in them, however great is the honor they do me.

It is indeed a stern question which his words suggest, whether, now that I have come to the end of my days, I have used aright whatever talents God has given me, and as He would have had me use them, in building up religious truth, and not in pulling down, breaking up, and scattering abroad. All I can say in answer to it is, that from the day I became a Catholic to this day, now close upon thirty years, I have never had a moment's misgiving that the communion of Rome is that Church which the Apostles set up at Pentecost, which alone has "the adoption of sons, and the glory, and the convenants, and the revealed law, and the service of God, and the promises," and in which the Anglican communion, whatever its merits and demerits, whatever the great excellence of individuals in it, has, as such, no part. Nor have I ever, since 1845, for a moment hesitated in my conviction that it was my clear duty to join, as I did then join, that Catholic Church, which in my own conscience I felt to be divine. Persons and places, incidents and circumstances of life, which belong to my first forty-four years, are deeply lodged in my memory and my affections; moreover, I have had more to try and afflict me in various ways as a Catholic than as an Anglican; but never for a moment have I wished myself back; never have I ceased to thank my Maker for His mercy in enabling me to make the great change, and never has He let me feel forsaken by Him, or in distress, or any kind of religious trouble. I do not know how to avoid thus meeting Mr. Gladstone's language about me: but I can say no more. The judgment must be left to a day to come.

In the remarks that follow I shall take the order of my Sections.

## SECTION I.

My first reason for writing in answer to Mr. Gladstone's Expostulation was his charge against us, "that Catholics, if they act consistently with their principles, cannot be loyal subjects." And he withdraws this in his new Pamphlet (*Vaticanism*, p. 14), though not in very gracious language. "The immediate purpose of my appeal," he says, "has been attained, in so far that the loyalty of our Roman Catholic fellow-subjects in the mass remains evidently untainted and secure."

My second reason was to protest against "his attack upon our moral uprightness." Here again he seems to grant that, if what I say can be received as genuine Catholic teaching, I have succeeded in my purpose. He has a doubt, however, whether it does not "smack of Protestantism" (*Vat.*, p. 69). He does not give any distinct reason for this doubt; and, though I shall notice it in its place, I think it but fair to maintain as a plain principle of controversy, that it is the accuser who has to prove his point, and that he must not content himself with professing that the accused parties have not succeeded to his satisfaction in disproving it.

Lastly, as springing out of these two charges and illustrating them, was his exaggerated notion of the force, drift, and range of the Vatican definition of the Pope's infallibility and supremacy. Here again I consider he leaves my interpretation of it without reply, though apparently it does not content him. Some of the objections to what I have said, which he throws out *obiter*, as well as some made by others, shall now be noticed.

I have said, apropos of the prospect of a definition of the Pope's infallibility in the times of Pitt and Peel: "If [the government] wanted to obtain some real information about the probabilities of the future, why did they not go to headquarters? why not go to Rome? . . . It is impossible that they could have entered into formal negotiations with the Pope, without its becoming perfectly clear that Rome could never be a party to such a pledge as England wanted, and that no pledge from Catholics was of value to which Rome was not a party." To my astonishment Mr. Gladstone seems to consider this a fatal admission. He cries out: "Statesmen of the future, recollect the words! . . . The lesson received is this: although pledges were given, although their validity was formally and even passionately asserted, although the subject-matter was one of civil allegiance, 'no pledge from Catholics was of any value, to which Rome was not a party'" (p. 39).

I deny that the question of infallibility was one of civil allegiance, but let that pass; as to the main principle involved in what I have said, it certainly does perplex and confuse me that a statesman with Mr. Gladstone's experience should make light of credentials, and should not recognize the difference between party opinion and formal decisions and pledges. What is the use of accredited ministers and an official intercourse between foreign powers, if the acts of mere classes or interests will do instead of them? At a congress, I believe the first act of plenipotentiaries is to show to each other their credentials. What minister of foreign affairs would go to the Cesarowitch, who happened to be staying among us, for an explanation of an expedition of Russia in upper Asia, instead of having recourse to the Russian ambassador?

The common saying, that "Whigs are Tories out of place," illustrates again what is in itself so axiomatic. Successive ministries of opposite views show in history, for the most part, as one consistent national government, and, when a foreign power mistakes the objections which public men in opposition make to the details, circumstances, or seasonableness of certain ministerial measures, for deliberate judgments in its favor, it is likely, as in the case of the great Napoleon, to incur eventually, when the opposition comes into office, great disappointment, and has no one to blame but itself. So again, the Czar Nicholas seems to have mistaken the deputation of the peace party before the Crimean war for the voice of the English nation. It is not a business-like way of acting to assume the assurances of partisans, however sincerely made, for conditions of a contract. There is nothing indeed to show that the Holy See in 1793 or 1829 had any notion that the infallibility of the Pope, even if ever made a dogma, would be so made within such limits of time as could effect the *bonâ fide* character of the prospects which English and Irish Catholics opened upon Mr. Pitt or Mr. Peel. The events in Europe of the foregoing half century had given no encouragement to the Papal cause. Nor did Catholics alone avow anticipations which helped to encourage the latter statesman in the course, into which the political condition of Ireland, not any kindness to the Irish religion, primarily turned him. There were Anglican ecclesiastics, whom he deservedly trusted, who gave it to him as their settled opinion, as regards the Protestantism of England, that, if the emancipation of Catholics could but be passed in the night, there would be no excitement about it next morning. Did such an influential judgment, thus offered to Mr. Peel, involve a breach of a pledge, because it was not fulfilled?

It was notorious all over the world that the North of Catholic Christendom took a different view of Papal infallibility from the South. A long controversy had gone on; able writers were to be found on either side; each side was positive in the truth of its own cause; each hoped to prevail. The Gallican party, towards which England and Ireland inclined, thought the other simply extravagant; but with the Ultramontane stood Rome itself. Ministers do not commonly believe all the representations of deputations who come to them with the advocacy of particular measures, though those deputations may be perfectly sincere in what they aver. The Catholics of England and Ireland in 1826 were almost as one man in thinking lightly of the question, but even then there were those who spoke out in a different sense and warned the government that there was a contrary opinion, and one strong both in its pretensions and its prospects. I am not bound to go into this subject at length, for I have allowed that the dominant feeling among our Catholics at that day was against the prudence or likelihood of a definition of Papal infallibility; but I will instance one or two writers of name who had spoken in a different sense.

I cannot find that Mr. Gladstone deals with my reference to Archbishop Troy, whose pastoral bears the date (1793) of the very year in which, as Mr. Gladstone tells us (*Vat.*, p. 48), a Relief Act was granted to Ireland. The Archbishop, as I have quoted him, says: "*Many* Catholics contend that the Pope . . . is infallible; . . . others deny this. . . . *Until* the Church shall *decide* . . . either opinion may be adopted."

This is a very significant, as well as an authoritative passage.

Again: Father Mumford's *Catholic Scripturist* is a popular Address to Protestants, in the vernacular, which has gone through various editions in the seventeenth, eighteenth, and nineteenth centuries. The edition from which I quote is that of 1863. He says (p. 39): "Whether the definition of a council alone, defining without their chief pastor, or the definition of the chief pastor alone, defining without a council, be infallible or no, there be several opinions amongst us, in which we do and may vary without any prejudice to our faith, which is not built upon what is *yet* under opinion, but upon that which is delivered as infallible."

Again, Bishop Hay is one of the most conspicuous prelates and authoritative writers amongst us of the eighteenth century. In his *Sincere Christian*, published between 1770 and 1780, he treats of the infallibility of the Pope at considerable length, and in its favor. He says, p. 188 (*ed.* 1871), that that doctrine "is not proposed to us as an article of divine faith, nor has the Church ever made any decision concerning it. Great numbers of the most learned divines are of opinion that, in such a case, the Head of the Church is infallible in what he teaches, but there are others who are of a contrary opinion." He proceeds: "On what grounds do those divines found their opinion, who believe that the Pope himself, when he speaks to the faithful as head of the Church, is infallible in what he teaches?" and he answers: "On very strong reasons both from Scripture, tradition, and reason." These he goes through *seriatim;* then he adds, p. 194: "What proof do the others bring for their opinion, that the Head of the Church is not infallible? They bring not a single text of Scripture, nor almost one argument from tradition to prove it."

I might add that the chief instrument in rousing and rallying the Protestant sentiment against Catholic emancipation was from first to last the episcopate and clergy of the Church Established ; now, if there was any body of men who were perfectly aware of the division of sentiment among Catholics as to the seat of infallibility, it was they. Their standard divines, writing in the vernacular, discharge it, as one of their most effective taunts, against their opponents, that, whilst the latter hold the doctrine of infallibility, they differ among themselves whether it is lodged in an Ecumenical Council or in the Roman See. It never can be said then that this opinion, which has now become a dogma, was not perfectly well known to be living and energetic in the Catholic communion, though it was not an article of faith, and was not spoken of as such by Catholics in this part of the world during the centuries of persecution.

Mr. Gladstone, as his mildest conclusion against us, is inclined to grant that it was not an act of duplicity in us, that in 1826 our Prelates spoke against the Pope's infallibility, though in 1870 they took part in defining it; but then he maintains it to be at least a proof that the Church has changed its doctrine, and thereby forfeited its claim to be "semper eadem." But it is no change surely to decide between two prevalent opinions ; however, if it is to be so regarded, then change has been the characteristic of the Church from the earliest times, as, for instance, in the third century, on the point of the validity of baptism by heretics. And hence such change as has taken place (which I should prefer to call doctrinal development), is in itself a positive argument in favor of the Church's identity from first to last ; for a growth in its creed is a law of its life. I have already insisted upon this; also in former volumes, as in my *Apologia* and *Difficulties of Anglicans*.

## Section 3.

As Mr. Gladstone denied that the Papal prerogatives were consistent with ancient history, I said in answer that that history on the contrary was the clearest witness in their favor, as showing how the promises made to St. Peter were providentially fulfilled by political, etc., changes, external to the Pope, which worked for him. I did not mean to deny that those prerogatives were his from the beginning, but merely that they were gradually brought into full exercise by a course of events which history records. Thus it was a mistake to say that Catholics could not appeal in favor of the Papal power to history. To make my meaning quite clear, as I hoped, I distinctly said I was not speaking theologically, but historically, nay, looking at the state of things with "non-Catholic eyes." However, as the following passage, translated from the *Études Religieuses* shows, it seems that I have been misunderstood, though the writer himself, Père Ramière, does me the justice and the favor to defend me, and I here adopt his words as my defence. He says:

"To express that providential concentration in the hands of the Pope of an ecclesiastical power previously participated in more largely by the Episcopate. Father Newman makes use of a legal term which should not be taken literally. He says that the Pope is *heir by default* of the universal hierarchy of the fourth century. The learned editor of the *Voce della Verità* finds fault with that expression, which, according to him, implies that the Pope holds his authority from the hierarchy: but Father Newman excludes that interpretation, for he derives the fulness of pontifical authority from the promise made by Jesus Christ to St. Peter."

## Section 4.

I say that "were I actually a soldier or sailor in her Majesty's service in a just war, and should the Pope suddenly bid all Catholic soldiers and sailors to retire from her service, taking the advice, etc., . . . I should not obey him." Here I avail myself of a passage in Canon Neville's recent pamphlet (*A few Comments, etc.*, Pickering), in which he speaks with the authority belonging to a late theological Professor of Maynooth:

"In the impossible hypothesis of the Pope being engaged in a war with England, how would the allegiance of English Catholics be affected? . . . how would it be, if they were soldiers or sailors? . . . Some one will urge, the Pope may issue a mandate, enforced by an annexed excommunication, forbidding all Catholics to engage in the war against him. . . . The supposed action of the Pope does not change the question materially. . . . The soldiers and sailors would not incur it, because '*grave fears*' excuse from censure [excommunication], censures being directed against the contumacious, not against those who act through fear or coercion. . . . It is a trite principle, that mere ecclesiastical laws do not bind, when there would be a very grave inconvenience in their observance; and it denies as a rule to any human legislator (*e.g.*, the Pope) the power of making laws or precepts, binding men to the performance of actions which, from the danger and difficulty attendant on their fulfilment, are esteemed heroic" (pp. 101–2).

## Section 5.

I have said, "The Pope, who comes of Revelation, has no jurisdiction over Nature"—*i.e.*, the natural Law. Mr. Gladstone on the other hand says: "Idle it is to tell us, finally, that the Pope is bound by the moral and divine law, by the commandments of God, by the rules of the Gospel: . . . for of these, one and all, the Pope himself, by himself, is the judge without appeal" (p. 102). That is, Mr. Gladstone thinks that the Pope may deny and anathematize the proposition, "There is one God": and may proceed to circulate by Cardinal Antonelli a whole Syllabus of kindred "erroneous theses" for the instruction of the Bishops. Catholics think this impossible, as believing in a Divine Providence ever exercised over the Church. But let us grant, for argument's sake, that a Pope could commit so insane a violation of the Natural and the Revealed Law: we know what would be the consequence to such a Pope. Cardinal Turrecremata teaches, as I have quoted him, that "were the Pope to command anything against Holy Scripture, or the articles of faith, or the truth of the Sacraments, or the commands of the natural or divine law, he ought not to be obeyed, but in such commands to be ignored." Other, and they the highest Ultramontane theologians, hold that a Pope who teaches heresy *ipso facto* ceases to be Pope.

After stating that there are cases in which the Pope's commands are to be resisted by individual Catholics, I have challenged Mr. Gladstone to bring passages from our authoritative writers to the contrary: and I add: "they must be passages declaring not only that the Pope is ever to be obeyed, but that there are no exceptions to this rule, for exceptions ever must be in all concrete matters." Instead of doing so Mr. Gladstone contents himself with enunciating the contradictory to what I have said. "Dr. Newman says there are exceptions to this precept of obedience. But this is just what the Council has not said. The Church by the Council imposes Aye. The private conscience reserves to itself the title to say No. I must confess that in this apology there is to me a strong, undeniable smack of Protestantism" (p. 69).

Mr. Gladstone says "there is to me"; yes, certainly to him and other Protestants, because they do not know our doctrine. I have given in my Pamphlet three reasons in justification of what I said; first that exceptions *must* be from the nature of the case, " for in *all* concrete matters," not only in precepts of obedience, rules are but general, and exceptions must occur. Then, in a later page, I give actual instances, which have occurred in the history of Catholic teaching, of exceptions after large principles have been laid down. But my main reason lies in the absolute statements of theologians. I willingly endure to have about me a smack of Protestantism, which attaches to Cardinal Turrecremata in the fifteenth century, to Cardinals Jacobatius and Bellarmine in the sixteenth, to the Carmelites of Salamanca in the seventeenth, and to all theologians prior to them; and also to the whole Schola after them, such as to Fathers Corduba, Natalis Alexander, and Busenbaum, and so down to St. Alfonso Liguori, the latest Doctor of the Church, in the eighteenth, and to Cardinal Gousset and Archbishop Kenrick in the nineteenth.

On the subject of the supremacy of Conscience a correspondent has done me the favor of referring me to a passage in the life of the well-known M. Emery (Paris, 1862), Superior of St. Sulpice. It runs as follows:

"The celebration of Napoleon's marriage with the Archduchess of Austria occasioned another difficulty about which M. Emery had to explain himself, not to the government, but to some cardinals who wished to know his sentiments. The question was whether or not the cardinals, who, to the number of twenty-six, resided in Paris, could conscientiously assist at the religious ceremony of the marriage. Some days before that ceremony, M. Emery, having been consulted about it by Cardinal della Somaglia, who seemed to regard assisting at it as unlawful, answered him that *if, as a matter of fact, he was so persuaded, he could not in conscience assist at the ceremony, for one is never permitted to act against his conscience.* But he added that assisting at it did not seem to him essentially unlawful," etc.

It got about in consequence that he had denied that any cardinal could with a safe conscience be present at the religious ceremony. This led Cardinal Fesch to write him a letter asking for an explanation, inasmuch as a cardinal had distinctly stated "that M. Emery had confirmed that cardinal in his opinion that he could not, in conscience, assist at the Emperor's marriage"; whereas, Cardinal Fesch proceeds, "even yesterday, at three in the afternoon, M. Emery, for the second or third time, said to me that he was altogether of the contrary opinion, and that he considered that the cardinals could assist at the ceremony." In consequence, he asked for "a categorical answer" from M. Emery.

M. Emery in consequence wrote letters to both cardinals to show his consistency in the language he had used in conversation with each of them, insisting for that purpose on the distinction which has led to the introduction of his name and conduct into this place, viz., that every man must go by his own conscience, not by that of another. He says to Cardinal Somaglia: "You told me that after the most careful investigation you were convinced that *you could not go to the marriage without wounding your conscience*. I was bound to tell you, and I did tell you, that *such being the case*, you should by no means assist at it, because I was persuaded, as *you were*, that one never could, that one never should, act against his conscience, *even when erroneous*." He adds: "Not that the inconveniences arising from absence could authorize assisting at it, if assistance were otherwise illicit, but that those inconveniences are a very strong reason for the most careful examination possible, as to whether or not one's presence really would be licit, and whether one's conscience formed on the subject is not erroneous" (t. 2, pp. 249–254).

In the event Cardinal Somaglia kept to his view, contrary to M. Emery, and did not attend the marriage ceremony.

## SECTION 6.

Speaking of the proposition condemned in the Encyclical of 1864, to the effect that it is the right of any one to have liberty to give public utterance, in every possible shape, by every possible channel, without any let or hindrance from God or man, to all his notions whatever, I have said that "it seems a light epithet for the Pope to use, when he called such a doctrine of conscience a *deliramentum*." Presently I add, "Perhaps Mr. Gladstone will say, Why should the Pope take the trouble to condemn what is so wild? but he does," etc.

On this Mr. Gladstone remarks (*Vat.*, p. 21, 22): "It appears to me that this is, to use a mild phrase, merely trifling with the subject. We are asked to believe that what the Pope intended to condemn was a state of things which never has existed in any country in the world. Now he says he is condemning one of the commonly prevailing errors of the time, familiarly known to the Bishops whom he addresses. What bishop knows of a State which by law allows a perfectly free course to blasphemy, filthiness, and sedition?"

I do not find anything to show that the Pope is speaking of States, and not of writers; and, though I do not pretend to know against what writers he is speaking, yet there are writers who do maintain doctrines which carried out consistently would reach that *deliramentum* which the Pope speaks of, if they have not rather already reached it. We are a sober people; but are not the doctrines of even so grave and patient a thinker as the late Mr. J. S. Mill very much in that direction? He says: "The appropriate region of human liberty comprises first the inward domain of consciousness; demanding liberty of conscience in the most comprehensive sense, liberty of thought and feeling, absolute freedom of opinion and sentiment on all subjects practical or speculative, scientific, moral, or theological. The liberty of *expressing* and *publishing* opinion may *seem* to fall under a different principle, since it belongs to that part of the conduct of an individual which concerns other people; but, being almost of as much importance as the liberty of thought itself, and resting in great part on the same reasons, *is practically inseparable from it*, etc., etc. . . . No society in which these liberties are not on the whole respected is free, whatever may be its form of government" (*On Liberty*, *Introd.*) Of course he does not allow of a freedom to harm others, though we have to consider well what he means by harming: but his is a freedom which must meet with no "impediment from our fellow-creatures, so long as what we do does not harm them, even though they should think our conduct foolish, perverse, or wrong." "The only freedom," he continues, "which deserves the name is that of pursuing our own good in our own way, so long as we do not attempt to deprive others of theirs, or impede their efforts to obtain it. Each is the proper guardian of his own health, whether bodily, or mental and spiritual."

That is, no immoral doctrines, poems, novels, plays, conduct, acts, may be visited by the reprobation of public opinion; nothing must be put down, I do not say by the laws, but even by society, by the press, by religious influence, merely on the ground of shocking the sense of decency and the modesty of a Christian community. Nay, the police must not visit Holywell Street, nor a license be necessary for dancing-rooms: but the most revolting atrocities of heathen times and countries must for conscience' sake be allowed free exercise in our great cities. Averted looks indeed and silent disgust, or again rational expostulation, is admissible against them, but nothing of a more energetic character.

I do not impute this to Mr. Mill. He had too much English common sense to carry out his principles to these extreme but legitimate conclusions; he strove to find means of limiting them by the introduction of other and antagonist principles; but then that such a man held the theory of liberty which he has avowed, and that he has a great following, is a suggestion to us that the Holy See may have had abundant reason in the present state of the Continent to anathematize a proposition which to Mr. Gladstone seems so wild and unheard of.

### SECTION 7.

I have said that the Syllabus is to be received from the Pope with "profound submission," and "by an act of obedience"; I add, "but not of faith," for it "has no dogmatic force." I maintain this still. I say, in spite of Professor Schulte, and the English

Catholic writer to whom Mr. Gladstone refers (p. 32), I have as much right to maintain that the implicit condemnation with which it visits its eighty propositions is not *ex cathedrâ*, or an act of the Infallible Chair, as have those "gravest theologians," as Bishop Fessler speaks, who call its dogmatic force in question (*Fessler*, p. 91). I do not know what Fessler himself says of it more than that it is to be received with submission and obedience. I do not deny another's right to consider it in his private conscience an act of infallibility, or to say, in Mr. Gladstone's words (p. 35), that "utterances *ex cathedrâ* are not the only form in which Infallibility can speak"; I only say that I have a right to think otherwise. And when the Pope by letters approves of one writer who writes one way, and of another who writes in another, he makes neither opinion dogmatic, but both allowable. Mr. Gladstone speaks as if what the Pope says to Father Schrader undoes what he says to Bishop Fessler; why not say that his letter to Fessler neutralizes his letter to Schrader? I repeat, when I speak of minimizing, I am not turning the profession of it into a dogma; men, if they will, may maximize for me, provided they too keep from dogmatizing. This is my position all through these discussions, and must be kept in mind by any fair reasoner.

I grant the Pope has laid a great stress on the Syllabus; he is said in 1867 to have spoken of it as a "regula docendi"; I cannot tell whether *vivâ voce*, or in writing; anyhow this did not interfere with Fessler's "grave theologians" in 1871 considering the Pope was not in 1867 teaching dogmatically and infallibly. Moreover, how can a list of proscribed propositions be a "rule," except by turning to the Allocutions, etc., in which they are condemned? and in those Allocutions, when we turn to them, we find in what sense, and with what degree of force, severally. In itself the Syllabus can be no more than what the Pope calls it, a syllabus or collection of errors. Led by the references inserted in it to the Allocutions, etc., I have ventured to call it something more, viz., a list or index *raisonné;* an idea not attached to it by me first of all, for Père Daniel, in the October of that very year, 1867, tells us, in the *Études Religieuses,* "One should ask of the Syllabus itself only that degree of clearness which is proper in a good table of contents" (p. 514).

But, whether an index or not, and though it have a substantive character, it is at least clear that the only way in which it can be a "rule of teaching" is by its telling us what to avoid; and this consideration will explain what I mean by receiving it with "obedience," which to some persons is a difficult idea, when contrasted with accepting it with faith. I observe then that obedience is concerned with doing, but faith with affirming. Now, when we are told to avoid certain propositions, we are told primarily and directly not to do something; whereas, in order to affirm, we must have positive statements put before us. For instance, it is easy to understand, and in our teaching to avoid the proposition, " Wealth is the first of goods "; but who shall attempt to ascertain what the affirmative propositions are, one or more, which are necessarily involved in the prohibition of such a proposition, and which must be clearly set down before we can make an act of faith in them?

However, Mr. Gladstone argues, that, since the Pope's condemnation of the propositions of the Syllabus has, as I have allowed, a claim on the obedience of Catholics, that very fact tells in favor of the propositions condemned by him; he thinks I have here made a fatal admission. It is *enough*, he says, that the Syllabus "unquestionably demands obedience"; that is, enough, whether the propositions condemned in it deserve condemnation or not. Here are his very words: "What is *conclusive* . . . is this, that the obligation to *obey* it is asserted on all hands; . . . it is *therefore* absolutely superfluous to follow Dr. Newman through his references to the Briefs and Allocutions marginally noted," in order to ascertain their meaning and drift. . . . "I *abide* by my account of the *contents* of the Syllabus" (p. 36). That is, the propositions may be as false as heathenism, but they have this redeeming virtue, that the Pope denounces them. His judgment of them may be as true as Scripture, but it carries this unpardonable sin with it, that it is given with a purpose, and not as a mere literary flourish. Therefore I will not inquire into the propositions at all; but my original conclusion shall be dogmatic and irreformable. Sit pro ratione voluntas.

I have declined to discuss the difficulties which Mr. Gladstone raises upon our teaching respecting the marriage contract (on which I still think him either obscure or incorrect), because they do not fall within the scope to which I professed to confine my remarks; however, his fresh statements, as they are found (*Vat.*, p. 28), lead me to say as follows:

The non-Roman marriages in England, he says, "do not at present fall under the foul epithets of Rome. But why? Not because we marry . . . under the sanctions of religion, for our marriages are, in the eye of the Pope, purely civil marriages, but only for the technical . . . reason that the disciplinary decrees of Trent are not canonically in force in this country," etc.

Here Mr. Gladstone seems to consider that there are only two ways of marrying according to Catholic teaching; he omits a third, in which we consider the essence of the sacrament to lie. He speaks of civil marriage, and of marriage "under the sanctions of religion," by which phrase he seems to mean marriage with a rite and a minister. But it is also a *religious* marriage, if the parties, without a priest, by a mutual act of consent, as in the presence of God, marry themselves; and such a vow of each to other is, according to our theology, really the constituting act, the matter and form, the sacrament of marriage. That is, he omits the very contract which we specially call marriage. This being the case, it follows that every clause of the above passage is incorrect.

1. Mr. Gladstone says, that English non-Roman marriages are held valid at Rome, *not* because they are contracted "under the sanctions of religion." On the contrary, this is the very reason why they are held valid there; viz., only because parties who have already received the Christian rite of baptism, proceed to give themselves to each other in the sight of God sacramentally, though they may not call it a sacrament.

2. Mr. Gladstone says, "our marriages are in the eye of the Pope *purely civil* marriages." Just the reverse, speaking, as he is, of Church of England marriages. They are considered, in the case of baptized persons, sacramental marriages.

3. Mr. Gladstone says, that they are received at Rome as valid, "*only for the technical*, etc., reason that the disciplinary decrees of Trent are not canonically in force in this country. There is nothing, unless it be motives of mere policy, to prevent the Pope from giving them [those decrees] force here, when he pleases. If, and when that is done, *every marriage thereafter con-*

cluded in the *English* Church, will, according to his own words, be '*a filthy concubinage.*'" This is not so; I quote to the point two sufficient authorities, St. Alfonso Liguori and Archbishop Kenrick.

Speaking of the clandestinity of marriage (that is, when it is contracted without parish priest and witnesses), as an impediment to its validity, St. Alfonso says: "As regards non-Catholics (infideles), or Catholics who live in non-Catholic districts, *or* where the Council of Trent has not been received, . . . *such a marriage is valid*" (tom. viii. p. 67, ed. 1845). Even, then, though the discipline of Trent *was* received in England, still it would not cease to be a Protestant country, and therefore marriages in Protestant churches would be valid.

Archbishop Kenrick is still more explicit. He says: "Constat Patres Tridentinos legem ita tulisse, ut hæreticorum cœtus jam ab Ecclesia divulsos non respiceret. . . . Hoc igitur clandestinitatis impedimentum ad hæreticos seorsim convenientes in locis ubi grassantur hæreses, non est extendendum" (*Theol. Mor.*, t. 3, p. 351).

Such being the Catholic rule as to recognition of Protestant marriages, the Pope could not, as Mr. Gladstone thinks, any day invalidate English Protestant marriages by introducing into England the discipline of Trent. The only case in which, consistently with the Council, any opportunity might occur to the Pope, according to his accusation, of playing fast and loose, is when there was a doubt whether the number of Protestants in a Catholic country was large enough to give them a clear footing there, or when the Government refused to recognize them. Whether such an opportunity has practically occurred and has ever been acted on, I have not the knowledge either to affirm or deny.

## Section 8.

I say in my pamphlet: "But if the fact be so that the Fathers were not unanimous, is the definition valid? This depends on the question whether unanimity, at least moral, is or is not necessary for its validity."

It should be borne in mind that these letters of mine were not intended for publication, and are introduced into my text as documents of 1870, with a view of refuting the false reports of my bearing at that time towards the Vatican Council and Definition. To alter their wording would have been to destroy their argumentative value. I said nothing to imply that on reflection I agreed to every proposition which I set down on my *primâ facie* view of the matter.

One passage of it, perhaps from my own fault, Mr. Gladstone has misunderstood. He quotes me (*Vat.*, p. 13) as holding that "a definition which the Pope approves is not absolutely binding thereby, but requires a moral unanimity, and a subsequent reception by the Church." Nay, I considered that the Pope could define without either majority or minority; but that, if he chose to go by the method of a Council, in that case a moral unanimity was required of its Fathers. I say a few lines lower down, waiving the difficulty altogether: "Our merciful Lord would not care so little for His people . . . as to allow their visible head and such a large number of Bishops to lead them into error." Père Ramière, in his very kind review of me in the *Études Religieuses* for February, speaks of the notion of a moral unanimity as a piece of Gallicanism; but anyhow it has vanished altogether from theology now, since the Pope, if the Bishops in the Council, few or many, held back, might define a doctrine without them. A council of Bishops of the world around him, is only one of the various modes in which he exercises his infallibility. The seat of infallibility is in him, and they are adjuncts. The *Pastor Æternus* says: "Romani Pontifices, prout temporum et rerum conditio suadebat, *nunc* convocatis œcumenicis conciliis, *aut* rogatâ Ecclesiæ per orbem dispersæ sententiâ, *nunc* per synodos particulares, *nunc* aliis, quæ Divina suppeditabat Providentia, adhibitis auxiliis, ea tenenda definiverunt, quæ sacris Scripturis et Apostolicis Traditionibus consentanea, Deo adjutore, cognoverant."

Nor have I spoken of a subsequent reception by the Church as entering into the necessary conditions of a *de fide* decision. I said that by the "Securus judicat orbis terrarum" all acts of the rulers of the Church are ratified. In this passage of my private letter I meant by "ratified" brought home to us as authentic. At this very moment it is certainly the handy, obvious, and serviceable argument for our accepting the Vatican definition of the Pope's Infallibility.

I said in my first edition, at page 306, that the definition at Ephesus seemed to be carried by 124 votes against 111; as this was professedly only an inference of my own, I have withdrawn it. Confining myself to the facts of the history, which are perplexed, I observe: The Council was opened by St. Cyril on June 22 of the current year, without waiting for the Bishops representing the great Syrian patriarchate, who were a few days' journey from Ephesus, in spite of the protest on that account of sixty-eight of the Bishops already there. The numbers present at the opening are given in the Acts as about 150. The first Session, in which Nestorius was condemned and a definition or exposition of faith made, was concluded before night. That exposition, as far as the Acts record, was contained in one of the letters of St. Cyril to Nestorius, which the Bishops in the Council one by one accepted as conformable to Apostolic teaching. Whether a further letter of St. Cyril's with his twelve anathematisms, which was also received by the Bishops, was actually accepted by them as their dogmatic utterance is uncertain; though the Bishops distinctly tell the Pope and the Emperor that they have accepted it as well as the others, as being in accordance with the Catholic Creed. At the end of the acts of the first Session the signatures of about 200 Bishops are found, and writers of the day confirm this number, though there is nothing to show that the additional forty or fifty were added on the day on which the definition was passed, June 22, and it is more probable that they were added afterwards (*vid.* Tillemont, *Cyril*, note 34, and Fleury, *Hist.*, xxv. 42). And thus Tillemont, *ibid.*, thinks that the signatures in favor of Cyril altogether amounted to 220. The Legates of the Pope were not present; but they had arrived by July 10. The Syrian Bishops arrived on June 26th or 27th. As to Africa, then overrun by the Vandals, it was represented only by the deacon of the Bishop of Carthage, who sent him to make his apologies for Africa, to warn the Council against the Pelagians, and to testify the adherence of the African Churches to Apostolic doctrine. The countries which were represented at the Council, and took part in the definition, were Egypt, Asia Minor, and Thrace, Greece, etc. The whole number of Bishops in Christendom at the time was about 1,800; not 6,000, as St. Dalmatius says at random. Gibbon says: "The Catholic Church was administered by the spiritual and legal jurisdiction of 1,800 bishops, of whom 1,000 were seated in the Greek, and 800 in the Latin provinces of the empire." He adds: "The numbers are not ascertained by any ancient writer or original catalogue; for the partial lists of the Eastern churches are comparatively modern. The patient diligence of Charles à S. Paolo, of Luke Holstein, and of Bingham has laboriously investigated all the episcopal sees of the Catholic Church."

To the same purport Father Ryder of this Oratory wrote, after my first edition, in answer to Father Botalla, S.J., as follows:

"As regards the Council of Ephesus, there are few points on which learned men are less agreed than its precise numbers. The names given at the opening of the first Session (June 22, 431), in which Nestorius was condemned and St. Cyril approved, amounted to 159; standing aloof from those and protesting against this precipitation in not waiting for the Antiochenes, were sixty-eight. . . . Five days afterwards the Antiochenes with the Patriarch John at their head, about twenty-seven in number, arrived, and then and there anathematized St. Cyril and all his adherents, declaring null and void all they had done. This condemnation is signed by forty-three. The forty-three consists, besides the Antiochenes, of some who had signed the deposition of Nestorius and some of the sixty-eight protestors. The larger part of the sixty-eight, we may presume, went to swell St. Cyril's party, for we find 198 signatures to the deposition of Nestorius. Subsequently to this, in various official documents, the majority refers to itself as 'about 200,' 'over 200'; but we have no signatures beyond the 198. On the other hand, we possess a document of the minority of July 17, containing fifty-three signatures. Afterwards the proportions of the schism were still more serious. . . . John of Antioch's twenty-seven were delegates and representatives of the whole Antiochene Patriarchate, except Cyprus. Thus, on leaving Ephesus, John was able to hold a Council at Antioch, and condemn Cyril with far larger numbers than before. . . . They cannot be well set at less than 100. . . . [And elsewhere], large portions of the Episcopate had no knowledge, or an utterly confused one, of what had been going on at Ephesus. St. Isidore, one of Cyril's own clergy, expostulates with him for his tyranny; and the works of Facundus and Liberatus show how deeply seated was the opposition of the African Church to the doctrine of Cyril."

SECTION 9.

It has been objected to the explanation I have given from Fessler and others of the nature and range of the Pope's infallibility as now a dogma of the Church, that it was a lame and impotent conclusion of the Council, if so much effort was employed as is involved in the convocation and sitting of an Ecumenical Council, in order to do so little. True, if it were called to do what it did and no more; but that such was its aim is a mere assumption. In the first place, it can hardly be doubted that there were those in the Council who were desirous of a stronger definition; and the definition actually made, as being moderate, is so far the victory of those many bishops who considered any definition on the subject inopportune. And it was no slight fruit of their proceedings in the Council, if a definition was to be, to have effected a moderate definition. But the true answer to the objection is that which is given by Bishop Ullathorne. The question of the Pope's infallibility was not one of the objects professed in convening the Council; and the Council is not yet ended.

He says in his *Expostulation Unravelled:* "The Expostulation goes on to suggest that the Council was convened mainly with a view of defining the infallibility, and that the definition itself was brought about, chiefly for political objects, through the action of the Pontiff and a dominant party. · A falser notion could not be entertained. I have the official catalogue before me of the *Schemata* prepared by the theologians for discussion in the Council. In them the infallibility is not even mentioned; for the greater part of them regard ecclesiastical discipline." P. 48 he adds: "Calamitous events suspended the Council."

I have referred to Bishop Fessler's statement that only the last sentences of Boniface's *Unam Sanctam* are infallible. To this Mr. Gladstone replies (p. 45) that the word "Porro," introducing the final words to which the anathema is affixed, extends that anathema to the body of the Bull, which precedes the "Porro." But he does not seem to have observed that there are two distinct heresies condemned in the Bull, and that the "Porro" is the connecting link between these two condemnations, that is, between the penultima and final sentences. The Pope first says: "Nisi duo, sicut Manichæus, fingat esse principia, *quod falsum et hæreticum judicamus* . . . porro, subesse Romano Pontifici, omni humanæ creaturæ declaramus, definimus, et pronunciamus omnino esse de necessitate salutis." That the Latin is deficient in classical terseness and perspicuity we may freely grant.

I say in my pamphlet: "We call 'infallibility' in the case of the Apostles, inspiration; in the case of the church, *assistentia*."

On this Mr. Gladstone says: "On such a statement I have two remarks to make; first, we have this assurance on the strength only of *his own private judgment*, p. 102." How can he say so when (p. 328) I quote Father Perrone, saying: "*Never have Catholics* taught that the gift of infallibility is given by God to the Church after the manner of inspiration"?

Mr. Gladstone proceeds: "Secondly, that, if bidden by the self-assertion of the Pope, he will be required by his principles to retract it, and to assert, if occasion should arise, the contrary." I can only say to so hypothetical an argument what is laid down by Fessler and the Swiss bishops, that the Pope cannot, by virtue of his infallibility, reverse what has always been held; and that the "inspiration" of the Church, in the sense in which the Apostles were inspired, is contrary to our received teaching. If Protestants are to speculate about our future, they should be impartial enough to recollect that if, on the one hand, we believe that a Pope can add to our articles of faith, so, on the other, we hold also that a heretical Pope, *ipso facto*, ceases to be Pope by reason of his heresy, as I have said.

Mr. Gladstone thus ends: "Thirdly, that he lives under a system of development, through which somebody's private opinion of to-day may become matter of faith for all the to-morrows of the future." I think he should give some proof of this; let us have one instance in which "somebody's private opinion" has become *de fide*. Instead of this, he goes on to assert (interrogatively) that Popes, *e.g.* Clement XI. and Gregory II., and the present Pope, have claimed the inspiration of the Apostles, and that Germans, Italians, French have ascribed such a gift to him; of course he means theologians, not mere courtiers, or sycophants, for the Pope cannot help having such till human nature is changed. If Mr. Gladstone is merely haranguing as an orator, I do not for an instant quarrel with him or attempt to encounter him; but if he is a controversialist, we have a right to look for arguments, not mere assertions.

THE END.

www.ingramcontent.com/pod-product-compliance
Lightning Source LLC
Chambersburg PA
CBHW032134160426
43197CB00008B/641

Walter James Malden

**The Conversion of Arable Land to Pasture**

Walter James Malden

**The Conversion of Arable Land to Pasture**

ISBN/EAN: 9783744749824

Printed in Europe, USA, Canada, Australia, Japan

Cover: Foto ©berggeist007 / pixelio.de

More available books at **www.hansebooks.com**

THE

# CONVERSION OF ARABLE LAND TO PASTURE

BY

W. J. MALDEN

AUTHOR OF "FARM BUILDINGS," "TILLAGE AND IMPLEMENTS,"
ETC., ETC.

LONDON
KEGAN PAUL, TRENCH, TRÜBNER & CO., Ltd.
PATERNOSTER HOUSE, CHARING CROSS ROAD
1898

# CONTENTS.

### CHAPTER I.
THE INFLUENCE ON FARMING, STOCK-KEEPING, AND THE NATION . . . . . . 1

### CHAPTER II.
THE FUTURE OF AGRICULTURE . . . . 21

### CHAPTER III.
SUITABLE GRASSES FOR PERMANENT AND TEMPORARY PASTURES . . . . . 39

### CHAPTER IV.
PERMANENT PASTURE . . . . . . 61

### CHAPTER V.
TEMPORARY LEYS . . . . . . 81

### CHAPTER VI.
LAYING DOWN LAND TO TEMPORARY PASTURE . 100

## CHAPTER VII.

MANAGEMENT OF TEMPORARY PASTURES . . 119

## CHAPTER VIII.

UTILIZATION OF THE CROP . . . . . 137

## CHAPTER IX.

GENERAL PRINCIPLES ASSOCIATED WITH PERMANENT PASTURE-MAKING: INFERIOR GRASSES AND WEEDS . . . . . 156

## CHAPTER X.

THEORIES, EXPERIMENTS, AND PRACTICES RELATING TO PASTURES . . . . . 174

# THE CONVERSION OF ARABLE LAND.

## CHAPTER I.

### THE INFLUENCE ON FARMING, STOCK-KEEPING, AND THE NATION.

THE feature about Britain which most strikes the foreigner when he first comes to England is the garden-like and well-cared-for appearance of the country. Centuries of care, hard work, skill and enterprise have been bestowed on the land, and out of forest and waste neatly-arranged fields have been developed, supporting commodious homesteads, villages and towns, all of which trace their origin to the produce of the fields. Perhaps there can be no more bitter reflection to an Englishman when he passes through the country than the knowledge that the work laid down by his fathers must to a great extent be abandoned; for with all our apparent prosperity, the land, the great workshop of the country in days gone by, can no longer be cultivated so as to give its full return. Not that the land cannot produce what it did, and not that those who would work it have less skill than of yore, for at no time in the world's history has there been so great an accumulation of skill and knowledge among farmers as that held by British farmers to-day; but because countries more favourably situated produce grain more cheaply than it can be produced at home, no matter what skill is brought to bear upon it. Grain is the mainstay of agriculture, because on the extent to which it is grown depends the quantity of land left at the farmer's disposal to crop with other products for which there is only a limited demand, and on which but a slight increase in production reduces the profit so as to render them unremunerative to the grower. This stage has been reached in England.

The unprofitable condition of agriculture has been realized by most people for some time past, though perhaps nothing has more clearly expressed it than a paper read by Mr. Martin Sutton at the Farmers' Club, where, when dealing with the necessity for converting arable land to pasture, he brought forward many causes which had tended to reduce it to its present deplorable condition, and gave sound advice to farmers for alleviating the losses they now sustain. Mr. Sutton pointed out that it was to pastures—permanent in some instances, temporary in others—that the farmer must look for the lightening of his expenses. If this good advice were followed, there is reason to believe that the farmer would lose less; but it must prove a serious blow to the labourer, and the country would be the loser to a very considerable amount on every acre diverted from arable culture, small as the annual return from an acre of grain is at present prices.

How vast the change which has taken place in farming within a quarter of a century actually is, was pointed out by Mr. Sutton. In Great Britain the total cultivated area is returned as 32,629,855 acres, of which 16,405,069 acres are given as pasture, and 16,164,786 acres as arable—an increase of permanent grass from 1871 to 1894 of 4,392,213 acres. A footnote in Mr. Sutton's "Permanent and Temporary Pastures" gives information that is not obtained from official returns. "It must unfortunately be admitted that a proportion of this vast acreage has been allowed to go to grass, unaided, in consequence of the inability of owners or occupiers to cultivate the land." In this is much truth. A large proportion of the land that has been withdrawn from cultivation "tumbled down." It was exhausted of fertility so long as any sort of grain crop could be got off it; the crops feebly struggled against the weeds, and finally, perhaps after a wet winter, when it lay water-logged in the spring, it appeared hopeless to do anything with it; it was therefore left for nature to deal with, and it has lain there ever since growing couch and other weeds, but little of such grasses and herbage as entitle it to be called permanent pasture. Very often this was land that for fifty years had a paid rental of from twenty-five to thirty-five shillings per acre, but which now is not worth the rates, taxes or tithes, to which it is subject—in fact it cannot be let to pay. The increase in cattle and sheep is in no way commensurate with the large increase in the acreage of grass; and this is the more striking when it is remembered how enormously the importation of feeding stuffs has increased. The fact is the farmer has been losing money all round; he cannot stock the land to the full; the cattle have to go to pay other expenses, and he cannot re-stock.

It is doubtful if there is any increase in the output of meat due to those additional four and a half millions of acres of grass beyond that which could have been raised without them, with the aid of the imported feeding stuffs. The country is under-stocked from end to end, and had the previously existing pastures been fully stocked, and the feeding stuffs been devoted to animals carried on them, as much meat would have been raised. Meanwhile those pastures would have been improved, and rendered capable of carrying still more stock in the future. Our own idea is that far more than the present head of stock might have been carried without the assistance of one acre of that four and a half millions, and also without the aid of by far the larger part of the imported feeding stuffs. The country is therefore losing the four and a half millions of acres. Under the old four-course system farmers used to say that to make a fair living (and they reckoned 1*l*. per acre per annum a fair return) the two corn crops should each give 10*l*. per acre. This is 20*l*., without taking into consideration the root and seed crops. Putting the expense of the cleaning and thorough working of the land necessary to take it through the rotation against the value of the root crop; and allowing two tons of hay, at 3*l*. per ton (not overmuch for a

## The Influence on Farming 9

crop which can be cut twice in a season), the farmer could handle 26*l*. in the four years, or 6*l*. 10*s*. an acre throughout his farm. To the country the full value of the root crop had to be considered even though the farmer may not have made a penny profit from it—although of course he often made a considerable sum by the consumption of the crop. The country got the benefit from it, because practically all that went to produce it was the outcome of labour and the soil, as there was little purchased from abroad. A twenty-ton crop of roots would feed 400 sheep of eight stone weight for 400 weeks; this at 4*d*. per week gives over 6*l*. 10*s*. per acre; consequently the return on the rotation was 33*l*., or 8*l*. 5*s*. per acre per annum. At this rate the four and a half million acres withdrawn from arable culture, and set to grow grass to support animals which, had the farmer's capital not been exhausted through the unremunerative condition of other portions of his calling, could have been supported on the pasture existing previously to their withdrawal, entail a loss of over 35,000,000*l.* per annum. Not an inconsiderable loss even to a wealthy country.

It may be urged that we have had the largely increased importation of feeding stuffs to help us, but they have helped us very little in regard to output. The country paid a pound for every pound's worth imported. We lose the arable cropping, and gain little, if anything, in output of meat, notwithstanding the increase of pasture and of feeding stuffs imported. Perhaps one of the most hopeless features in connection with land going to grass is that there were 350,000 fewer cattle, and 1,400,000 fewer sheep in the country in 1894 than in 1893, notwithstanding the fact that feeding stuffs were imported at a lower price than at any previous time. It does not appear from this that farmers benefit from the cheap importation of feeding stuffs to so great a degree as some would have us suppose.

And yet with good reason farmers are advised to change their system of farming, and turn their arable land to pasture. When it comes to such a state of affairs that the best remedy is to turn from the greater evil to the less, things are indeed bad. The great drawback to turning arable land to pasture is that farmers have been top-weighted by foreign competition so severe and so long continued that only a small proportion are in a position to reap advantage from it. The want of capital to stock the new grasses must effectually check many who would from doing it. Where is a man, already pressed, to find the money to stock from 20 to 100 acres? He could, perhaps, work the land with fewer horses, less labour, less machinery; he may sell some of his horses and machinery, but they will not go much farther than the expense of seeds for laying down the land. Rent, rates, taxes, and a whole lot of incidental expenses will remain, so that he has little to turn into cash to make purchases. As things go he sees nothing before him but a gradual loss of capital. It is only those with capital at command who can hope to reap full advantage from the change.

Taking all things into consideration an acre of well-farmed land returns to the farm labourer 30s. for the work he does on it. As many pence are sufficient where the land is under grazing, as the farmer can do practically all that there is to be done except on special occasions. Assuming that four and a half million acres of land have gone from the plough to grass, and that this is grazed, the agricultural labourer loses 6,000,000l. yearly. Is it any wonder that he leaves the rural districts, and goes directly or indirectly to swell the ranks of the unemployed in towns? The loss in amount of wages is not only felt through the quantity of land turned to grass within the past twenty years, but the want of capital prevents farmers from employing all the labour they would on that portion still under cultivation. A lighter labour bill, whatever its consequences, becomes a necessity when ready money is not available, and saving in this outlay is easily effected. Fewer hands are employed, less work is given to the land, and doubtless comparatively few farms carry the hands they did in the days of prosperity. On the sixteen million acres still under arable cultivation in Great Britain the smaller amount of labour employed on each acre must represent some millions of pounds less going into the pockets of the labourer yearly.

Sixteen million acres remain in the balance. Will this go also? Grain, meat, vegetables, anything the English farmer can grow, can be supplied from abroad at a cheaper rate than he with

## The Influence on Farming 15

English handicaps in the way of rates, tithes, taxes, and other necessities requisite for the support of a high-class shop-keeping nation, is able to produce them. If we take each important item the position is easily seen. In grain we are badly beaten. In meat we are running at such a low margin of profit that last year the decrease in cattle was 350,000, in sheep 1,400,000. Recent advices say that the Argentine is preparing to send carcases, equal to those imported for 18*l.* from North America, at 12*l.*, so the future profit looks doubtful to us. Already milk, hitherto considered unimportable, is a daily arrival. Butter, and its poor relative, margarine, are coming in ever-increasing quantities, so dairying does not look so very hopeful. Potatoes, we have recently been told, are more promising because the English farmer imports comparatively less than he did. We, however, fail to see great cause for rejoicing. In 1878, the year before the depression in agriculture is generally stated to have commenced, 508,000 acres were grown; in 1894, 504,000 acres. The greater freedom of cultivation which has opened up an almost unlimited extent of land suitable for potato cultivation, has not increased the acreage. Granted that some improvement in the cultivation and in the varieties grown has taken place, resulting in a greater yield, there is no reason to suppose that this has increased abnormally within the past fifteen years. There were Champions and Magnum Bonums in those days. What has occurred is that the increase in supply has been sufficient to keep the markets in an over-supplied condition, and except in years when, through disease, frost, or other exceptional reasons, prices have received a special impetus upwards, the normal price has not been sufficiently good to induce the foreigner to grow main-crop varieties with the view of putting them on our markets. If it does not pay the foreigner with cheap sea-rates, free importation, cheap labour, and lower taxation, to grow them, it does not pay the English grower. The satisfaction the English grower gets out of the luxury of supplying potatoes that once were supplied by the foreigner is therefore not very great, especially when he remembers that the early potatoes, which are those which would be most remunerative if his climate would allow him to produce them, are imported, so that he loses the very high prices which once were his. Altogether it appears to be a sort of negative satisfaction. The exceptional prices of 1895 were due to the May frosts, disease, and the winter frost, a combination of circumstances which rarely occurs. We do not say that under ordinary circumstances all the half million acres of potatoes are grown at a loss, but a great proportion are. Those who grow the choicest varieties after the best methods naturally do best, as they realize the highest prices, but the demand for the best is more or less limited.

The palmy days of market gardening have to a great extent disappeared owing to increased home and foreign competition.

No matter to what the farmer turns to help himself, he is only catering for an already over-stocked market. A few more chickens and eggs and a few more specialities are well enough in their way, but very slight increase in the supply of any one rapidly reduces them to the point where no profit is reached. As things go, according to the experience of those most intimately concerned, a large portion of the sixteen million acres of arable land still being worked is losing money. If it continues to lose, it must cease to be worked. At 6*l*. per acre this practically means that 100,000,000*l*. annually would be withdrawn from the income of the country, almost all of which is absolute profit. With it goes all the capital represented in the improvement of the land, in its buildings, cottages, &c., a sum not well comprehended. Turn it to grass. Some of it may be saved in this way, but in providing more food for stock, and raising more meat, the question arises, What price will meat fetch when more meat is produced? What is to prevent grass from being over-stocked when already there is so much under-stocked?

# CHAPTER II.

### THE FUTURE OF AGRICULTURE.

THE future always leads one forward more hopefully; if it does not, things are indeed in a bad way. Whilst there is any glimmer of light through the mist, hope is ready to see it in a brighter day beyond. The present is always with us; the future never comes; but hopes may be realized in the future. It is certain that existing circumstances cannot carry British agriculture far into the future. There must be changes. The changes will have to be made both by the farmer and by those who do not farm. The farmer must make his business one in which the outgoings are reduced to a minimum. There was a time when a man who made two blades to grow where one had grown before was considered a patriot. Now, one class of patriot has come to the conclusion that the land is of so little importance that it must "go." A ray of hope is that, with greater knowledge of the benefits a nation receives from its land, this class of patriot will become smaller, and that those who realize how badly agriculture fares, and how serious its loss would be to the nation, will give it their practical support. The farmer in his lights has been doing his best to adapt himself to the changing circumstances. The strong prejudices which were the stock arguments of not many years ago, have disappeared almost entirely, and are only

## The Future of Agriculture 23

found in those districts where nature has been kinder in the disposal of soil and climate, and in providing the soil with breeds of cattle or sheep peculiarly adapted to it. We know a few such districts; in these the extremes of climate have not been felt throughout the past fifteen or twenty years in anything like the degree that has been experienced in the greater portion of the country, and here men have been able to continue their prejudices without suffering in the same way that those less favourably placed have done. As a rule, however, farmers have realized that there is no harm, and nothing which injures their business reputation, in going outside the beaten track. Those who have best faced the times have struck out in fresh directions, and others see that they must do so also. Without losing any of their general astuteness, farmers have changed in a remarkable manner, and with anything like encouragement they are prepared for further change, though, with the ever-increasing supply of foreign produce, it must be patent to those who know little of farming, that the inducement to effect change is hardly sufficient to make them enthusiastic about it. Changes cannot be effected on the farm without considerable outlay of capital, or the waste of existing capital, any more than a draper or milliner can change his business to a tailor's, or an ironmonger his into a wheelwright's. If, then, farmers are a little slow in making changes, it is now more often due to the exercise of business caution than to ignorance and prejudice.

There is little doubt that alterations are frequently not made because of the terms of the agreements farmers hold with their landlords. It may be urged that in these days landlords are glad to let their land on any reasonable terms, so long as they can get a rent. There is a great deal of truth in this, especially where it affects poor landlords. There are, however, landlords holding even large estates to whom it is not a matter of serious issue whether they get any profit from their estates, but who hold the peculiar notions with regard to farming that they inherited in bygone days, and these are not men with whom it is easy to get a change of lease. Then, again, a farmer may be in a bad financial position, and not well equipped to make terms favourable for himself. In fact, there are thousands of farmers holding leases and agreements they signed years ago, which include clauses they would like altered, but which from causes best known to themselves they prefer not to urge. A man may effect various permanent improvements on the farm; among them he may put down land to pasture; he may treat the land fairly as between tenant or landlord; he may do no injury to it; yet when he presents his claim for unexhausted improvements, a counter claim is put in on the ground of breach of contract in accordance with his agreement. The breach may be that he changed his cropping—had not such and such a proportion cropped in a particular manner. He may have been doing it for years and no objection have been lodged, but, although he has done no harm, he must sacrifice that which he has done for the permanent good of the farm he is leaving.

It is this which has caused the recent Agricultural Holdings Acts to be such a dead letter. While guarding the landlord's interests so that malicious injury is not effected, it is important, in view of the greatly changed conditions of farming, that items in these musty leases which are prejudicial to both landlord and tenant should be dispossessed of the power of preventing tenants from turning the land to better account. In the long run it would be better both for the landlord and the tenant. Doubtless many thousands of acres out of cropping to-day would have been paying substantial rent if the tenant had felt he might exercise his own judgment, and change his system of farming without incurring serious liability by so doing. The landlord should, of course, be guarded against the unscrupulous squatter who steps into a farm to exhaust it of any available fertility, and then moves on. If tried tenants had been allowed to make the changes that their experience with the particular land warranted, and had not been tied hard and fast to leases possessing no elasticity to meet altering circumstances, it would have been far better for the landlord. The absurdity, and want of business principle in providing one form of lease to meet the varying conditions of land—hill or valley, clay or gravel—which existed on some large estates are so apparent that it is evident that such dealing could only have been instituted at times when competition for land was very keen, and men were careless what they accepted so long as they could get the land.

Farming has been too princely. In this we mean there has been too great expenditure in directions where corresponding returns could not be expected. "Model" farm buildings have been responsible for much unnecessary outlay. Perhaps one of the worst days' work an ambitious man has had has been when he has been taken to look at a show-farm, where everything about the premises had been arranged with perfect taste and judgment: Halls for cattle, boudoirs for dairies, palaces for stables, neatly-furnished cubicles for piggeries, enlarged dolls' houses for poultry, and everything in the same proportion. Very pretty to look at, but nothing that money—if there is plenty of it to waste—cannot buy. Anybody can have such a place if he will spend the money on it; but what purpose does it serve? It does not indicate good farming any more than does growing big crops by extravagant outlay. The unfortunate part of the matter is that both these forms of extravagance have been too often regarded as indicating skill, and have had many imitators. The fact of the existence of these "model" homesteads was bad, because it bred the desire for something on the same lines, and to satisfy the demands of their tenants landlords had to play a sort of game of brag as to who could go farthest. That many went too far is known only too well on estates in all parts of the country. Something more simple could have been contrived which would have answered the purpose of the farmer equally well.

Fattening cattle beyond a certain degree has been a source of loss, almost, though certainly not quite such a source of loss as selling them as fat when they were only three-fifths fat. However, it is not always for want of judgment, but because necessity wills, that a farmer sells his stock at the time they are entering on the most profitable phase of their existence. There is no excuse for the man who makes blubber in days when candles are displaced by gas, oil, and electricity. He simply indulges his own vanity, and of course he must pay for it. Cattle, and all live stock, require to be fat to fetch the best price, but beyond a certain condition their food is wasted. It is not good farming to make animals fatter than they can be made so profitably. There was some excuse in the days when wheat was fetching 3*l*. per quarter, as, with moderate tillage, dung made by extravagantly fed animals was likely to produce wheat in return which would show a profit. The lower the price to which wheat falls the less inducement is there to make dung by extravagant means, as the dung is used to raise lower-priced crops.

The future of farming must involve carefulness in every direction. Luxurious notions must be allowed to slide. A change from arable land to grass will render many of the princely homesteads unsuitable for the new conditions. These homesteads will have to be converted into more suitable farms, each according to its present accommodation and the extent to which the system of farming is altered. It is unreasonable for farmers to expect that landlords will make great outlays; and farmers must be satisfied with such reasonable changes as will allow them to carry on their business. Little inconveniences must be overlooked, and everything turned to the best account. Barns may be turned into suitable cattle byres or sheds with very simple fittings. Central feeding passages with tram rails, &c., may be done without. An ordinary floor manger, with simple ties, is all that can be asked reasonably for. There is not much that English farmers have to learn from Irish farmers, but after seeing the extravagant feeding houses in England, the interest on the outlay of which often amounts to the profit of several bullocks, one cannot be otherwise than struck with admiration at the large number of cattle that are conveniently, comfortably, and profitably housed in the inexpensive simply-fitted sheds which are met with on moderate-sized farms in some parts of Ireland. Different indeed are these to the general run of cattle sheds in England. Such princely cattle halls as that at Bemerton, near Salisbury, are of course exceptional, but the waste of building a house at the cost of two or three thousand pounds, to hold eighty or ninety cows, cannot be too strongly deprecated. In this case, from 25*l*. to 30*l*. was spent to shelter each animal. Very few have considered how much is spent per animal on a large number of the high-class homesteads in

England. If they did, they would be much astonished. Therefore, we say, in making alterations in premises, it is necessary to exercise great caution in respect to the outlay, especially as there is a vagueness as to the profit which will be realized in the new order of things.

A change in cropping from arable to grass tends in one important direction, that of reducing the heavy cost of carriage of produce. When the produce can walk to market, instead of being carried there on wheels, a saving is effected. There are times when carting can be done with but little expense to the farm, but such times are exceptional. It cannot be too readily remembered that when once anything is put into a cart expenses commence with it. It is greatly in favour of mixed farming, even when the tendency is strongly on the side of grass, that the corn grown upon the arable can be fed with great advantage on the grass. Instead of carting corn to market, and carting back another form of feeding stuff, that which is at home is saved the cost of cartage, and the profit of the buyer of the corn and the profit of the dealer on the feeding stuffs are saved.

The excessive charges of railway companies check the profit the farmer would get, as the preferential rates at which foreign produce is carried act as a handicap to him. It is distinctly unfair for railways to do this; it is harder because proportionally railways are lightly rated, and it is still harder because railways, which pay so little towards the school rates, obtain the services of young men and lads who have been educated almost entirely at the expense of the English farmer. A gleam of light is that sometime railway rates will be adjusted so as to render matters fairer towards the farmer.

Light railways are held out as a boon in the near future. There are some districts where such railways would be a decided gain, but, as a rule, the larger railways have tapped the districts where any considerable amount of carriage is to be obtained. No one, of course, would refuse to have a railway brought close to his door, if he paid only a slight proportion of the charge, but it is emphatically unfair to tax others so that he may be more conveniently situated. Before rushing into a wholesale system of new railways, the most important step appears to be to ascertain whether the land throughout the country within three miles of a railway is in a paying condition. If not, what good is to be expected from opening up other districts? What under-supplied market are they going to supply, when all markets are already overstocked? Anything additional will only tend to lower them. Light railways will not in themselves make English agriculture prosperous.

# CHAPTER III.

### SUITABLE GRASSES FOR PERMANENT AND TEMPORARY PASTURES.

Having reached the point where we must begin to deal with the methods of treatment of arable land which is to be converted into grass, it is advisable to detail a few of the features of the plants which are found most suitable for that purpose. The descriptions will be brief because the characteristics must be dealt with when treating with mixtures suitable for particular purposes.

Rye Grass.—The Italian and the Perennial are the two species of rye grass which deserve the greatest attention from the farmer. There are a great number of varieties of these grasses, especially of the latter, but for most practical purposes these two are all that need be considered, though for shortest leys the annual ryegrass is valuable as producing a large amount of feed in a short space of time. The Italian is biennial—sown in one season, it comes to maturity in the next, and produces a fair amount of growth the second year. True, some plants live on a year, sometimes two, longer; but from a practical standpoint it may be considered of no value after its second year. In water meadows, especially on the edges of the grips where the soil is worn from time to time by the action of the water, it may be seen growing from year to year, but how far this is due to seed falling on it, cannot be easily proved. For a single year's ley it is of the greatest value, coming into growth very early, and producing several crops in the season if it is cut each time as soon as it is well-grown, but not allowed to ripen its seed; producing, of course, most crops in a moist season; in fact, it so loves moisture that we have seen crops of it on the Bedford Irrigation Farm, measuring three feet in height, as the result of one month's growth. It grows on almost any soil. Mr. Sutton mentions that "fair results have been obtained from heaths dressed with marl and farmyard manure. It flourishes in warmth and moisture, and in rich damp soils the growth is extremely rapid. It starts earlier in the spring and grows later in autumn than any other grass"—a good record. When it is added that all stock relish it, and that it makes excellent hay, it is not difficult to see that it is of the greatest value in short temporary pastures. When sown alone three bushels are required per acre, and it is best sown in February and March for spring seeding, in September and October for autumn seeding, though it may be sown at any convenient time from February to October, when desired. The seed, which is comparatively light, owing to the husk and long awn which prevents it settling down solidly, should weigh over 18 lbs. per bushel, improving in accordance with its weight up to 22 lbs. Care should be taken that it is free from seeds of inferior grasses, such as couch or twitch, tall oat grass, Yorkshire fog, the poorer brome grasses, &c., and of weeds,

## Suitable Grasses

such as crowfoot, rib-grass, docks, &c. The same obnoxious weeds should be guarded against in samples of seeds of all grasses, especially such as Perennial rye grass and Meadow Fescue, where, on casual observation, they are not easily recognizable, though they may be detected with little trouble if the sample is looked into closely.

To those who are not accustomed to look at samples of seed, and do not readily recognize foreign matter in them a small magnifying glass or lens proves of great service. A description of the seeds of grasses that should not be present in any sample, but which unfortunately are found too commonly, may help buyers to notice them. The seed of couch may be recognized from Italian rye grass, because instead of the awn appearing to be an extension of the keel-like rib which runs along the back of the seed, the rib is much less marked, and the awn (as far as there is one) is only the husk which has shrunk and partly rolled itself up to a sharp point, and is not, strictly speaking, an awn at all. The seed of couch is longer, and gradually tapers to a point from near the base. The seed of the tall oat grass, which is also common in badly cleaned samples, should be looked for, as it produces the objectionable onion couch. It is much larger than the rye grasses, and may be seen on casual observation. It is very similar in appearance to a small wild oat. In colour it is usually brown on the back; and out of the back, near the base, springs a stout long awn, about twice the length of the seed. This awn is

## Suitable Grasses

straight and spiral about half its length, after which it generally turns off abruptly. At the base are a number of fine hairs similar to those seen on the wild oat. The seed of the soft brome grass is often met with. It is a coarse thick seed with a short awn. Being twice the size of the Perennial rye grass, it is easily noticeable. The outer husk is coarse, and if the seed is viewed lying on its back the kernel appears to lie deep down in the husk. The kernel is somewhat flat and sole-shaped, and is covered by a thin skin which has strongly serrated edges. The seed of Yorkshire fog is very dissimilar to those before mentioned. It is short, and is surrounded by a thin husk of a light colour; under a small magnifying glass it appears to be similar in shape to a beech-nut which has partly split showing the kernel inside. The two last-mentioned are largely sown when the sweepings of the hay-loft are used.

Permanent rye grass is admirably suited for long or short leys. A few years since there was a crusade against its being employed for permanent pastures, but the error of the advocates of its non-employment for this purpose has been shown, and it is rare now for any field to be laid down without it. We were victims to laying down fifty acres in three fields without it; two of those fields are under the plough again, after having given most unsatisfactory results. All round it is doubtful if we possess a grass of such great general value. Sown in a crop one year it produces great bulk in the following, and does well, if manured, for two more. It then generally goes back, but this is usually for want of manure. On most soils it does not as a rule die out when sown in a mixture of seeds intended to produce firm pasture, but it grows less as the surface of the soil becomes exhausted of its manure; the application of manure immediately causes it to spring up again to vigour. As the soil of a new pasture becomes enriched with the decaying roots of plants, the rye grass wakes up to use the fertility thus engendered, and as years go by it increases its hold again. As seen in the investigation of old pastures made by Dr. Fream, it almost always becomes the predominant grass in the best pastures throughout the country. It is most frequent in pastures carried on good rich soils, and is less frequent and grows less robustly as the soils become thinner and dryer. On waterlogged soils it does not thrive. It possesses no feature which detracts from its value. It does not grow in coarse unsightly tufts; it has a rich verdant green colour; is highly nutritious; gives excellent hay easy to make; is relished by horses, cattle and sheep alike; and forms a good turf above and below ground. The seed is sufficiently vigorous not to be smothered at seeding so readily as are some of the smaller seeded grasses, and is easy to harvest and to thresh. When growing, the plants of the Perennial and Italian rye grasses may be easily distinguished. In the case of the Perennial it will be seen that the young leaves are folded flat on the mid-rib throughout their whole length when emerging from the

## Suitable Grasses

purple sheath at the base of the plant; whereas in the case of the Italian, the young leaves curl round somewhat corkscrew fashion. When in ear, the awns of the Italian distinguish it from the awnless perennial. The best seed weighs from 24 lbs. to 28 lbs. per bushel. From 24 lbs to 26 lbs. is that usually sold as the choicest, and any extra weight is not of special value. From 22 lbs. to 24 lbs. is sound and good, but below that it cannot be relied upon.

TIMOTHY OR CAT'S-TAIL is another valuable grass for alternate husbandry, or for permanent pasture. It has increased in popularity of late years, though it has long been a favourite in America and Canada, whence a considerable quantity of Timothy hay has been sent to England during the past four or five years. Sown in temporary pastures it gives a good return for several years. As it is essentially a late grass, it is not so suitable for use in a single year's ley to mix with clover, as it matures later, and Mr. Sutton recommends it to be sown with cowgrass, when the two will be at their best at the same time. It, however, makes coarse hay, which requires chaffing when the grass has been left late before cutting. Its hardiness is a strong point in its favour. If late in maturing, it affords nutritious autumn and winter grazing. When mown with the view of getting good aftermath, it should be cut early. It is particularly suitable for clay and moist soils, and luxuriates in peat soils. The seed, which readily falls from the husk, weighs 50 lbs. per bushel, and it is very easy to detect foreign matter or weeds in it.

MEADOW FOX-TAIL ranks first as a permanent grass, though it does not come to maturity sufficiently quickly for its value to be obtained in short leys. A somewhat similar grass—the black-bent or mouse-tail—resembles it only in outward appearance, for instead of being highly nutritious and capable of producing abundant herbage, it is one of the worst pests on heavy arable land, and has no feeding value. Several other grasses belonging to the same family resemble it in the flowery head, but have no value to the farmer. Meadow Fox-tail comes into flower as early as the middle of April, and produces so much herbage early in the season, that fields in which it is plentiful are always amongst those on which farmers can turn their most forward stock as they are fit to seed sooner than those where it is not so plentiful. It does not do its best except on rich moist soils. One of the richest fields we know, in the parish of Thorney, near Peterboro', is composed to a great extent of this excellent grass; the soil of this field is rich fenland resting on clay. On burning soils it makes very little show, but where circumstances are favourable to it, that is on all good soils, it is the most highly-prized grass we have. The seed is light, the heaviest samples not exceeding 12 lb. per bushel, and is more often obtained at eight or ten pounds. Being small and light, it requires careful seeding, as if buried deeply it will not germinate.

MEADOW FESCUE is a valuable grass,

but it rarely appears to form a large portion of the grasses in a pasture. It was very much boomed a few years ago, and was strongly recommended by its supporters as being better suited than perennial rye grass for sowing on land to produce permanent pasture. There are many reasons for supposing that those who advocated it mistook the herbage of rye grass for meadow fescue, which it somewhat resembles, though the marked midrib down the rye grass is only slightly marked in the meadow fescue. Nor is it preferable to rye grass in temporary mixtures. It is, however, the most valuable of the broad-leaved fescues, of which the various-leaved ranks next. There are many narrow-leaved fescues, the Hard Fescue being the best among these. It is well worth a place in a mixture for most soils, for if it establishes itself it provides valuable food. It is found on almost all sheep pastures, often occupying an important place in them. Sheep's Fescue grows freely on Down land, and is found largely among the sheep pastures of the Highlands. It is unimportant in rich pastures as it is shouldered out by stronger varieties, it being the smallest of cultivated grasses. Though small it is nutritious, and it thrives on poor, thin soils, such as those mentioned, where no other grass would give so good a return.

ROUGH COCK'S-FOOT is a valuable grass for either temporary or permanent pasture. On dry soils and in dry climates its growth is stunted, and an objection is often lodged against it that it produces a tussocky form of growth which is unsightly in newly laid pasture. My own opinion of the value of the grass has been greatly raised by seeing what a prominent place it takes in the best Irish pastures. Even on comparatively new ones it proves valuable. The tussocky habit of growth disappears when the pasture becomes well established, as instead of keeping in a bunch it ramifies through the turf and mixes well with other grasses. It is exceedingly well suited to temporary pastures, where its great growth of rich feeding grass proves very valuable. In hay it is coarse, and should be cut early ; and its coarseness makes it rather a farmer's than a market hay. On dry soils it should be sown in small quantities, but on rich moist soils it may be sown more abundantly. The seed weighs 18 lbs.

per bushel and possesses considerable vigour.

ROUGH-STALKED MEADOW GRASS and smooth-stalked meadow grass are the two Poa grasses found most useful. Mr. Sutton recommends the former for strong moist soils, and the latter for drier soils. They are not well suited for temporary pasture. The grasses are very similar in appearance, and the only reliable point of distinction is the shape of the ligule. In the smooth variety it is rounded, in the rough pointed.

DOG'S-TAIL is found so frequently in old pastures that it cannot be so valueless as some would have it estimated. It is found on our pastures of moderate feeding value, but it is there because the amount of fertility in the soil will not carry the better grasses. By doing away

## Suitable Grasses

with the dog's-tail, room would not be made for grasses which would give a better return. The fittest stand. Manure the soil to encourage better grasses, and the dog's-tail will be less in evidence. It makes a good bottom, and helps to form a turf of roots. As a portion of it goes to seed when grazed, there is no need to sow it thickly, as in course of time it will spread to the required degree.

SWEET VERNAL is a grass of low-feeding value. It, however, takes up small room in a pasture, and, as it possesses more than any other grass the peculiarly sweet aroma of new hay, it is valuable in hay as imparting to it a pleasant smell.

FLORIN, or Creeping Bent Grass, is valuable in moist situations, but it is practically valueless in dry places. Other plants of the family Agrostis are weeds, and useless.

The CLOVERS most valuable for farm purposes are the red, white, alsike, yellow and cowgrass. The red is especially valuable for temporary leys, and may be sown in quantity in mixtures for permanent leys. Cow-grass, which is often regarded as only a variety of the former, is more perennial in growth. It is known as a single-cut clover, as it comes to the scythe but once in a season, whereas broad produces two, and we have taken three crops in a wet season. White clover is unfitted for hay as it rarely grows tall enough, but it produces thick herbage of a most nutritious nature. Sown by itself, or in temporary pastures, it is very valuable, and there are few really valuable permanent pastures where it does not form a considerable portion. Trefoil is not of great value, though it has its place in temporary mixtures on thin soils. Alsike is a single-cut clover, growing a big crop for a year or two. It is often sown in permanent mixtures, but is rarely found in established pastures.

SAINFOIN AND LUCERNE are two extremely valuable leguminous plants, particularly for soils where lime is present in the subsoil. They may be laid down alone with great advantage, or may be sown in temporary mixtures. Well cared for, a crop of either will stand many years, but if they die out from exhaustion it is no use to plant the same land with them again for some time. Lucerne is the Alfalfa of the Argentine. There is a great and commendable increase in the quantity of these crops being sown, lucerne especially thriving without a chalk subsoil, once thought essential. We have seen a ten-year ley as good as ever after ten years' cropping on fen peat resting on clay, and have seen a twenty-year ley on a mixed light soil in Norfolk.

# CHAPTER IV.

### PERMANENT PASTURE.

A PERMANENT pasture, as distinguished from a temporary pasture, is grass land which has reached that stage where there is a kind of turf of grass above ground, and a turf of roots below. Until the roots form into a matted turf of at least one and a half inches, the characteristics of permanent pasture are not shown above ground. In a temporary pasture the individual plants as sown are distinguishable; in a permanent pasture they have merged together so that it is difficult, in very old pastures impossible, to detect which blades belong to particular plants. The roots in a temporary pasture are but thinly collected, and the soil about them has changed little in colour. The roots of an old pasture continue to be matted together to a depth of as much as six or eight inches at times, and the colour of the soil has darkened from the decay of previous generations of roots. The age of pastures may be approximately arrived at if the sod is examined. On gravelly land, no matter how many stones there are on the surface when the seed is sown, these are gradually buried by the matting of the roots and the growth of plants above them; worms too are continually at work passing the herbage through them, thus bringing the undigested portion to the surface and there leaving it in the form of worm casts. The immediate surface soil thus becomes completely altered. A large amount of fertility becomes stored in it from time to time, and this becomes available for the use of succeeding generations of grasses.

The difference between permanent and temporary pastures is this: Temporary pastures have to rely entirely on the soil for support. Permanent pastures are able to find additional sustenance from the food collected, which is in the form of humus or decayed vegetable matter, this being the remains of previous generations of grasses grown there. It is for this reason that old pastures are said to be self-supporting. This is true only in degree. On very old pastures so much fertility is stored up that the omission to apply manure is not strongly marked for a year or two; whereas the omission in the case of a temporary pasture is at once apparent. It is obvious that the storing of fertility can only be done at considerable cost, and it is here that the expense of making a pasture is directed. Break up the pasture, and set free the stored-up fertility, and then the extent of the storage becomes apparent. In making a pasture, therefore, it is necessary to store up fertility. The longer the pasture is down, the greater is the amount of fertility stored. Even in a short ley an appreciable amount of fertility is stored away, and the setting free of this renders it unnecessary to apply heavy dressings of manure to support a corn crop—one of the points in favour of temporary leys. When once a pasture is self-supporting —though this must not be traded upon too much—it is found that for a small outlay a big return is made, provided, of course, that drainage and other matters are attended to. But it is not reached without considerable outlay at first. At these times, when it is necessary to avoid outlay, the value of permanent pasture is understood. It is to be regretted that there is such a large proportion of existing pastures in a less prosperous condition than they should be, through want of better and more generous treatment.

The laying down of arable land to permanent pasture is a simple act in many ways, but the want of success attending the labours of many who try to bring it about shows that it is not altogether an haphazard performance. The widely different circumstances which have to be dealt with in preparing a soil

F

such as is found on thin chalk downs, and one found in the heavy clay districts, point to the necessity of practising different methods. A difficulty in connection with laying down permanent pasture is that you do not necessarily reap what you sow. A permanent pasture grows just that herbage which the particular form of fertility, the mechanical and chemical condition of the soil, and the climate, are capable of producing. The aim should be to reach the point where the pasture becomes permanent, with as little loss and as much gain as possible. The experiments at Rothamsted and Kidmore show that the nature of the herbage on the same soil, and existing under exactly similar conditions, can be entirely changed by the application of the comparatively few pounds' weight of artificial manure applied annually. On a larger scale the same thing is seen in the fields around us. Two fields lying alongside each other often show great difference in the grasses which go to make up their pasture. One which has been generously treated carries grasses which are capable of fattening a bullock per acre, while the other, exhausted by frequent mowing and unaided by manure, will hardly carry a yearling. The grasses in these two fields differ entirely. Each supports the varieties it is capable of carrying. If the poor field is subjected to manuring, the poor grasses are driven out by the better; if the rich field is subjected to an exhausting process for a few years, the higher class grasses become stunted, and the poorer grasses increase and smother the good ones. In practice good pastures usually keep good, because, if any animals receive extra food whilst grazing, it is those which are nearest to the butcher; the poor keep poor because they get no help.

The reason why many fields are so slow in coming to pasture is that, before being seeded, they have generally been exhausted of their fertility—in fact, brought to such a point that they can only carry inferior grasses. When this happens, the efforts of the seedsman to supply good seeds are of little avail. All he can do is to supply sound seed of such character as seems most likely to suit the soil in its exhausted condition. The young plants come up and search for food; if there is none suitable they cannot prosper, whereas weeds and inferior grasses thrive and choke them out. The seedsman can give a field the best possible start; the farmer holds the success of the crop in his hand. This must be borne in mind when making preparations for laying down. When seeds are sown in a cereal crop on land for some time subjected to an exhausting system of farming, there is little left for the young grasses to seize upon when the corn crop has taken out what it wants; it must be manured. In these times, when every penny is a consideration, men are loth to give up a crop which will give them a return, even though it is a small one per acre, and few will be induced to lay down the land from fallow. Unless a farmer can afford to manure his seeds during their early years, he follows a very doubtful method in laying down the poor land with seeds in a corn crop. It is better to lay down in a green crop, such as turnips or rape. In this way the rent and part of the expenses of working the land are saved, as the root crop can be fed off by sheep, which will manure land. When this is practised the roots should be got in as soon as the land is ready for them. The seed should be sown broadcast, not too thickly, and the grass seeds should be put in immediately. If this is done, the latter will be well established by the time the roots are fit to feed. The treading of the sheep does good to the grasses, as the tightening of the surface conduces to their rooting more firmly. The sheep should not be allowed to feed off the roots too closely, and if a piece of root is left in the ground it soon decays, affording nourishment to the young plants which will quickly fill in the gap the root made whilst growing.

The preparation of the land for seeding varies of course in accordance with the nature of the soil and the conditions under which it is to be sown down. The object is to get a clean seed-bed with a fine surface. It is sometimes argued that because twitch, or couch, dies out of pastures in course of time, it is immaterial whether it is destroyed previously to the land being sown, or whether it is allowed to grow among the young seeds. If it were only because the hay from it would, through the ripened seed, contaminate the remainder of the farm where the hay is fed, it would be sufficient cause for its extermination; but the fact that for some years it would be taking up a large quantity of nourishment, and storing the greater part of its thick roots underground, where it would become but slowly available, shows the mistake in leaving it there. It is far better to kill it on the land, and let it lie, for if this is done it rapidly becomes food for the young grasses. It is better to leave it than to burn it, if it can be killed without burning.

A fine surface is necessary, because grass seeds are so small that they do not possess the power of forcing their way through a depth of soil; and also because, if deeply buried, they will not germinate at all. Very few grass seeds will grow where buried more than half an inch; therefore the surface must be both smooth and solid, otherwise the seeds slip between the clods, and, for

## Permanent Pasture

practical purposes, are lost. Discretion has to be used as to whether the seed shall be harrowed or rolled in. Several considerations regulate this: the condition of the surface with regard to moisture and roughness, the tendency of the land to bind, and the immediate probabilities of the weather, all require to be considered. On land which binds when rain falls on it after being freshly moved, the greatest care is necessary, for if rolled under such conditions it is liable to set and harden, so that when a spell of dry weather follows, the seeds sown often germinate and malt, after which, of course, they are useless. The aim should be to get the land worked and cleaned previously, then to get it in a fairly consolidated condition, after which the seed may be sown, and lightly harrowed in by bush-harrows, or the lightest seed harrows. Sometimes the seeds are best merely rolled in, as in cases in which the surface lies in small clods which yield to a light roller, and afford sufficient covering for the seed in breaking down; however, except on very light land, rolling is dangerous, when there is risk of rain following immediately. Seeds are best sown by means of a broad cast machine, the ordinary harrow being well adapted for it. Except when a cup or force feed distributor is used, it is necessary to sow the coarse seeds at one operation, and the small ones by themselves in another operation. With the smaller seeds the clovers may be included.

The time for sowing seed depends on the circumstances under which the grass is to be grown. If in wheat, they may be sown in February, or as soon as the land will harrow. On a firm wheat bed they may be harrowed freely. In spring corn they may be sown at the time of seeding the corn, being sown just before the last light harrowing. If the land is weedy, the corn may be allowed to get up sufficiently to permit harrowing or hoeing, and the seeds may be then put in. Seeds sown early in spring stand the best chance of establishing themselves before the summer droughts. When sown among roots they must be sown when the weather is favourable; it will be rather late and precarious, but not prohibitively so. Autumn seeding should be done in September or October; if left later, the plants stand a chance of being injured by severe cold.

As to mixtures suitable for seeding, better cannot be devised than those offered by the larger and more reputable seed firms, who supply the several varieties separately, so that the buyer may be satisfied that he is purchasing what he orders. The only reservation to this is that we do not recommend expensive mixtures containing an exceptional number of varieties. In most cases these have been devised to meet the idiosyncrasies of those who have taken a special fancy to particular varieties to the exclusion of others. The aim should be to get a mixture which, while producing a good head of grass in the first years, will be at the same time working towards the establishment of the pasture. The return of these years must not be altogether lost sight of, even when striving to secure the permanency of the grass. Still, a few of the smaller and finer grasses may be included, so that if circumstances are favourable, or when the circumstances become favourable, they will have their chance of developing. Where the land is rich in lime, the quantity of clovers should be increased, as they are of the greatest value in a pasture, and soils which carry them freely are the quickest to become pastures, and are least expensive whilst so doing. In most cases pastures consist of a considerable quantity of clovers and grasses. Often the clovers seem to have almost entirely disappeared when the pastures have been down a few years, but as the conditions improve they generally come back again, and there is no better indication of a turf having been formed than that the white clover has re-established itself. Before the white clover comes back, the yellow trefoil is at work, doing what it can to add nourishment to the soil. The land is not rich enough to carry the white clover, but gradually the trefoil has to give way, and in course of time, if the pasture is well treated, it disappears, or makes but little growth.

During the first few months coarse weeds should be kept down. If in a corn crop this must be restricted to pulling out weeds, such as docks. If sown alone on a fallow, the weeds may be brushed with a scythe. At whatever time sown, it is a mistake to let any plants seed, as they are weakened by so doing. Young cattle are excellent feeders of young seeds, as they do not crop too closely. Sheep should be kept off until the pastures are at least three years old, and it is better to leave them longer under most circumstances. Nothing, however, does so much good to a pasture of four or five years or more as close folding with sheep fed on additional food to that grown on it. Grazing with cattle, by which the land becomes manured and the plants are induced to keep close to the ground, is the best method of treating young grasses during the first few years. Any feeding stuffs given during this time will be well repaid by the increase of grass and meat. If hay is taken off, manure in proportion should be returned; manure of a mixed nature is best. Farmyard manure is especially good, as the decaying straw helps to make that fine vegetable mould that is so necessary about the roots, and induces worms to work, a most important feature in the making of a pasture. Lime is highly beneficial, as it induces the clovers to grow. Nitrate of soda has a marked effect on the grasses, though this is at the expense of the clover. Bone meal is a good all-round manure, influencing both the grasses and clovers. Kainit is beneficial in the same way as clover. Superphosphate, added to other manures, does much good where land requires phosphates. Sulphate of ammonia is beneficial to the grasses, and is less injurious to clovers than is nitrate of soda.

# CHAPTER V.

## TEMPORARY LEYS.

It is a significant fact that those districts in which temporary leys of some years' duration prevail are among the most prosperous at the present time, while those where the shortest are followed fare the worst—generally in the eastern counties. This is almost tantamount to saying that those who went ahead most in matters agricultural are suffering the most. It is an unpleasant reflection that the greatest skill and energy should meet with such a reward, but undoubtedly those who—properly, whilst corn-growing was most remunerative—kept their land at high pressure, are those who are worst placed now. The man who took things more easily, and neither laid out so much money nor required so much skill and knowledge in his work, fares best. Climate undoubtedly had much to do with the matter. Where it was wet, corn did not ripen so well, and less was risked in corn-growing. If corn is not grown frequently, the land must lie in grass longer, for there is no profitable rotation to follow. In the dry climate and lighter soils of the eastern counties, long leys do not answer so well as they do in the moister climates of the west and north. Soil and climate have not altered, so these will have some influence on the length of time a pasture can be profitably left down now. In Ireland, in districts where it cannot be said that the knowledge of agricultural matters is great, the low price of corn has not told so severely as it has in England, where there is a much greater knowledge. Contrary to the general impression, Irish agriculture, on the whole, is prosperous, and this is due to the length of time to which pastures are left down. In parts of Ireland where the knowledge of farming is greater, and where more energy is devoted to the working of the farm, the long leys are also the main source of prosperity. Where grass seed is grown for exportation it is still greater. On these farms the outlay is exceedingly small, the labour bill and the expenditure on implements being phenomenally little. Carts, implements, and tools together are worth but a few shillings per acre; and more are not really needed, as the work is done satisfactorily with these. It may be taken generally that, where long leys prevail, agriculture is comparatively prosperous. The natural inference is that more should follow on these lines, and there is no better advice than that this should be done.

But the whole thing cannot be undertaken at once. If land is to be set to grow grass, there must be something to eat it. Where are these animals to come from? The grass is not wanted for hay, as the supply is sufficient already. What is to eat it? Already there is more grass than can be consumed by the stock in the country. If, say, two million acres were turned to grass temporarily, one of the first effects would be to raise the prices of store cattle, for the mere fact of turning land to grass will not cause cattle to come to eat it. Simultaneously, or before the land is laid down, stock must be raised to eat it. Farmers must bear this in mind before launching out too far. There are only 25,000,000 sheep in the country now—there were 30,000,000 in 1878, notwithstanding the effect of foot-and-mouth disease during several preceding years; cattle have increased, but not to the extent which the extra pasture and the large importation of feeding stuffs warrant. Our advice, therefore, is to change, but to change gradually. The alterations in systems of farming must chiefly affect those who, up to the present, have not adopted long temporary leys. The rotations which provide for one grass crop in four or five years are those which require the greatest alteration. The four-course system admits but one grass or seed crop in one year; the extension of the period that the seeds should hold the ground for two years at once makes it a five-course system, and this, under the name of the Berwick rotation, is common in Scotland. This rotation may be regarded as a sound one, as with four cultivations, two corn crops and three green crops are produced. It is one that is suitable for very general adoption.

Except, however, where great care is exercised in selecting seeds, leys do not hold well in the dryer districts on thin soils for more than one year, and provision should be made to meet them. In Scotland, where moisture is fairly constant, rye-grass is a more valuable crop than in the drought districts of the south of England. In Scotland it is regarded as a fairly good preparation for a crop; in dry districts it is not. On soils where the rye-grasses do not hold well, more responsibility is thrown on the clovers, and to ensure better results a larger proportion of cow-grass and alsike should be sown, as they make a good show in the second year. It is probable that on these hot soils it would be found better to go in for more frequent seedings rather than attempt long leys. Instead of the rotation mentioned, it is certain that more would be grown if it were changed as follows:—Wheat or barley-grass seeds (chiefly Italian and perennial rye-grass), barley or oats, clovers, roots. This necessitates two seedings, but the return more than counterbalances the extra cost; clover would come once in five years, and this would be too frequent to take red clover or cow-grass. So each five years it should be alternated with red clover, and either white clover or alsike. In this way the danger from clover sickness would be avoided. The same principle would be adopted under other existing rotations where experience shows that leys of more than one year cannot be relied upon: it merely means the insertion of another seed crop at any convenient period, and the working of the farm is upset only to a very small extent. Where the climate and soil permit longer leys they are, of course, more advantageous, the chief drawback being that the greater length of time they are down the fouler the land becomes, as small pieces of couch grow into larger patches, which, if very bad, require a great amount of work to destroy them. Long leys also encourage insect pests. Leys afford great harbourage to insects, such as wireworms, and several kinds of moths; the latter lay their eggs upon the foliage, and where they hatch the grub attacks the crop. These, however, do not seriously affect the value of leys.

In moister climates longer leys become more appropriate, and for some years show a profitable return. In some parts of Ireland we have seen good leys at five years, although the mixtures sown have included nothing more than rye-grass and red and white clover. Such leys, however, have been on good limestone soils, where the white clover has established itself thoroughly, and has appeared to have become permanently fixed. So well have some of the leys done, that at the end of five years it looked almost a pity to break them up, for, owing to the great clover growth, they had become better established than many we have seen in less favourable circumstances at ten or twelve years. Conditions, however, are not so favourable as a rule, and the difficulty of making the ley stand has to be met by seeding with grasses which are of a more perennial nature than those employed in one year's ley. Timothy and Cock's-foot are the most suitable, as they take a strong hold on the ground, and produce big crops. The seeding must also be thicker. In the case of a three years' ley, fox-tail and hard fescue may be added where the land is in good condition. Yellow trefoil helps to fill in the bottom in the first season, and answers well. In longer leys mixtures of strong growing grasses and clovers must be employed, but these will rarely do much good after the third year, unless they are treated liberally with manure. Where long leys are intended, the land must not be exhausted too much by cuttings, but they must be fed off by stock.

Lucerne and sainfoin allow of special opportunities for making long leys, as where soil is favourable they possess the property of holding the land for a number of years. A proportion of these should be sown in all pastures intended for long leys. They prove of greatest value, however, when employed separately. Lucerne does not do particularly well in mixtures intended for long leys, as it is liable to be crowded out by other grasses. Some little surface stirring also seems to be beneficial to it. It requires to be considered as a crop for arable land, for then it does best. For this reason it should be drilled in rows a foot or more apart, and be kept free from weeds by hoeing, especially early in the year, for when once well up it is able, through its robust growth, to smother the weeds.

One of the present features of the seed trade is the extension of the quantity of the lucerne seed grown. Even in counties where it has not hitherto been grown, except on a very small scale, it is being sown freely. A great point in its favour is the power it possesses of withstanding drought. This is due to its deep rooting, and its success is largely owing to the nature of the sub-soil in which, to a great extent, it feeds. The fen soils appear as unlikely as any for its prosperity, as it is little dependent on the organic matter in the soil, but if the peat overlies clay, or, better still, a rice loose sub-soil not far from the surface, it does well. Any open sub-soil containing a quantity of lime, whether in the form of chalk or limestone, is suitable, and the plant will establish itself. It becomes a matter for manuring subsequently, and this should not be spared, as the plant is able to give an enormous return, because it produces several crops in a favourable season. We know a field which has averaged three crops yearly for twenty years, and has received nothing but farmyard manure. On soils weak in lime or potash these should be applied. Hitherto it has been considered as essentially a crop of the chalk soils, but it has been shown to be well adapted for a much greater variety, and it would be highly advantageous for it to be more frequently grown. A bushel of the seed shelled from its peculiar pod weighs 64 lbs. Drilled in March or April at the rate of 10 lbs., or sown broadcast up to 16 lbs. per acre, it soon gets a strong hold, and will make good growth by autumn. It should be kept down from five to seven years, but if smothered out by weeds, or if the soil is unsuited to it, it will give out before.

Sainfoin is especially suitable for chalky soils, and does fairly well in most others when the soil is not too wet or heavy. The amount of lime present largely influences its durability. In

Hampshire and the adjoining Down districts it is reckoned that land which has not carried sainfoin for twenty years should remain profitable under sainfoin for seven years. Much of the land, however, has been cropped with it frequently, and the length of a ley is more often only four or five years. In the eastern counties it is rarely left more than two years, sometimes only one. As it does not come to its best before the second year, it seems injudicious to destroy it so young. Sainfoin grows well when sown broadcast, and differs from lucerne in that it does not suffer from the presence of other plants near it, and does not require hoeing; it can therefore be sown in a corn crop, as it usually is. It is, in fact, most often sown with grass seeds, especially rye-grass, so that in the first season, when the sainfoin will not give a full cut, a good sward is obtained. As the sainfoin gets more firmly established, the grasses gradually weaken. It is not an uncommon practice to mix a little trefoil with the seed to help to make a full plant in the first year. Although there is not much feeding value in trefoil it does good by sheltering the soil from the sun. It is best to mow sainfoin the first season, after which grazing is more advantageous. However, it makes such excellent hay for sheep that in sheep districts it is sure to be mown fairly frequently. Manuring and top-dressing aid very much in keeping it in a growing and healthy condition, and in this way its profitable duration may be much extended. It is, of course, necessary to sow a crop like this, which is to be down for a number of years, on clean soil. It is usual to sow four bushels of unmilled seed (in the pod) or 20 lbs. of milled seed to the acre.

Seeds, when composed entirely of clover, are usually left down only one year, having been sown in a corn crop in the spring of the year preceding. One important reason for not leaving clovers down longer is that it induces the land to clover-sickness, and the clover plant is more liable to fail on the next occasion when it is sown. Broad clover is most affected by clover-sickness, and white clover often grows well under conditions which, from the presence of the eelworm, would be fatal to the red. Broad or red clover gives a splendid return, whether in the form of hay or as green fodder. Its peculiar adaptability to grow among grass seeds is a point highly in its favour for mixing with seeds for temporary leys. As a rule, from 12 to 16 lbs. are sown per acre, when no other seeds are sown with it. The amount of seed depends very much on the quality used. We had a good illustration of this in 1895. The seed bought in the case referred to weighed over 70 lbs. per bushel, and only 8 lbs. per acre were drilled; the plants were as thick and strong as could be desired, although there were over 40 acres sown in three fields possessing very different types of soil.

White clover, though unsuited for hay, is very valuable sown alone or in mixtures; it is rarely of much value when sown alone after the first year,

Those who produce fat lambs find it unequalled for laying on meat. It is, however, rather dangerous at times, as it has a tendency to "blow" the animals. To avoid this danger the sheep should not be turned into it when they are in a hungry condition, otherwise they eat ravenously, and it ferments instead of digesting. Clovers should not be fed when they are stale. Clovers become stale when fed by sheep, the manuring appearing to make them rank and unhealthy; if, however, a crop is mown off, the injurious tendency is avoided, therefore as far as possible grazing should be alternated with mowing.

# CHAPTER VI.

## LAYING DOWN LAND TO TEMPORARY PASTURE.

THE seeding of temporary leys is spring work. If there is any circumstance which makes it better to lay down permanent pasture without a corn crop, it does not apply to short leys. Short leys are crops of the immediate future. Permanent leys relate to the more indefinite future. As the profit is to be looked for in the first years of the ley, it is important to get the young plant thoroughly established in the year it is sown, so that in the next year it may give a full return. Seeds sown in the autumn rarely do this, and the earlier the seeds are established in the spring the better, as they come on earlier and stronger the next season. The corn crop must not be entirely sacrificed to the seeds. Wheat suffers little at harvest when the seeds are well grown, but a big growth of seeds in barley proves vexatious, as long after the barley has matured and is fit for the stack, the green stuff at the butts remains green, and often holds a considerable amount of water. On very weedy land, particularly on that much infested by annual weeds, it is often desirable to hoe the barley before the seeds are sown. In some districts the seeds are sown immediately before hoeing, and are hoed in during the operation of destroying the weeds, and this is a good plan under the special circumstances. In a wet spring there is little trouble in getting the seeds to grow, but it is a far more difficult matter to get a plant in a dry spring. Seeds sown broadcast in such seasons lie dormant a long time, or perhaps germination is set up by the little moisture turned up by the harrows, but for want of continued moisture the young shoots die off, and the seed is worthless. The best method for securing plants in persistently dry seasons is to horse-hoe between the corn-rows, and immediately—not in a few hours, but at once—follow this with the seed drill set so that the seed falls in the moist track made by the hoe, and then roll it in. The seed thus lies in the moisture, and as the land is rolled, the moisture is

## Laying down Land

prevented from escaping freely, but keeps consistent through the supply brought up by the capillarity of the soil. The little track lies in a shallow furrow, so that in event of the light showers falling, the wet is conducted to it. Where possible, however, the seed is best sown broadcast, as the plants are then better distributed about the ground, and it is less expensive.

The preparations for seeding a temporary ley are necessarily very simple, and as a rule amount to little more than procuring a fine surface; in fact, it is generally sufficient to sow the seeds on the surface, merely harrowing them in. When sown in winter-wheat the seed can rarely be buried too deeply by ordinary seed harrows, but in spring-sown corn great care must be taken. If the surface lies in large, loose clods, it is very easy for the seed to fall to a depth which will prevent it germinating. The surface must be brought down to a fine condition, and it may then be necessary to tighten it with a roller. The corn crop must not be sacrificed by the land being made to " cap " through injudicious harrowing, or rolling when it is in a wet condition. The harrowing or rolling, or, for that matter, the abstinence from both, if circumstances demand it, are subjects for determination in the field. The heavy soils which are among those where it is most important to stay the plough, are very liable to "cap," and the aim of the farmer must be to lightly cover the seed with soil, but not to do it in such a way as to render the land liable to be injured by drought subsequently.

There is no absolute rule as to harrowing or rolling, and it must always be a matter of discretion settled in the field. It is, however, important to urge carefulness, for often, even when there are no seeds sown, a well-worked and good corn seed-bed is ruined at the time of sowing the corn, by want of judgment in ordering the last operations. When the weather is fair anyone can sail a boat; it is the catchy weather that proves the sailor's skill; so it is in farming; there are plenty of fair-weather farmers, but the foul-weather farmers are not so common. In genial weather nothing is more simple than the process of sowing grass seeds.

Except in market-garden districts there are few men who can sow small seeds with any degree of evenness, but seed distributors, which sow with all needful accuracy, are not difficult to get. The ordinary seed-barrow answers most purposes, although where there is great variation in the size of the seed it is necessary to sow it in more than one operation, otherwise the small seeds are run out as soon as the box is filled, and the large ones left to be sown subsequently. This, of course, prevents anything like even distribution, and must be guarded against by going over the ground twice, or more, if necessary, according to the varying size of the seeds. When this is done it is advisable to cross the drafts, so that, if there has been any irregularity in the steering of the barrow, the gaps will be filled in. Windy days should not be chosen to sow small light seeds. The machine for which Messrs. Cotton recently obtained the Royal Agricultural Society's silver medal, combining a roller and a seeding machine, is a useful addition to the machinery of the farm.

As a rule, mixtures for temporary leys need not be very complex. The great aim should be to grow as many leguminous plants as the land will carry, without making it clover-sick, and therefore unable to produce clovers in the next rotation. Long leys of clover tend to make the land clover-sick, because the lime and potash in an available form as food for clovers become exhausted, and on many soils it takes a long time for them to accumulate in sufficient quantity to support another crop. When the supply is short the young clover plant loses vigour, and is attacked by the stem eel-worm, which soon destroys it. The advantage of growing clovers and other leguminous plants is that they possess the power of taking from the atmosphere nitrogen, which grass is unable to assimilate therefrom. The nitrogen thus acquired is as valuable as that for which a high price is paid when purchasing nitrate of soda, sulphate of ammonia, and other nitrogenous manures. The plant is enriched by it, and some portion goes into the hay, while the other is stored in the roots, which, when they decay, give it up to the soil. The value of a good clover stump or root is recognized everywhere on account of its manurial effects; consequently, it is easy to understand how important it is to grow clovers and to do all that is reasonable to encourage them. The varieties of clover which are to be sown should be regulated to some extent by the purpose to which the leys are to be put. If grazing is the chief object in view, more clover should be sown, as that affords excellent sheep pasturage. Where hay is required, a greater quantity of broad clover and cow-grass are wanted. These should always be in good quantity, except when there is reason to believe that the land is specially liable to clover-sickness. When this is the case, white clover and alsike should be sown more freely. Of the other important leguminous plants, lucerne and sainfoin, an account of the circumstances under which they thrive, and may be used profitably, has already been given. Although the inferior clovers and leguminous plants, such as trefoil, bird's-foot trefoil, and yellow suckling, do not give a good return, there are circumstances in which they may be profitably sown in small quantities, and, as a rule, a sprinkling of each in mixtures for leys on light, poor land, where the better clovers do not grow freely, is not out of place. The cost of the seed is small, and they help to make a sole to the turf, and do not injure the hay. Where clover is grown in considerable quantity, it is important to see that it is free from dodder, as that parasitic pest spreads with great rapidity, destroying all that comes in its way, and, if left to seed, renders the soil unsafe to carry clover for some years, as the seeds lie dormant for a long time. Careful sifting is the only safe way of insuring against it. If it appears, the patches should be carefully and thoroughly destroyed by burning.

The most simple seeding for short leys

## Laying down Land

is a mixture of rye-grass and clover. A bushel of rye-grass and 8 lbs. of red clover is a common seeding where clovers thrive better than rye-grass. Where rye-grass thrives better than clovers, two bushels of rye-grass and from 4 to 6 lbs. of red and white clover is found a good mixture. This is a full seeding of its kind. Rather less of either may be sown; in fact, it is found that in the place of a 50-lbs. mixture 40 lbs. is usually enough. Where a more general mixture is sown, including some of the smaller seeded strong-growing plants, like timothy, the quantity may be reduced very materially, and from 30 to 35 lbs. of seeds are sufficient. It is, of course, important to use grasses of high germinating powers and of good stock. By dint of careful selection our great seed firms have done much to improve the quality and yielding powers of the important grasses, and the improvement in these grasses is, perhaps, more advantageously felt when they are used for temporary leys than when used for permanent pastures. This is only natural, as the grasses undergo little change in the short time they are down. If they are not of good type, the soil has a poor chance of influencing them. Grasses grown in particular climates, or on particular soils, have more or less distinctive features, though, perhaps, this is not so noticeable as in the case of clovers. American red clover seed is not nearly so large as well-grown English, nor will it produce anything like the same growth. It is, in fact, a dwarf variety of English clover. On

## Laying down Land

occasions when the quantity of home-grown seeds has run out, we have bought small lots of American to finish the field, and then the difference has been most marked, for it has never at any cutting given so great a yield. Low-priced clover seed is rarely cheap, because it is priced low for one of the following reasons:—Inferior stock, presence of weeds, weakness of germinating power. The best means of guarding against a weak stock, particularly in the case of red clover, is to buy bold, well-coloured seed. The presence of the seeds of dock, plantain, and other plants materially affects the value of a sample of red clover; small seeds of dock and plantain also are found in white clover and alsike, and in addition to these are those of sorrel, forget-me-not, and others, which, from their size and weight, are very difficult to take from the sample. The most frequent weed-seed found in white clover, however, is that of the wild geranium. We have seen samples containing fifty per cent of this adulterant. It is somewhat difficult to detect when only casually looked for, as it is about the same size, colour, and shape; more closely observed it is seen to be of rather darker colour, approaching chestnut, and to be more rounded and plumper instead of heart-shaped. Under a magnifying glass it is easy to detect. So careless, however, are some buyers, that I know of markets where large quantities are sold where not one buyer in twenty could tell what it is, or has even noticed its presence, although in those same markets scarcely a sample is sold with less than ten per cent. present, and far larger quantities are common.

Red clover should be bold and well tinged with purple; brown seeds are dead; yellow are often of weak germinating power. White clover should be a pale golden yellow; when brown and withered they are useless. Alsike should be a dark green; when light green the germination is weak; brown are dead.

When buying grass seeds from firms of good repute there is little fear on the point of adulteration. Low-priced articles have a fascination for many people; the consequence is they buy in the lowest and dearest market, and sow what they have no wish to reap. It is impossible in a short space to speak of the adulteration of all grasses, and so describe them, especially without the aid of illustrations, in a way that would make them recognizable. Our best advice is for those about to buy grasses to obtain a sample of each one, and under the magnifying glass (one at a shilling is quite powerful enough) learn to know what its features are. If there are two different seeds, it is obvious that one must be a stranger and has no right there. The trouble of learning to distinguish the seeds of the ordinary grasses sown is so very little that there is no excuse for a man not taking so simple a precaution against adulteration. If a man has not this knowledge, he should buy on guarantee and let someone else analyze for him. It is so very simple, however, that any one may soon become expert in detecting the presence

## Laying down Land

of foreign seeds or other matter. Seen under magnifying power, the several seeds are as easy to distinguish as oats from barley. The germination is a simple matter, but there is some little art in taking a fair sample; this should be taken from the main heap, not from the sides where the lighter seeds naturally fall, but by inserting the hand well into the heap.

Farmers rarely possess machinery suitable for cleaning grass seeds as thoroughly as they should be cleaned. The modern winnowing-machine with wire-wove sieves is not equal to the old-fashioned Cooch winnower with perforated sieves. Small grass and clover seeds require a wind separation combined with sifting power. When first going over a famous seed-store we were much struck to see so many of the Cooch winnowers at work among the special machinery. For ordinary purposes machines of this type, fitted with sieves of suitable size, will clean clover and most of the ordinary grasses.

# CHAPTER VII.

### MANAGEMENT OF TEMPORARY PASTURES.

PERMANENT pastures depend for their success in no small degree on the treatment to which they are subjected during the time they are acquiring their permanent characteristics. The aim in this case is to establish a plant which will stand for an indefinite period. Temporary pastures, of course, are of shorter duration, and there is, naturally, less chance of treating them improperly. At the same time there are right and wrong methods of treatment, which influence their value. When grasses are sown down in a corn crop there is little to be done until autumn; docks and thistles may be drawn or cut up, but beyond this they must be left until the corn crop is harvested. The hoe or spud should not be used for cutting up weeds, as the young seeds are destroyed in the operation. A docking-iron for the docks, if they will not draw by hand, and a weed-hook for thistles, are all that are permissible. Where seeded without any other crop an opportunity is afforded to keep in check, by means of the scythe, other weeds which would prove injurious; however, it is the annual weeds which make most show, and so far as the temporary leys are concerned, they do not often do serious injury; when, however, they are allowed to seed, they prove troublesome in succeeding corn crops, and this should be prevented. Cutting with a scythe, or a slight brush with a mowing machine, set high so as to miss most of the grass, is usually sufficient. Charlock is the worst weed in most districts, and it is very important that it be not allowed to seed. In early-sown seeds it comes to maturity, but in autumn-sown grass it rarely produces seed, and is killed down by winter. Seeds afford a good opportunity for keeping this pest in check, and it should not be lost, even if the charlock has to be pulled.

Young seeds, according to the season at which they are sown and the amount of growth they make during the summer months, may, or may not, be fit to graze in the autumn. Except when the land is heavy and wet, good, rather than harm, is done by grazing. The earth is trodden firmly up to the roots, causing the plants to become better established and less likely to be injured by frost. Many people object to autumn feeding, but so long as the animals do not tread the land so to leave saucer-like depressions, which hold the water during winter, the treading does good. It is advisable not to stock young grasses too hard, but light stocking does good rather than harm. Treading by sheep does far more good than is effected by rolling, as the roller works more unevenly, and a proportion of the plants are not affected; whereas sheep pinch in the earth about the roots of all plants.

Where there is much clover in the ley it is necessary to be careful, when the plant is fresh and growing, that the sheep feeding it do not become hoven or blown. Injury from this cause is more prevalent in spring than in autumn, but occasionally it occurs in the latter season. If sheep become blown, which is indicated by their distended sides, particularly the left side, they should be at once removed; and it is advisable to keep them moving for some little time, so that the gases which have generated may work off. If an animal has become very bad, and there is fear of its bursting, its stomach should be punctured by a trocar, but as this is not often available, a long knife may be used. Frothing at the mouth is a preliminary symptom of hoven. Where the leys consist mainly of grasses there is little to fear from hoven.

Little can be done in the way of

keeping the land clean after the first year beyond destroying docks and thistles, unless patches of couch are dug out in the autumn. A few years ago the autumn forking of the leys to take out the couch patches and docks was a common practice on almost all well-managed farms. Where land is carefully worked and kept clean by skilful tillage and hoeing, the digging out of small patches of couch which may have eluded other implements, is a profitable operation, as it renders unnecessary extra cleaning after the ley is broken up. Where the forking out can be done for a shilling or two an acre, it is well worth doing, but of course where a field is smothered by innumerable patches, the expense of digging is so great that it is better to leave the cleaning to be done

## Management of Pastures

during the fallowing operations connected with the root crop. It is, of course, useless in those instances where quantities of couch seed is sown among the seeds purchased. As before stated, carelessly-purchased seeds contain more impurities, such as seeds of couch, which may often pass notice because the buyer does not know one seed from another. In the first year the young patches of couch are not bigger than can be dug out with a fork at one dig; but in the following year, if left untouched, they are two or three feet in diameter, and increase proportionately in subsequent years until the field becomes so foul that, if for no other reason, it is necessary to break it up. This should impress buyers with the necessity for care in purchasing. It is strange that with couch going to seed in every hedge-row and ditch side, a vast number of people who have farmed for half a lifetime cannot recognize it. It is scarcely to be wondered at that they buy inferior seeds, and in doing so make foul land. It is sad to think that many farmers who possess great skill in managing and cleaning land, undo the work of years by sowing grass seeds containing so much couch-seed, that by the time the ley-land is broken up, it is as foul again as ever.

Temporary pastures possess a remarkable property, namely, that both the grasses and clovers of which they are composed are able to add materially to the fertility of the land. As a rule, grass seeds are looked upon as being somewhat exhausting to the land, unless they are fed very frequently. They can, however, be made to add greatly to its permanent fertility. Grasses are particularly partial to nitrogenous manures, especially to nitrate of soda. If nitrate of soda is applied, practically the whole of it is utilized by the crop, as it is not easily washed out of the land even by winter rains. The nitrate thus utilized becomes organic nitrogen, and when the crop is fed the farm is enriched by it. Clovers, as has long been recognized, add to the fertility of the farm and to the land on which they grow. The crop taken off the land enriches some other portion of the farm; and the root or stump contains so much nitrogen that the land is richer after the crop than before it was grown. This was recognized, but it was not known why it produced this result until within recent years. Now, however, it is known that nitrogen is taken from the atmosphere, and as it is proved that the amount of nitrogen acquired is largely dependent on the amount of potash and lime available, the value of applying these manures is understood.

Perhaps one of the most remarkable features in the changes which have come over farming within the past few years is the altered views which farmers, as a rule, hold as to the value of artificial manures. It was considered a sign of astuteness, even among otherwise smart farmers, to decry their use, and the man who had the best collection of terms, such as jumping powders, stimulants, &c., was considered the smartest. By understanding the properties, uses, and methods of applying them, their real value has been discovered, and now comparatively few farmers fail to recognize their value as *bonâ fide* aids to fertility. As aids to grass and clover-growing they have proved highly valuable; for, though they lack the mechanical properties of farmyard manure, they supply what worn-out, or less used-up, soils require to make them grow remunerative crops. No single manure is so beneficial to pastures as farmyard manure, and there is no part of the farm where we like to see it applied better than to the pastures; but it is expensive to make when the best stall-fed beasts fetch only 4s. per stone; and a good coating of it runs into a large sum per acre. A dressing of one hundred-weight of nitrate of soda, three hundred-weights of superphosphate of lime, and three hundred-weights of kainit, which can be applied for 16s. an acre, is a good full dressing to apply to a temporary pasture in the second year of its ley, when the first fertility set free by the tillage has been, to a great extent, exhausted; and it is at any time a liberal dressing for old pasture. Three loads of farmyard manure cost as much, and will not give nearly so good a return. As already stated, the produce raised by the artificial manure when consumed takes the form of organic manure, and, if fed on the farm, adds to its lasting fertility. Unless the crop is made into hay and sent off the farm, instead of the land becoming exhausted, the fertility is increased by the use of artificial manures. The constant use of nitrate of soda with no other help tends to exhaust the land of the constituents supplied by mineral manures, and, if persisted in for a long period, fails to realize as good a return as it should; it is most marked if the grass is mown and taken away. It acts less injuriously if the grass is constantly fed; in fact, if the land is rich in the mineral constituents, it may be used with great advantage for a practically unlimited time, provided the land is grazed. In temporary pastures kept down for two or three years only, exhaustion is not so noticeable, especially if a root crop is grown during the rotation, and it is fed on the land where it grew.

On short leys quickly-acting manures give the best results; on permanent pastures slower acting manures, such as bones, farmyard manure, and any decaying vegetable matter, have a good effect, but pasture-making without grazing is not a satisfactory process. If the crop is taken off every time it grows, a large return in the way of manure must be made. The beneficial effects of grazing and treading are also most marked, and tend to produce a close soil or sod which cannot be got when land is always under the scythe. The close sod, and general mixing of herbage, is not so essential in temporary leys, and greater latitude in the use of the scythe is permissible, provided the fertility exhausted in taking away the crop is made good by returning the equivalent in the form of manure.

Where clovers preponderate in a mixture, mineral manures should be used to increase their growth, and so as to increase the growth of the grasses with as little hindrance to the clovers as possible, it is better to substitute sulphate of ammonia for nitrate of soda, it being found that clovers thrive on sulphate of ammonia. In fact, almost all sulphates appear to act beneficially on clover, and sulphate of lime is sometimes found to give exceptionally good results. On moory and sour land basic-cinder proves of great value, and on heavy land generally does well. On light gravel soils it is uncertain, and in some experiments we carried out for several years on light gravel land, dressing varying from 500 to 2000 lbs. per acre made practically no difference to the yield. Where mixed with other manures it did better, but never more than moderately. Malt culms, soot, almost any manure, in fact, do good to grasses.

Mineral manures should be applied in autumn or winter; the beneficial effect of these manures is often lost for nearly a year, through their being sown late in the spring. They require to be washed into the soil early, otherwise they begin to work too late to do good in the year in which they are sown. If sown in March, and the weather remains dry through April and May, they do not become incorporated with soil sufficiently early.

Farmyard manure should be applied at different times according to circumstances. As a rule, long dung should be applied in autumn and early winter, and short dung in the spring; however, it is less important on grass land than on arable, as the roots prevent much loss which would occur were it applied

## Management of Pastures

where no crop was growing. It may be taken as a broad principle that long dung protects the plant through winter, sets the worms working, wastes little from soluble portions being washed into the drains, and becomes fit to be taken up by the crop early in spring. Short dung may lose a portion of its soluble matter if applied in autumn, but is quickly available if applied at the end of winter; it works into the soil readily. As stated before, however, the loss of manurial constituents is not serious, and any convenient season may be availed of. In some districts it is the practice to dung immediately after the first crop of hay is off; on burning soils this is done with advantage, as the manure acts as a mulching, and the prejudicial effects of drought are averted. Leys and pastures are so benefited by manuring that it is commonly said that any kind of manure does good, no matter when applied. This is more correct than many sayings.

# CHAPTER VIII.

### UTILIZATION OF THE CROP.

PASTURES or leys afford food all the year round, for though there are times when little can be grazed, hay and ensilage may be made to supply the animals during such periods. As rotations are increased in length by the addition of longer leys, the root crop becomes curtailed, and this alone makes an alteration in the system of farming. Stock, especially sheep, are diverted from the turnip fold to the pastures, and where it has been the custom to rely on roots for food for sheep in autumn they have to be kept longer on grass. There is nothing to object to in this, as it is cheaper to feed off pastures than to cut turnips. One naturally looks to sheep as the best means of feeding short leys, because fields which have been turned from arable to grass are rarely well enough fenced to hold bullocks, and sheep are better distributers of manure than cattle. On permanent pastures the heavy droppings of cattle affect the whole field in course of time, but on short leys they are patchy, and consequently the manuring is not so effective. At the same time temporary leys produce a large amount of excellent food, and are well adapted to carry young stock.

It is necessary, where leys are required to be fed while green, that they should not be allowed to become stale or soured by too constant manuring. When sheep feed off leys too frequently

## Utilization of the Crop

the growth is strong and apparently healthy, but the animals are liable to scour, while lambs and young sheep are apt to "go wrong." Every sheep-keeper knows what this means, and how difficult it is to get them round unless there is a plentiful supply of fresh food to turn them on, so too much care cannot be exercised. For some years, whilst conducting the experiments at Woburn for the Royal Agricultural Society, I had to weigh the sheep frequently, and it was a significant fact that they always did far better the first time over than in subsequent feedings, though, to all appearances, the food was as good at one time as at another. In the case of the white clover leys the sheep always did as well without any extra food in the first feeding as they did with it. The clover apparently supplied all that they required in order to lay on as much flesh as they were able. In the second feeding, however, there was always a wide gap between those which received cake and those which received nothing but clover. There is no reason to suppose that the clover possessed less feeding matter, but it was not so palatable or digestible, consequently the cake was required to correct the deficiency. As this occurred every year for several seasons, it could hardly have been accident. It may safely be taken that where clovers predominate in a ley there is great risk of souring, but there is less danger of it if the quantity of grass increases. On old pastures, probably owing to the greater amount of grass and the effect of the large accumulation of humus, the danger of injury from souring is very greatly lessened.

Where sheep-farming is largely carried out it is particularly necessary to avoid souring. This is always effectively done where mowing is made to intervene between the grazings. If it is not desired to make hay, there are two alternatives; the crop may be cut green, and so used for soiling cattle and horses in the yards, or it may be made into ensilage. In soiling, the cost of mowing and carting to the animals have to be set against the increased amount of food obtained by preventing loss by treading into the ground. This is very considerable in wet weather, and through the better thriving of the animals (particularly in very hot weather, when, through the discomfort of heat and the annoyance of flies, they rest badly) it may be taken that the cost of getting the stuff to the animals is met by the increased amount of meat laid on. Beyond this, valuable manure is made, and may be used with full advantage. When grazing in hot weather cattle make bad distributers of dung, as they collect under trees and in other sheltered spots where their dung does little good.

Ensilage is particularly valuable when the root crop is lessened on account of diminished acreage. We do not recommend expensive systems of silage, as the drawn-up heap is effective and calls for no outlay beyond labour. As food for ewes we know nothing better, and nothing which ensures a better flow of milk. Sheep take to it readily, particularly to that which is most heavily compressed and most acid. The lambs do well on the milk which is produced by their mothers when fed on ensilage. In winter, when roots are cold, especially when they are frozen and indigestible and often difficult to get, ensilage is especially valuable, as it is warmer. Cold roots lower the temperature of the animals eating them, and a large proportion of the food contained in them has to be devoted to sustaining the animal heat. Ensilage cut fresh from the heap is comparatively warm. With hay, ensilage, and the pastures themselves, sheep can be kept at small expense, and there is no need to go to the root heap.

Hay-making should be commenced when the grasses are still young. The quality of the hay is greatly improved, and, though there is not the bulk of hay, it is well counterbalanced by the greater growth of aftermath. Hay made from leys requires more careful handling than that from permanent pastures, as, owing to the larger quantity of clovers in it, the leaf is likely to be lost if knocked about. The tedding practised in grass hay-making is not permissible; it must be turned lightly by a rake or fork, without shaking or tossing. Instead of putting into windrows and running up into heaps for pitchings, it requires to be cocked in the same manner as corn.

Cattle are better adapted for grazing longer leys than shorter ones, because, if the fields are not already fenced, it is worth while to put down a temporary fence. The mixing of cattle and sheep when grazing is also advantageous. Cattle-grazing does not render the crop

## Utilization of the Crop

sour to sheep. Sheep after sheep without an intervening mowing is bad, but sheep graze safely after cattle. The alternation is therefore beneficial. Where cattle are grazed and corn or cake is given them, the corn troughs should be moved frequently so as to attract the animals to different parts of the field in order that the manuring may be evenly effected. Sheep troughs should also be moved daily.

It is very un-English to graze pigs on clover, but it is one of the cheapest ways of keeping them. Pigs like grass, but have a special preference for clover. They will eat it either when cut and soiled to them, or they are perfectly happy when they do their own cutting. With shade and water they thrive well, and there is no better method of keeping in-pig sows. The danger of slipping their young prematurely, which is experienced when sows are fed almost entirely on turnips, does not exist; and the exercise they get in moving, even in a comparatively small fold, keeps them healthy; in fact, there is no better way of insuring safe farrowing. Americans, who are skilled pig keepers, rely very much upon the clover patch for rearing and fattening their pigs. A few corn cobs and a supply of water are all they get in addition. No pork is made on cheaper lines.

Corn-growing England has not gone in for grass seed-growing to the extent it might. It has not accorded with the rotations in vogue, and the terms under which land has been rented precluded it. The greater freedom of cropping now allowed has opened a wider field, which those favourably placed should not be slow to utilize. The climate in many parts of England is not suitable for the production of all kinds of grass seeds, but most varieties can be grown profitably in one or another district. The arable land of England, so long subjected to the influence of the hoe and good cultivation, is in a better condition to carry clean seeds than is much of that producing grass seeds. Rye-grass growing is carried out in Ireland on land which has never known a hoe, and the crops are often infested with alien plants. Yorkshire fog, couch, onion couch, and brome grasses form no small portion of the grass crop which is to produce seed in the districts in Ireland where rye-grass seed-growing is an important and prosperous business; yet the Irish seed is put on the market cleaner than is that grown in France. On clean soils, in the fairly moist districts of England, the finest and cleanest rye-grass seed might be grown. The harvesting is very simple. The crop is cut, tied into sheaves, and left in the stock until fit to thresh. It may be threshed in the field, or be stacked and threshed at leisure. The seed falls out readily under the flail, and often little more is done beyond knocking the sheaf against a bar. The seed is hit with a stick held in one hand, while the sheaf is held in the other. The feeding matter of the hay left behind is not quite equal to what it is when the grass is cut young; but, if chaffed, it is a valuable fodder for horses, cattle, and sheep. When in Ulster, a farmer showed me a field, then in its second year, which looked like growing four or five cwt. of seed per acre, and twenty-five to thirty cwt. of hay. In the previous year he grew on this same land eight cwt. of seed, which he sold for 17*s.* per cwt., and thirty-five cwt. of hay, which he sold locally at 4*s.* per cwt., making in all 13*l.* 16*s.* per acre. This was not bad as things go nowadays. Those farmers who possess clean land, and a climate suitable for growing rye-grass seed, might do well by turning their attention to rye-grass seed-growing. It is an advantage that, when growing the seed, clover need not be entirely precluded from the mixture. The hay is improved by it, and if sown in moderate quantity does not materially affect the yield of rye-grass. Cocksfoot, timothy, and other similar grasses may also be grown with good success. With the prospect of more land going to temporary pasture, the demand for seed is likely to increase rather than decrease. Even for home growth on the farm a small patch of carefully-selected seed is well worth growing. Clean seed can thus be insured, for by pulling out weeds and grasses other than those desired, there can be nothing to render it unclean. It is, of course, important to sow good seed in the first instance, and in small patches. For growing stocks artificial manures are preferable to farmyard manure, as the latter often contains hay seeds, which, on growing, at once make the stock untrue.

Clover-growing for seed purposes is rightly considered in conjunction with the disposal of the crop. In speaking of clover seed it is usual to allude to it as maiden, or second-cut seed. The maiden is that which is produced from the spring growth; the crop being allowed to grow and ripen before being cut or fed off. This ripens in summer. Where a crop of hay or a grazing is taken and the second crop allowed to go to seed, it is called second-cut seed. This ripens in autumn, and as the weather is not reliable at that season it is often difficult to harvest. It frequently occurs that there is a very large acreage ploughed in as manure after lying wet so long as to be worthless for other purposes. As a rule, maiden seed is the best coloured and the finest, but is also most liable to contain seeds of weeds, as weeds such as plantain and dock ripen under ordinary conditions at the same time as clover. In the second cut this is to a great extent avoided. Clover requires a sunny climate, as without it the growth of foliage is made at the expense of flowering. Crops of moderate size are better suited to produce a good yield of seed than are very heavy ones, because they flower more evenly, and the crop is less liable to be laid or storm-broken. Clover seed never ripens simultaneously throughout the crop, but usually at three periods. The top seed is generally light, the middle seed often is the best, and the last to ripen is too late to wait for. A considerable amount of discretion is required to decide when the crop shall be cut, as there is no definite rule as to which ripening is the best. The aim is naturally to catch all three ripenings, and this is most easy on a moderate crop in sunny weather, as they then come nearly together. Clover requires very careful handling, as when dry the seeds fall out with the least blow. White clover is most difficult to get, as the best crops are grown on short stems, and unless the land is level it is sometimes impossible to cut off all the heads; and when the heads are cut it is difficult to gather them together. It is often necessary to collect them with a daisy-rake early in the morning whilst the dew is on the ground. To attempt it when the seed is dry would be useless, as it would all thresh out. When cut, the sward of any kind of clover should be made into small " horse-head " cocks, and these should be turned occasionally, increasing them as the material dries by putting one to another. Large cocks should not be made at any time, for the pressure of sticking a fork into them would knock out a large quantity of seed. They should not be bigger than a long-tined fork will gather without pressure. The loads should be built so that no portion of the material is outside the body of the cart or waggon, as there would be considerable loss, particularly in the case of white clover. The crop must be absolutely dry at the time of stacking, so that heat is not generated, as heated seed is spoiled in colour, and, if badly heated, germination is destroyed. Fine weather should be chosen to thresh the seed, and it is generally advisable to wait until frost comes. The cob, or seed heads, which come down an ordinary threshing-machine where the chaff of corn falls, is the part to secure. If a clover-rubbing machine is not working simultaneously with the threshing, the cob must be stored in a dry place, care being taken that it is not trodden upon or consolidated more than is absolutely necessary. A considerable amount of winnowing is required to clean the seed, though, from its lightness, it is necessary to winnow lightly. By saving one's own clover seed the risk of getting inferior foreign seed is avoided. As a rule, the districts best fitted for grass seed-growing are too moist for clover seed-growing, and *vice versâ*. This is, of course, not a hard and fast rule, and the two sometimes may be grown alongside, but wet districts cannot be relied upon for clover seed-growing, and dry districts are not favourable for the fullest crops of grass seed.

# CHAPTER IX.

## GENERAL PRINCIPLES ASSOCIATED WITH PERMANENT PASTURE-MAKING: INFERIOR GRASSES AND WEEDS.

It is more easy to realize the conditions under which permanent pastures thrive when the circumstances under which they were formed are borne in mind. No such thing as a permanent pasture existed at one period of the earth's history, for there was no vegetation of any kind; yet by the process of evolution, from low forms of plant life they have gradually come into existence without the aid of man. At the present

## Permanent Pasture-making

time we have in England exemplifications of pastures which have been formed with little outlay of labour on the part of man. Take the thin chalk downs which are covered with a permanent pasture, poor, it is true, still permanent. The same on heaths. Many of our richest pastures are undoubtedly self-made, except that the land was probably cleared of its forests. We see around us to-day pastures in course of development. Land which was cultivated a quarter of a century ago fell out of cultivation and was allowed to take its own course. Couch grass and other weeds held the ground, but where the land had a reserve of fertility these are gradually, in most cases slowly, giving way to more nutritive grasses and other herbage, accumulating plant food year by year, and thus forming the early stages of permanent pasture. The rapidity with which these become capable of carrying sufficient stock to show an appreciable return depends on the nature of the soil with regard to its texture and the amount of food contained in it, its freedom from stagnant water, and the assistance rendered by manuring, or the feeding of extra food upon the ground.

A good example of the change from barrenness to a higher state of fertility is shown in the case of a tiled roof. New tiles present a perfectly clean surface free from vegetation, yet in course of many years we find them grass-grown. In the first instance some minute plant of low order, it may be of a fungus type, begins to grow, and this goes on almost imperceptibly for years, but gradually it thickens. Why? Because generations of the tiny growth have died down and left their remains to supply food for successive generations. In course of time the roof becomes covered with a deep covering of moss, and after this grasses of poor quality are found intermixed with it, and if left long enough the decay of the plants produces a thin soil, capable of producing grasses of better quality. This roughly indicates what has taken place in nature, and illustrates how, as the soil is formed or improved, higher forms of vegetation are carried.

The capability of soils in a particular condition to carry certain grasses is well exemplified in the experiments on old pastures at Rothamsted. A few acres of such were set apart for experiments, and each plot has been manured with a dressing containing more or less of the several constituents of plant food. Although the pasture through the whole of the plots experimented upon was nearly as similar as possible at the time the experiments commenced, they differ now in a marvellous degree both in appearance and in the varieties of grasses which compose them. Some are luxuriant and carry herbage of highest feeding values, others appear poverty-stricken and none but inferior grasses can be found, while others produce heavy crops of coarse and profitless grasses. Permanent pasture of the best feeding value is not, however, entirely composed of grasses; leguminous plants and other miscellaneous herbage, in fact, often form its most important feature.

## Permanent Pasture-making 161

They, moreover, perform an important part in the formation of new pastures.

This brings us to a question which may naturally arise. Why is one pasture field better than another? It is richer in fertility, the soil is healthier in the matter of drainage, the pasture is older and therefore more self-supporting. To lay down a field which is what is known as worn out with regard to fertility, and not to supply manure to it, is to invite failure. This is most marked on heavy soils where the mechanical conditions are also unfavourable. The land is not in a condition to supply food for a heavy crop of nutritious plants, and it is impossible for it to carry them. It can only produce a light crop of grass, or under some conditions a larger crop of grasses of poor quality. Land in poor condition will sometimes produce a heavy growth of poor grasses such as Yorkshire fog, the feeding value of which is small, as nearly the whole of such a plant is indigestible woody fibre, which has about as much feeding matter as saw-dust. The mechanical condition of a heavy soil is altered when it is covered with a thick pasture, and this accounts for good rich pastures such as are found on heavy land. The thick mass of fibre prevents the land from cracking in time of drought, and the surface water drains through it more easily. In the case of a previously almost purely inorganic soil there is a considerable accumulation of vegetable matter to supply the pasture with food it cannot find on land newly laid down.

## INFERIOR GRASSES AND WEEDS.

Although it has been pointed out that in course of time the varieties of grasses found in a pasture are those which find the conditions of soil and climate most suitable to their growth, it is obviously absurd to sow seeds of worthless or inferior grasses, as they produce little that is of value, and take the place of more valuable varieties. Some years would be occupied while the better varieties were obtaining mastery over the inferior ones. The sowing of inferior varieties is therefore as unwise as unprofitable. Among the inferior grasses may be included the whole family of Bromes.

The soft brome (*Bromus mollis*) is most commonly found in pastures. It is also frequently found in fields of rye-grass and other grasses from which seed is taken. The seed is thus mixed with the better kinds, and, unless carefully screened, is sown with it. Those who are acquainted with rye-grass seed need have little difficulty in detecting its presence. All brome-grass seeds are coarse. Soft brome is larger than rye-grass, being longer and much wider. The hard, flat kernel seems to lie deep in the sheath of husk. The seed is narrow at both ends, but bulges widely at about two-thirds its length, and contracts somewhat suddenly at the top. The kernel, as seen when slightly magnified, is covered by a thin husk, which has serrated edges. The edges of the large sheath-like portion of the husk are serrated also. The piece of stem attaching to the base is short, somewhat thick, and slightly hairy. A definite keel runs down the back, and is continued so as to form a stout awn; when viewed from the back the seed is suggestive in shape of a small boat, as ribs run from end to end. The whole of the back is hairy, but the hairs are stronger at the top than at the bottom. Other brome-grasses are coarse, and the seeds are easily distinguishable from those of the grasses the farmer is likely to want to grow.

Yorkshire fog (*Holcus lanatus*) is one of the commonest grasses in permanent pastures. It is found very commonly in hay-lofts, and those who prefer to sow seeds from this source to buying them should be careful to examine closely for these. The seed is small, and might be taken for that of one of the finer grasses. Brome-grass seeds are also common in the sweeping of hay lofts, but they are more readily noticeable. Both germinate freely and strongly, so that if sown they are sure to establish themselves, whether the finer seeds do or not. Apparently a good plant of seeds is secured, but it is the sort of plant which should not be there ; and a heavy growth is obtained, but it has practically no feeding value. As a rule, the seed of Yorkshire fog is found with the outside husk attaching, and when magnified it looks like a small beech-mast of very light colour, as the shape is somewhat similar and the exterior has the same roughness. This roughness is not so apparent to the naked eye. The seed appears closely like beech-mast when cut in an unripe condition, and is more open, as it is riper. No portion of the attached stem is visible.

## Inferior Grasses and Weeds 167

The kernel is covered with a fine smooth husk and is comparatively small.

Another seed found in badly-dressed samples of seed is that of the Onion Couch (*Arrhenatherum avenaceum bulbosum*). This is due to the fact that in many districts where rye-grass seed is grown the onion couch, as it is often called, is very commonly met with. It is very closely allied to, and is the only variety of the ordinary tall oat-grass, is a free-growing plant of fairly food feeding value, though this variety is poor in feeding properties. The seed is sufficiently distinct for it to be easily distinguished from rye-grass seed. It is very similar to the seed of the wild oat, but much smaller. The seed is attached to the stem at its base, consequently the broken piece of stem seen in many grasses is not present. In colour it is usually rather brown at the back, and from the back, near to the base, springs a long stout awn, about twice the length of the seed. This awn is straight and spiral about half its length, after which it generally curves slightly. At the base of the seed there are numerous fine hairs, as in the wild oat. The seed appears shrivelled towards the top, where it comes to a somewhat sharp point.

The seed of couch-grass, scutch, twitch, and innumerable other local names (*Triticum repens*) is frequently met with in mixtures of rye-grass; in fact, it is found so frequently that a not uncommon idea prevails that rye-grass turns to twitch. The seed is larger than that of Perennial Rye-grass, and is proportionately longer and narrower. It comes to a more acute point at the top, and the piece of stem adhering to the seed is nearly cylindrical. The inside edges of the husk are seen, when magnified, to be slightly hairy. The back is keel-shaped and comparatively smooth. It is usually, but not always, awnless.

Hassock-grass or tussock-grass (*Aira cæspitosa*) is prevalent in wet pastures. The seed does not appear very frequently in samples or mixtures, because it rarely grows on land where grass seed is cultivated but that of *aira flexura* is. It is most frequently found as an adulterant in samples of Rough-stalked Meadow Grass. It should be eradicated when it does appear; its presence is a sign of excessive moisture; consequently, superabundant moisture should be got rid of by drainage. The tufts should be cut off by an adze to allow the better grasses to fill in. Some years ago I ploughed over about an acre of pasture which was largely composed of hassock-grass, and which would have cost a considerable sum to get rid of by ordinary methods; this cut the top root, and leaving it exposed for a few weeks weakened it so that when the turf was turned back into its original position, the better grasses gained possession of the land and the hassocks entirely disappeared. I rather frightened the authorities by ploughing up an acre in the middle of a grass field, but a little reflection would have shown them that good, rather than harm, must result. It was quite sufficient for them, however, that it was against custom. A piece of

## Inferior Grasses and Weeds 171

worthless ground was made as good as the rest of the field for the outlay of a few shillings spent in labour.

There are several varieties of Bent Grass (*Agrostis*), but only one Fiorin (*Agrostis alba, var. stolonifera*) is of value. The seeds of agrostis are very small, and in ordering fiorin the purchaser should be careful as to the honesty of the firm he is buying from, or a worthless weed will be sown instead of a more useful one. It is not much use to sow fiorin on any but moist soils; it does little good on dry soils. The risk of paying for poor seeds and getting a crop of weed is so great that it is hardly worth the risk.

Docks, both land and water, are objectionable in meadow land, as beyond being unsightly and useless as food, the seeds are conveyed to other parts of the farm, thereby causing trouble. They should be got out by means of a docking iron—a fork with a ball on the underside at the top of the prong to lever them out of the ground. Sorrel is a sign of want of lime in the soil. It indicates acidity, which is neutralized by the use of lime. Daisies, moss, and other weeds common in poor pastures are present because of want of better manuring; except perhaps for a short time occasionally during winter, moss is not seen where the clovers are growing plentifully and the better grasses thrive. Daisies are met with on lawns where the grass has been cut and taken away for many years, and no manurial return made; or on poor pastures generally. They disappear to a great extent as the

## Inferior Grasses and Weeds 173

soil becomes richer. Bone meal, superphosphate, kainit, and sulphate of ammonia as manures are the best means of getting rid of them, as the better herbage which they induce ousts them. Harrowing is useful in destroying moss, as it kills a portion which thus becomes converted into manure; but harrowing alone is not sufficient to permanently get rid of it. The cause of its existence remains until the soil is made more fertile. Harrowing and rolling act beneficially on grass by giving it the only cultivation possible without really disturbing the turf.

## CHAPTER X.

### THEORIES, EXPERIMENTS, AND PRACTICES RELATING TO PASTURES.

THE discussion of features which have been brought into notice on various occasions may now be profitably dealt with. One of the theories which attracted most attention was that known as the De Laune theory, in which it was urged that the want of success which so frequently attended the laying away of land to pasture was due to the fact that seeds of indifferent varieties of grass were sown, and a special crusade was made against Perennial Rye-grass, which was described as being comparatively worthless. It was stated that " the grasses most pernicious to newly-formed pastures are first and principally rye-grass in all its varieties, and Yorkshire fog or soft, woolly grass (*Holcus lanatus*)." As a matter of fact, Perennial Rye-grass is one of the most nutritious grasses we have, and, moreover, it forms by far the greater portion of the grasses found in our richest pastures; it is hardly beside the mark to say that it is the most prominent grass in all good pastures. It must not, however, be confounded with Italian rye-grass, which is of great value for temporary pastures, but useless to those which are to become permanent. In the thorough and careful tests which Dr. Fream carried out in connection with the herbage of old pastures, reported upon in vol. xxiv., part 2 of the Journal of the Royal Agricultural Society, some striking facts were shown. Twenty-five sods were taken from the richest pastures of the United Kingdom and transplanted into garden soil. Care was taken that several inches of soil were left attached to each sod, so that there could be no admixture of soil or species of grass which would affect the results. As I saw these sods planted, and they were under my eyes up to the final examination, I am able to testify to the carefulness in every detail connected with the experiment, and the thorough reliability of the results obtained. In twenty-four out of twenty-five of these pastures rye-grass formed an important feature; but in the one from the county of Derby it did not appear at all. This, however, was admittedly one of the weakest pastures tested, for it was previously described as being "not sufficiently strong to graze steers or oxen." Notwithstanding this, Perennial Rye-grass constituted 36 per cent. by weight of the grasses in twenty-five turfs, *Agrostis vulgaris* being next with 17 per cent.; and no other grass was found to the extent of 10 per cent. In fifteen of the pastures rye-grass was found to the extent of over 75 per cent. of the total weight of grass; and in only three was it less than the average of the next prominent grass in the series. This makes the case a strong one for Perennial Rye-grass, and indicates that it must be generally regarded as necessary.

It was urged very strongly by the supporters of the De Laune theory that Meadow Fescue (*Festuca pratensis*) should

N

form a large portion of the seed sown to form a permanent pasture, but in only three instances out of twenty-five was it represented, and then barely to the extent of 1 per cent. in weight on the whole. This was apparently a case of mistaken identity, the blades of rye-grass having been regarded as those of meadow fescue, to which there is some resemblance, though closer examination shows that the mid rib of the former is strongly marked, while it is scarcely discernible in the latter. The young blades striking up from the heart of the Perennial Rye-grass plant are folded flat, while in the case of the meadow fescue they are twisted round, appearing in a cylindrical form somewhat similar to those of Italian rye-grass.

The objection to Perennial Rye-grass

## Theories Relating to Pastures

was formed because it grew too freely at first, but subsequently diminished in size. The fact is, rye-grass is highly nutritious and requires plenty of rich food to thrive upon. When land is first sown it eagerly takes up the food at its disposal and produces heavy crops during the first two or three years. By this time the available food becomes exhausted, and unless additional food in the form of manure is supplied, it cannot produce the growth it does under more favourable conditions. It does not waste its time, but turns to profitable account the food at its disposal, and this is what a grass ought to do. The first cuttings are very valuable, and because Perennial Rye-grass effects in two or three years what other grasses take several years to accomplish, this should not be regarded as a failing, but as a point strongly in its favour. Rye-grass does not die out; it only becomes stunted in growth; apply suitable manure, and it will grow again as strongly as ever. However, many who sow rye-grass mow it, and take off the crop, returning little to the soil, and then find fault because it does not continue to grow as freely as at first. How can it? You cannot produce bricks without straw. It has been stated in a previous chapter that land carries the varieties of grasses which thrive under special conditions. When land is poor good grasses wane, and others of inferior feeding value, such as Yorkshire fog, thrive. This is well illustrated in a field sown with rye-grass. As the food supply becomes deficient, rye-grass gives way to inferior varieties.

## Theories Relating to Pastures

The worst period in the life of a pasture is from the third to the tenth year, or a little longer, in accordance with the fertility of the soil. If liberally manured, the grass will grow freely every year, and produce good crops; if not, as is usually the case, it progresses slowly. Every year, however, adds something to the fertility stored up in the soil. The rootlets gradually die, and thus act as manure to succeeding generations of plants. The soil thus becomes altered in its consistency and texture. Such conditions are more favourable to the growth of Perennial Rye-grass; the stunted plants gradually gain vigour and increased fertility, as was shown in Dr. Fream's experiments. This may be confirmed by examining any rich old pasture; they take the most prominent position among the grasses of the pasture. In examining a pasture to estimate its value the frequency with which the fresh green blades of rye-grass appear, and the vigour which they show, must be regarded as the most valuable guide. This is most important when white clover is found growing freely among it, for it is absolutely certain that when this combination is found, the pasture is one of exceptionally high feeding properties.

It has been shown that rye-grass is a profitable grass only when there is a fair amount of fertility in the soil, and other grasses are profitable only when the same conditions prevail. At the same time it is advisable to sow a small quantity of seeds of other good grasses, so that they may be present to take advantage of conditions which may be specially favourable for them. Even in the best pastures other good grasses beyond Perennial Rye-grass are met with, and it is advisable to give all a chance.

In the making of a pasture it is particularly important to encourage the development of clovers. Clovers naturally enrich the soil, and add to its fertility by taking nitrogen from the atmosphere. Grasses take their nitrogen from the soil. The difference is significant. It has for a long time been recognized that the clovers "come" in an old pasture, and that they do this gradually. At first when sown they grow freely for a year or two, and then, like rye-grass, they grow less freely. The reason is the same—the food they most require becomes exhausted. The manure most essential to the growth of clovers is of a very different nature to that of grasses. A large quantity of nitrogen is required for the development of grasses, while it has little effect on clover. Lime and potash are of first importance, because without the clovers they cannot abstract from the atmosphere the requisite nitrogen. Clovers and all leguminous plants are provided with small nodular growths on the roots, and these are small laboratories inhabited by minute bacteria which have the power of extracting nitrogen from the air; but these little workers require lime and potash to carry on their work. Without them they starve, and as they supply no nitrogen to the plant it cannot make growth; on the work of the bacteria depends the existence of the clover plant. It is therefore essential that these manures shall be supplied if the land does not contain sufficient within reach of the plants. As nitrogen is the most expensive element in manures, the advantage of getting the clover plant to work on behalf of the farmer is easily understood. The amount of nitrogen thus absorbed enters the plant, and if that plant is consumed by animals, a large portion of it is returned to the soil as food for the grasses; but a considerable portion of the nitrogen is stored in the clover roots, and as these die, that stored in them also becomes available. It is found that it is much more easy to get a permanent pasture on good soils where lime and potash are available than on other soils, and it is the presence of these which greatly regulates the power of land to "take to grass." Loams in which there is a liberal supply of lime take readily. Sandy land with little lime is slow, and the pasture is with difficulty made to produce food for strong cattle. Thin chalk soils with an ample supply of lime, but with little potash, produce weak pastures, as shown on Down land. Heavy clays which possess lime and potash in abundance, if well drained, can be made to carry good pastures, though the mechanical condition is not so favourable as where the soil is somewhat lighter, as on heavy loams. Want of drainage, however, destroys the chance of good pastures.

As soils rich in nitrogen carry grasses of higher feeding value than do those which contain but little, so soils rich in potash and lime carry more valuable

## Theories Relating to Pastures 187

clovers than those deficient in them. Thus on a rich pasture white clover is met with in considerable quantity, while on poor soils, and on new pastures from their third to the twelfth years, the small trefoils are most commonly found. These lowly trefoils must not be despised, as they are doing the work of storing up nitrogen from the atmosphere, and when the soils become richer they will give way to the white clover. It is of course better that the soil should be well stocked with plant food suitable for both grasses and clovers, as then both will produce heavy growth, and the root formation will be proportionately greater. The reason why feeding off pastures, instead of mowing the crop and taking it away, is obvious. The advantage of feeding cake on it is equally readily seen, especially in the case of rich food such as cotton cake, which contains a large percentage of nitrogen and potash.

Pastures are economizers of nitrogen in yet another way. A considerable quantity of nitrogen in combination is brought to the ground every year, being carried down by rain, dew, and snow. This varies according to the situation with regard to the presence or absence of large towns, whose chimneys vomit out huge quantites of smoke containing nitrogen in different forms. An average of analyses made in nine places in different parts of Europe showed that as much as 10·23 lbs. of nitrogen were brought down on to every acre. As little as 1·86 lb. per acre was measured at one station, and over 20 lbs. at another. At Rothamsted

## Theories Relating to Pastures 189

it is about 4 and 5 lbs. As there are 15½ per cent. of nitrogen in nitrate of soda, the equivalent of about 70 lbs. of nitrate of soda falls where 10 lbs. of nitrogen are thus brought down. This, of course, falls on arable land also, but arable land is more wasteful of its nitrogen, no inconsiderable portion being washed out in drainage. Pastures waste but little in this way; the roots ramify the soil in every direction, and the humus has an effect in retaining the nitrogen. It is for these reasons that such full results are obtained when manure is applied to grass land.

A serviceable work was done by the supporters of the De Laune theory in calling attention to the fact that some of the larger growing grasses are possessed of considerable feeding properties. An idea prevailed among many that only the finer varieties were highly nutritious. So many of the coarse grasses, such as Yorkshire fog, the brome-grasses, &c., possess' but little feeding value, and all tall or coarse growing grasses were entered in the category. Three of those specially advocated, Meadow Fox-tail, Cat's-tail, Cock's-foot, are well worth encouraging in situations where they are likely to thrive. The prejudice against coarse grasses, however, affects them when it is desired to sell the hay, which deteriorates from their value for mowing.

THE END.

www.ingramcontent.com/pod-product-compliance
Lightning Source LLC
Chambersburg PA
CBHW032134160426
43197CB00008B/637